CREATING TOMORROW'S ORGANIZATION

'The *virtual organization* is the ultimate results-centred enterprise. By using *Future Work* principles, it is able to produce results that are at least equal to those of its traditional competitor but leveraged from a smaller asset base. This gives it the potential to beat the competition hands down. Its results are real and will show up in the bottom line. But if you search for the traditional means of achieving these results – the massive empires of office buildings, headcount and organizational politics; with work constrained to fixed times and locations; and the madness of large scale commuting – you will not find them because they are not there.'

Readers may use the Internet to contact the authors with comments and suggestions about *Future Work* and information about the *Future Work* Forum at Henley on
http://www.henleymc.ac.uk/

To receive current information on developments in Organizational MetaLanguage™ contact
cto@metacorp.demon.co.uk

CREATING TOMORROW'S ORGANIZATION

Unlocking the Benefits of Future Work

David Birchall
and Laurence Lyons

FT

PITMAN
PUBLISHING

PITMAN PUBLISHING
128 Long Acre, London WC2E 9AN

A Division of Pearson Professional Limited

First published in Great Britain 1995

British Library Cataloguing in Publication Data
A CIP catalogue record for this book can be obtained
from the British Library.

ISBN 0 273 61094 5

3 5 7 9 10 8 6 4

Typeset by Pantek Arts, Maidstone, Kent
Printed and bound in Great Britain by
Biddles Ltd, Guildford and King's Lynn

*The Publishers' policy is to use paper manufactured
from sustainable forests.*

CONTENTS

FOREWORD

Much of our case study material comes from *The Future Work Forum at Henley* – a research initiative set up within Henley Management College in 1992 bringing together senior and prominent people across the whole area of *Future Work*. These pioneering companies and individuals include several major banks, national institutions, suppliers of communications infrastructure and leading IT suppliers, local and central government agencies and advisers, as well as leading academics and others with a special interest in the subject area. We have conducted original research into aspects of *Future Work*, we have provided the research methodology for OffNet (an EU Telework project), and we have given evidence to government. We were delighted to receive recognition of our efforts:

> **'We live in fast-changing times and informing ourselves and being brave enough to grasp the technology is perhaps the greatest barrier. In this connection, the Henley Management College is doing excellent work in bringing about something called the *Future Work* Forum. This is being actively supported by big players in industry and telecommunications itself, including British Telecom and Mercury.'**
>
> LORD LIVERPOOL
> House of Lords debate on Flexible Work, January 10, 1994

The results from our Focus Groups, Conferences, Syndicate Sessions – as well as informal discussions with people both in and around the *Future Work Forum at Henley* – have had a significant influence on our beliefs. They have been a key motivator and source of material for this book. We also bring to bear many years of first-hand practical personal professional and managerial experience working within, commentating on, monitoring and analyzing the development of organizations of all sizes, both private and public, and across many industries. Of course we have to say that responsibility for the views expressed here rests entirely with the authors, just in case the future does not unravel itself exactly as we foresee!

David Birchall
Laurence Lyons
Henley 1995

This graphic represents the ideas pioneered by
The *Future Work* Forum at Henley

FUTURE WORK FORUM
at Henley

- *Future Work* is about IT-enabled New Working Practices and their relationship to Business Strategy.

- *Future Work* is not just about advanced flexible office practices. It is about new ways of doing *all* kinds of work in *all* business functions and working differently across those functions.

- It covers all the emerging practices and opportunities that flow by detaching work from its traditional fixed place and rigid time. It is the key to global flexible operations.

- It is the concept upon which the *virtual office, virtual employee* and *virtual organization* are based.

- Its principles enable organizations to provide brand new services; to address markets or segments that are as yet untapped, and to work more closely with their partners and suppliers.

- *Future Work* is also the name of a new lifestyle. It simultaneously affects the working and non-working lives of the people who adopt it as well as those that are around them.

- It is a powerful and unassailable force that is being propelled by the imperatives of business productivity, quality of life, and global competition.

- Today's adopters of the business benefits will be among tomorrow's winners.

- *Creating Tomorrow's Organization* discusses the benefits and pitfalls, it provides case examples, approaches and theory as it guides the reader towards unlocking the benefits of *Future Work*.

ACKNOWLEDGEMENTS

There are a number of colleagues we would like to thank for their help and support with *Creating Tomorrow's Organization*. First of all, we would like to thank Richard Stagg and FT Pitman for sponsoring the book, Sally Green for her tireless help in editing it and Colin Reed for his graphic insights that translated our original sketches into ideas on the page. We are grateful to the *Future Work* Forum Management Team at Henley Management College, and all the Forum members, who contributed ideas and shared their experiences with us. We would also wish to thank Rhona Prichard at Henley Management College on whom we have relied for her administration *par excellence* especially in meeting tight deadlines and Yvonne Frost for conducting the BT-sponsored foundation research into the drivers and barriers in our subject area.

For reading early drafts and review copies of specific chapters, and for giving general encouragement and inspiration we are grateful to Anne Minter at the Centre for Strategic Cell Development, Ron Ardell at Metacorp Management Consultants and Lynne Canal.

We would also like to thank the following authors for their kind permission to reproduce texts and diagrams as follows:

Chapter 2, Fig 2.2, reprinted from B Lloyd, *Office Productivity – Time for a Revolution*, Long Range Planning, 1990, 23 (1) 66, with kind permission from Elsevier Science Limited, The Boulevard, Langford Lane, Kidlington, OX5 1GB, UK and B Lloyd, South Bank University, 103 Borough Road, London SE1 0AA, UK.

Chapter 4, page 66 opening quote, reprinted from SP Bradley, JA Hausman and RL Nolan, eds, *Globalization, Technology, and Competition: The Fusion of Computers and Telecommunications in the 1990s*, Boston, Harvard Business School Press, 1993, p. 12, with kind permission from Harvard Business School Publishing, Soldiers Field, Boston, Mass., USA.

Chapter 4, Fig 4.1, reprinted from G Morgan, *Creative Organization Theory*, California, Sage, 1989, with kind permission from Sage Publications Inc, 2455 Teller Road, Thousand Oaks, California, USA.

Chapter 4, Fig 4.3, reprinted from LS Sproull, K Kiesler, *Connections: New Ways of Working in the Networked Organization*, MA, MIT Press, 1991 with kind permission from MIT Press, 55 Hayward St, Cambridge, MA, USA.

Chapter 5, Ref 8, reprinted from S Davis, *Journal of Management Development*, vol 12, issue 6, 1993, pp 15–20, with kind permission from MCB University Press, 60/62 Toller Lane, Bradford, West Yorkshire, UK.

Chapter 5, Ex 5.5, undertaken by G Aichholzer and A Kirschner at the Institute of Technology Assessment (ITA) in Vienna, Austria, as part of the OffNet Project with the Telework '94 Action Plan of the EU and reprinted with kind permission from G Aichholzer & A Kirschner, Institute of Technology Assessment, A 1010 Wien, Postgasse 7/4/3/, Vienna, Austria.

Chapter 6, page 134 opening quote, reprinted from W A Pasmore, *Creating Strategic Change – Designing the Flexible, High Performing Organization*, New York, John Wiley, 1994, reprinted with kind permission from John Wiley & Sons Inc, 605 Third Avenue, New York, NY, USA.

Chapter 6, Ref 1, reprinted from JR Katzenback and DK Smith, *The Wisdom of Teams: Creating the High-Performance Organization*, Boston, Harvard Business School Press, 1993, p.45, copyright © 1993 by McKinsey & Company Inc.

Chapter 6, Ref 3, reprinted from JE McGrath and AB Hollingshead, *Groups Interacting with Technology*, California, Sage, 1994 with kind permission from Sage Publications Inc, 2455 Teller Road, Thousand Oaks, California, USA.

Chapter 7, Ref 2, reprinted from D Garvin, *Building a Learning Organization*, Harvard Business Review, Vol 71, issue 4, July/August 1993, pp 78-91, with kind permission from Harvard Business School Publishing, Soldiers Field, Boston, MA, USA.

Chapter 7, page 156 opening quote, reprinted from C Argyris, *Knowledge for Action – A Guide to Overcoming Barriers to Organizational Change*, San Francisco, Jossey-Bass, 1993 with kind permission from Jossey-Bass Inc, 350 Sansome Street, San Francisco, California, USA.

Chapter 7, Fig 7.2, reprinted from DA Kolb, *Experiential Learning; Experience at the Source*, New Jersey, Prentice Hall, 1984 reprinted with kind permission from Prentice-Hall Inc, Englewood Cliffs, New Jersey, USA.

Chapter 7, Ref 12, reprinted from T Peters, *Crazy Times Call for Crazy Organizations*, New York, Vintage Books, 1994 with kind permission from Vintage Books, a Division of Random House Inc, 201 East 50th Street, New York, NY, USA.

Chapter 7, Table 7.1, reprinted from proceedings of the EDEN Conference, Tallinn, Estonia, 1994, with kind permission from Jorgen Bang, Department of Information & Media Science, Aarhus University & Jutland Open University, Ndr Ringgade 1, DK-8000, Aarhus C, Denmark.

Chapter 7, Fig 7.5, reprinted from *Case Working Towards Year 2000*, with kind permission from Povl Dalsgaard, Drammensveien 124, PO Box 228, Skoien N 0212, Oslo, Norway.

'I am proposing simply that society should use [computers and telecommunications] to redesign its institutions, and to operate those institutions quite differently.'

STAFFORD BEER

Designing Freedom, John Wiley & Sons, London, 1974.

1

WORKING TOWARDS THE FUTURE

We are witnessing the end of the predominance of the large business organization in its present form. The only question that remains is: *how long will it take*? We believe that by the dawn of the twenty-first century, the emerging forces we describe in this book will have become sufficiently powerful and mature so as to determine the shape of what remains of 'the traditional organization' as we know it today.

THE 'FUTURE WORK' ARENA

The opportunities we describe are to be found at the intersection of three forceful drivers for change (Figure 1.1) and within the setting of a sustaining economic framework:

- The arena of *Information Technology* (IT), in which there is much opportunity for organizational improvement and development. But with opportunity comes the danger of applying pat solutions to non-existent problems, and launching projects that do not always recognize nor declare the full extent of their side effects, either inside the organization or elsewhere.
- The province of *People at Work*, where in all aspects other than direct manufacturing there is a promise of new personal freedom, as individuals are increasingly able to detach themselves from the traditional requirements of working at specific times and in fixed locations, as work becomes more knowledge-based.
- The sphere of *Business Strategy* where, in theory at least, the potential power released from carefully managing the fusion of the other two domains can now offer a completely new organizational form. The *Future Work Organization*, in its various forms, is of such a fundamentally new nature that it is capable of reaching business aspirations which until now have been considered unattainable or even unthinkable.

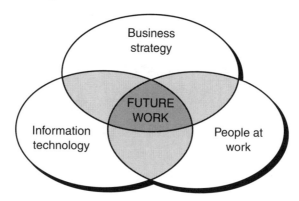

Figure 1.1 The *Future Work* territory

Within the area of overlap all three drivers fuse, reinforce, inform and support each other to prescribe the domain of *Future Work*. It is in this location that a management subject is now rapidly emerging. It promises to redraw boundaries both within and around the organization. As an area that will give rise to a completely new breed of organization, it is, at least for some organizations, a reason *in itself* to consider reinvention of the business. For organizations already pursuing a re-engineering or transformation plan, it promises to offer *stretch goals* – new and adventurous aspirations that should be added to the strategic agenda in order to keep one extra step in front of the competition.

We call these new organizations *Future Work Organizations*. New, innovative and adaptive varieties of organization will emerge from the concepts and principles we will develop throughout the book. We believe that their inception will be exhilarating and relatively painless, but they may surprise their competitors. Other *Future Work* organizations will be the successors of organizations that exist today. Some will result from reconstructed parts of businesses which will struggle to achieve *Future Work* and will fail.

A KEY ROLE FOR MANAGERS

A new age of *Future Work* will surface at the *organizational level* primarily through the collective initiatives of decision-makers within today's organization. They alone have the real power to do this. Governments may stimulate and legislate; individual workers may experiment with and even demand new working practices and structures, but *Future Work* can only be introduced and sustained through the commitment of the collective entity we call 'the organization' through the efforts of its managers and the drive of its executives..

Those managers who are yet to champion the transform towards *Future Work* are today employed by 'the organization'. It is 'the organization' that pays salaries and enters into work contracts. It is 'the organization' that owns and allocates assets, often including in its view its human resources. It is 'the organization' that provides funding for projects and programmes. *Future Work* will either flourish or fail depending

> **The messages from the *Future Work* movement are relevant to business owners, shareholders, suppliers, customers, directors, managers, employees and students of management.**

on how it is perceived, introduced and exploited in 'the organization' by its directors and managers.

Those organizations with the hardest challenge to face will be the traditional large businesses of today in their struggle to survive in some recognizable form into the long term. In these organizations, status-conscious middle managers who find it difficult to shed their traditional beliefs, especially those who believe and act as though they 'own' their people, will suffer the most discomfort during the process of change. They will fight a losing battle.

But those professionals and managers with a more open and achievement-centred approach will become the leaders and winners in tomorrow's new era of working. These champions of *Future Work* who are today within the traditional organization are our primary audience.

The messages from the *Future Work* movement are relevant to business owners, shareholders, suppliers, customers, directors, managers, employees and students of management.There are also important messages for government as the inevitable march towards *Future Work* has literally far-reaching, and possibly unexpected consequences. Some varieties of the *Future Work* organization have the power, through new transnational trading structures, to affect the very fabric of the world's economic geography radically. In the field of international competition, this is a subject we ignore at our peril.

EXECUTIVE SUMMARY

In this book, we set out to provide a modern executive insight into the new ways of organizing work. Armed with this book, directors and managers will be able to assess *Future Work* impacts relevant to their own organization. We have provided several pointers to help managers devise a suitable strategy for gaining the benefits from the emerging new organizational forms. More immediately, we provide a wealth of evidence – and hopefully inspiration – to help raise the profile of this new and vital subject even further towards the top of board agendas.

We also have much to say to those in medium and small organizations. These managers should not fear that their destiny will be determined wholly by the whims of a few of their large customers. We are of course aware of Electronic Data Interchange (EDI) which is the classic example of just this happening. In general, however, the smaller organization, perhaps being that much more flexible and fleeter of foot, has greater scope and ability for truly innovative change. Just like David and Goliath, the smaller are capable of outsmarting the larger players right across the supply chain, with a little thought, informed planning and appropriate tools.

As we enter the global marketplace we are becoming increasingly aware that current trading, employment, and business legislation are encrusted in anchored beliefs about work methods virtually unchanged and unchallenged since the inception of the Industrial Revolution. The need to break free from these legislative constraints, which have now become too narrow to accommodate properly future business opportunity, has become a national and international challenge which must be of uppermost concern to those in government.

Additionally, the environmental aspect of the subject – identifying a real and demonstrable opportunity to significantly reduce traffic congestion and pollution and to revitalise rural areas – is of concern to many outside the traditional organizational perimeter.

We hope to inform, to inspire, to alert, and in some cases to warn. There is much contained here, whether your interest is in managing the introduction of *Future Work* to transform your business into a *virtual corporation*, or simply to become informed about the potential for new and better ways of working and living. The chapters that follow are intended to give you a glimpse into a future that is grounded in the present. It will prepare you for improving your organization, your work and even your own style of life.

STRUCTURE OF THE BOOK

Chapters 1–3

The first three chapters set the scene and portray the subject within a 'Big Picture'.

Following the present chapter, **Chapter 2** describes *The Emerging Future Organization*. We begin with what we believe to be the heart of the matter – the opportunity to innovate organizational structure. Important drivers are identified that are today reforming structure and putting this topic at the centre of the management stage. We describe why we expect a series of structural 'dawn raids' on the near horizon as the first modern managers adopt *Future Work* principles. To end this chapter, the idea of the 'virtual' organization is presented, not necessarily as an aspiration, but as a badly-needed model to help managers to think in a strategic way, far beyond an approach of simply responding to competition.

Chapter 3 looks into *The Company and its Emerging Boundaries*. As the stage upon which *Future Work* and other transformations will emerge, it is important to review some strategic implications involved when creating a *company*. We are particularly interested in how views about *the company* may have to change or expand so that the opportunities we describe can be successfully sustained within it.

Chapters 4–7

These chapters go into much greater detail about the forms and opportunities that are becoming available.

Chapter 4 examines *Networking: the Future Organization Form*. It puts emphasis upon the impact of technology on the development of three forms of the networked organization – the stable network, the dynamic network and the internal network, using case studies to illustrate each. We look at the impact of networking on traditional organizations and traditional managers. We finish the chapter by highlighting some of the potential pitfalls.

Chapter 5 focuses on *Maximising Productivity in the Information Age: Moving to the Mobile Workforce*. Through practical case studies we look at how organizations are using IT to support the move to the more mobile and flexible workforce. It is making possible the location-independent workforce, but we stress that without an effective strategic approach business is unlikely to achieve the possible benefits. These benefits will result from sound implementation and include a radical rethink of the role of the traditional office – a topic covered in some detail.

In **Chapter 6** we look at one of the current hot issues facing many businesses – The *High Performance Distributed Teams*. Technology is making possible new ways of working by breaking down time and place dependence. But organizations need to extend their support of individual staff who work in this way and learn how to build and manage them into effective distributed teams. Increasingly, work in organizations is based around temporary project teams so an understanding of how to increase their output is vital.

Chapter 7 is devoted to *Learning in Organizations: New Approaches for Future Work Organizations*. Here we examine the need for learning at individual, team and organizational levels and how technology can support learning at each of these three levels. We support the proposition that organizations need to learn faster than their competitors. We also base our work around a competency approach to developing people and organizations. We show how IT has a major role to play in facilitating just-in-time training and development for the individual as well as supporting the development of the 'learning organization'.

Chapters 8 and 9

Our last chapters look at 'making it happen' with the emphasis on informing managers so as to prepare for and implement change.

Chapter 8 *Approaching Future Work*, prepares managers in today's traditional organization for introducing *Future Work* into their own organizations. It argues for a strategic rather than an opportunistic approach. It discusses the personal skills that managers will need as they begin to introduce the subject to their colleagues. We then introduce a completely new model of management that is sufficiently rigorous and robust to accommodate the advanced type of organizational transformation that *Future Work* brings about – a structural fabric with new boundaries in and around itself.

Chapter 9 *Managing the Transformation to Future Work*, starts by looking at the current approach to transforming organizations – Business Process Re-engineering (BPR). We explain how the re-engineering approach has represented an important step forward as it has tried to address some very real problems that the organization presents us with. We argue that *Future Work* transformation requires a rich or 'multidimensional' approach, and we suggest a model for achieving this. Finally, we provide managers with a set of practical tools to help them analyze and qualify their *Future Work* opportunities.

Table 1.1 Organization of the book

Elements of Future Work	Where found in this book
Emerging Opportunities.	Chapter 2
The Nature of the Company as the territory for *Future Work* introduction.	Chapter 3
The Network Organization as a new structural form.	Chapter 4
Individuals at Work.	Chapter 5
Teams at Work.	Chapter 6
Learning as the basis of new core organizational competence.	Chapter 7
Preparing Managers for *Future Work*.	Chapter 8
Introducing *Future Work* in the Traditional Organization.	Chapter 9

'How to grasp this opportunity to decentralize is, to me, the most urgent issue that confronts architects, urban designers, planners – and all the rest of us.

All those new technologies, in themselves, will not solve any of our problems. What we need to learn is how to use those new technologies creatively – how to shape them to our own purposes before they shape us to theirs (or to those of their manufacturers).'

PETER BLAKE

Chairman, Department of Architecture and Planning
Catholic University of America, Washington DC 'Urban Planning', *The Phenomenon of Change*, Cooper-Hewitt Museum, The Smithsonian Institute, Rizzoli, New York.

2

THE EMERGING FUTURE ORGANIZATION

INTRODUCTION

Tomorrow's dominant form of business organization will differ from that of today at its very foundation – in its structure. As the scope of work broadens from capital-intensive to knowledge-intensive, IT opens up new structural vistas.

In this chapter we will take a hard look at the impact of IT on some physical business assets – namely place, space and the resource of time. We describe why it is only now that technology is able to transform the traditional assets of the organization that have hitherto fixed work to specific locations and times. We explain how the emerging physical forms of organization are constructed from the resulting 'virtual assets'. We give examples of how *virtual organizations* are already being constructed from *virtual assets* and offering significant real benefits to businesses.

> **The virtual organization is able to produce results that are at least equal to those of its traditional competitor, but if you search for office buildings, headcount and organizational politics you will not find them, because they are not there.**

We also take our first look at the impact of *Future Work* opportunities within a traditional organization, discussing some difficulties in recognition and measurement.

THE IT TRIP-WIRE

At some time during the late 1980s in the West, we silently and unobtrusively crossed over a trip-wire and into a new era. There was no explosion, no fanfare. Rather than casualties, there were many beneficiaries. It is really only now, in retrospect, that we can appreciate what had actually taken place. Had we been able to determine the date of this event we might have instituted an annual celebration.

The trigger-point was in the relationship between business needs and the inability of IT to meet them (*see* Figure 2.1). In the past there had always been a positive gap between the needs of the business and what IT could offer. Businesses were then striving for increased efficiency and effectiveness.

To try to quantify the momentous scale of this potential we only need to look to Robb Wilmot, Chairman of OASIS and past Chief Executive of ICL, who in 1988 commented:

> **'Within five years the industry will be delivering more computer power annually than is currently in total use – if, and it is a big if, we are capable of absorbing it all.'**

ROBB WILMOT[1]
Long Range Planning

To appreciate the changing nature of the application of IT to the business world we find that:

> **'IT is a field that has changed radically in the past five to ten years. It has moved from being a tool of incremental operational improvement to being a means of achieving fundamental competitive advantage. It is changing the shape of industry. By the mid-1990s most industries will be information intensive.'**

JOHN L. CECIL AND EUGENE A. HALL[2]
The McKinsey Quarterly, 1989

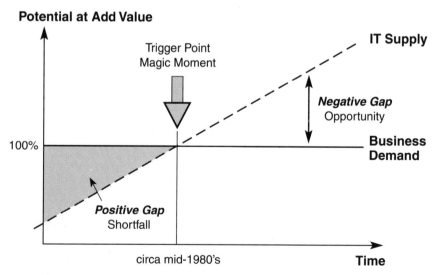

Figure 2.1 The era of the negative gap

Also, within the large companies instigating IT projects aimed at business improvement, came the complex problems of implementation and the deep disappointments of reality. All too often projects were late and over budget, and for the remainder that were not abandoned altogether, they often delivered results that were far below expectations, frequently requiring inordinate amounts of additional unbudgeted resources and unplanned support.

The maturity and atomization of technology

As with many technological waves that had gone before it, IT – a name that was coined as recently as the early 1980s to denote the convergence of computer and communications technologies – had reached a level of maturity through standardization to give rise to a new mass market. Among the most obvious standardization today is the Personal Computer (PC) with its now familiar operating systems, and the *PC network* providing an accessible and empowering channel of communication at work via electronic mail.

Another less obvious though very significant move towards standardization was the shift away from the bespoke application written by a special team of computer programmers, towards the new generation of standard software 'packages' that could be customized by users themselves – typically these are word processors, spreadsheets and databases. This approach avoided the costs of reinventing the wheel. It also reduced technical risk and encouraged continuous improvement as each package was effectively being tested every time it was used by each of its thousands of customers daily, so that any software errors (or bugs) would be identified and fixed in a later revision of the software. Most importantly, this trend has placed power in the hands of individual users who can now exploit the benefits for themselves. No longer was IT within the exclusive domain of a centralized Management Information Services (MIS) monopoly within the organization. As IT costs plummeted to a level within their discretionary spend limits, middle managers were flocking in droves to acquire personal computing for themselves, instigating new dialogues within many organizations. We can locate this atomization of boundaries in the context of a wider and general shift of power towards individuals, an important topic to which we return in Chapter 3.

Costs were driven down as the dynamics within the IT industry eroded the marketing differentiation of proprietary platforms, opening the floodgates to pervasive and affordable industry standard products, thus enfranchizing many new IT-users for the first time. With increasing IT literacy, a critical mass of understanding has grown up to provide a new and better-informed social – and hence management – context in which the technology has taken root and is now flourishing.

Exhibit 2.1 IT and the organization of work

MANAGEMENT BRIEFING
Essential Facts on Information Technology in Relation to the Organization of Work

In the early 1980s two powerful technologies converged – Computer Technology and Communications Technology. The result is Information Technology (sometimes called Information and Communications Technology).

The organizational implications for managers are:

- IT Computer Technology dramatically shrinks the time required to do certain work. Doing the same work in less time produces *efficiency* (once the fixed cost of the technology investment has been recovered).

- IT Storage and Retrieval Technologies enable us to record, to never forget and to quickly recover information. They provide *memory*.

- IT Communications Technology can be used to rapidly get information exactly where it is needed. In some cases it may remove the need for certain work to be done in fixed locations. This can increase *effectiveness*.

- When taken together, this powerful range of IT and business components can be configured to dramatically enhance the capacity for the organization to service its customers; work in partnership with its suppliers; improve the working environment for its employees; and improve the environment and quality of life in general. In some cases it is possible to change the very basis of competition and to transform the organization into doing something quite new.

- There are costs and risks involved in adopting IT.

- There are costs and risks involved in not adopting IT.

- So powerful is the technology that in some industries (e.g. insurance) it is possible to completely cut out the middle man ('disintermediation').

The Era of the Negative Gap

Now we live in the 'Era of the Negative Gap' in which the needs of a typical business may fall below the potential that IT has to offer. In simple terms it would be true to say that hitherto IT was catching up with business; *today business is having to catch up with IT*. There is now a surplus of available power. And the potential for exploiting this gap for competitive and profit advantage is phenomenal.

In many cases the potential to add value, to increase margins and boost profitability by *doing things differently* has been truly staggering. The growing number of *Future Work* case studies include companies up against a wall (as we shall see later in Exhibit 2.6 with New York Life the wall was demographic), or going to the wall (Silverstone's[3] Black Monday book publisher that went on to become the most profitable in its market), and where quite remarkable and unexpectedly brilliant results were obtained. Others have acted proactively and have stolen a lead on their competitors.

But this rapid switch in the economics of the supply and demand for 'IT business potential' is having other far-reaching effects, not the least of which has been the birth of *Future Work* allowing us to work independently of location and time.

> **In simple terms it would be true to say that hitherto IT was catching up with business; *today business is having to catch up with IT.***

Yet another and quite unexpected effect has been the expansion of the roles for HR, IT and Real Estate executives into the strategic planning of the business. We expect this to provide an opportunity, if not a need, to involve more people in the planning process. This need will be difficult to deny as competition speeds up. This is a topic we return to in Chapter 8.

ASSETS: THE FINAL FRONTIERS

The *where* and *when* of doing work is rooted in the distant past of the Industrial Revolution when it seemed sensible to anchor all work around the factory floor. Indeed, it was sensible as most of the information needed to process office work was readily to hand. Today a visit to any town centre will reveal floors and floors of prestigious office buildings totally dedicated to clerical and administrative work. The factories that produced the goods or services to which this work relates will be far distant. There is now also a recognition of 'knowledge workers', whose total added-value is in the intelligence that they provide to the business rather than any physical labour. Along with professionals, these people are the example par excellence of the location-independent worker. For them, work has shifted from hand to head, and can be undertaken anywhere.

The important questions for today's manager are shown in Exhibit 2.2:

Exhibit 2.2 Questioning the office

- Is the present office location still sensible?
- Is the current utilisation of offices acceptable?
- Is the very idea of an office still appropriate?

On location

Office buildings tend to be 'chunky'. They are often acquired (relatively easily), and disposed of (usually with difficulty) in units or chunks. Before long, and driven supposedly by the demands of work and the need to process it efficiently, the medium or large traditional organization finds itself exposed to a sprawling and growing portfolio of buildings.

The numbers are significant. Buildings and their servicing frequently appear as major items on balance sheets and income statements. Many companies have suddenly woken up to find themselves unexpectedly in the property business.

Chunky buildings are inflexible. They tend to be traded in units of floors rather than individual offices. Some companies have built their corporate logo into the architecture, asserting a greater confidence in a long-term relationship with the building than their more modest neighbours. Small or even medium-scale improvements in work patterns that would allow better space utilization will not improve the bottom line. There is an unavoidable fixed cost in owning a minimum chunk of floor.

But many of the assumptions behind the geographical blueprint of today's organization have disappeared. Technology and new work practices now make is possible to utilize space differently. Tools are available today to enable knowledge-workers to occupy significantly less office space than in the past. New offices that have been designed on

In the *era of the negative gap*, and within the global economy, all the traditional assumptions are under threat.

less than one half of the traditional floor space have been built and have worked well without any loss of productivity. The young and growing medium-sized companies are well positioned to take advantage of these savings in overheads.

Common factors often cited by companies in locating an office include:

1 Availability of staff.
2 Closeness of support services.
3 Good communications (roads, rail, airports).
4 Being physically close to the customer.

The location of business is also affected by government policy, as stresses and strains appear at the macro level. Over the decades we have experienced see-saw policies that have encouraged companies to locate out of and then back into inner-cities such as London.

In the *era of the negative gap*, and within the global economy, all the traditional assumptions are under threat.

The office as a space

Since the late 1980s, Bruce Lloyd[4] has been asking some awkward questions about office space. Some four years after publishing his findings in *Long Range Planning*, and after examining several companies in detail, Lloyd still argues that only between 5 and 10 per cent of real relevant work is done within office buildings (*see* Figure 2.2). The main differences between real relevant work and the total 365-day year include: the five day week; the eight hour day; vacation time; lunch time; sickness; late arrival and early leaving. He goes on to point out that, when compared with any other asset, the utilization is very small.

The real figure is therefore minuscule, as many companies will report that a significant portion of traditional office space is not used, as is evidenced by empty desks. Recent down-sizing has also left desks empty. The expensive and expansive reception areas in some buildings also eat up space, the return on which is often questionable. When this 'space' dimension is applied to Lloyd's time analysis, the actual return looks to be exceptionally small indeed.

Space as an investment

One of the most important implications of the poor utilization of office space is in its effect on capital investment decisions. The accounting measure, Return On Capital Employed (ROCE) is the ratio of earnings before interest and taxation to the average net assets the company holds over the

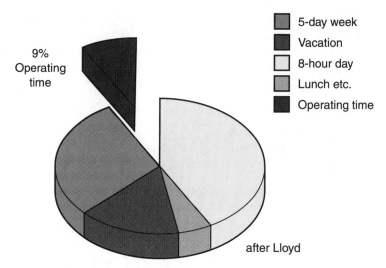

- 5-day week
- Vacation
- 8-hour day
- Lunch etc.
- Operating time

9%
Operating
time

after Lloyd

Figure 2.2 Utilization of the traditional office

accounting period – normally one year. Office buildings will feature on the Balance Sheet as part of those net assets if the offices are owned. Alternatively, they will show up as a large figure on the Income & Expenditure Statement (or P&L account) if they are leased. The costs of servicing the buildings will also show there. Each of these entries is significant as for many businesses the cost of people and space are among the high-ticket items in the accounts.

Companies develop their business through investment in new programmes and projects. When they do this they must make a decision about which projects to accept and which to reject. Very simply, it is possible to establish a *hurdle rate* which is a rate of return that the project must meet or exceed in order to be acceptable to the company for investment. All things being equal, a company will tend to invest in projects that exceed the hurdle rate in preference to those that do not. It is usual for this hurdle rate to be calculated on the basis of the company's *cost of capital*. This cost of capital simply measures how much it costs the company to borrow. It normally takes into account the fact that the money will come from a mixture of shareholders' and other investment sources by incorporating a weighted average in the computation. The result is often uplifted to take risk into account and reflect the possibility of the project failing.

If there are many projects running at the same time, the company is said to have a project portfolio. The performance of the portfolio as a whole can be taken into account in the capital investment decision, the logic being that the company wants to know whether a new project will match the return currently being generated from existing actual projects.

For our purposes, it is interesting to consider the effect of an underperforming property asset whose current return is below the company's project hurdle rate. In order for the business to meet its target return overall, it has to find a star project that will outperform by the same amount that the poor project is underperforming. If the poor project is a fixture in the portfolio and is of a large scale, this effectively means that the company's hurdle rate must be raised in order to compensate for it.

From what we have said above, the company's office space may well represent such a 'dud' project when set against the typical hurdle rate for a healthy company. The effect of a poor yield on office space may encourage a company to invest in short-term, or high-return, high-risk projects instead of some perfectly good alternative that just failed to meet the elevated target return. The opportunity to release capital implies a multiplier effect on the business's finances.

Innovation in office space may be able to make the finance director's dreams come true. If a business case along these lines could be made, it should be greeted with the same relish and fanfare as would a significant drop in interest rates. In financial terms, both these events would have a similar effect on investment decisions.

Traditional managers may argue that office space is not really a project within a portfolio, and cannot be properly regarded as such. They may say that the office is essential for doing business. They would argue that the office is an unavoidable expense: no office means that no work gets done, which means no business gets transacted. *We think not.* We believe that a review may turn out to be well overdue for very many businesses, especially today when the lifetime costs for new buildings have become a major concern for property investors in the light of their poor energy efficiency, running costs and even the cost of demolition.

Of these, the demolition of buildings may not seem to be especially problematical. But following the Bishopsgate bombing of the NatWest Tower in April 1993, Robert Miller and Jon Ashworth[5] in *The Times* reported almost two years later that 'the task of demolishing such an enormous structure, which was built with prestressed concrete, had never been undertaken before', and that an estimated £150m refurbishment was being undertaken instead. National Westminster Bank employed over 2,000 people at the Tower at the time of the blast. Thanks to their good neighbours, who temporarily hosted NatWest people in their offices, and also to a rapid acceleration of their own existing *Future Work* programme, this

> **Innovation in office space may be able to make the finance director's dreams come true.**

London bank survived a disaster and placed a question mark over the necessity for large chunky space.

In the era of the negative gap it may be possible at last to perform the alchemist's trick. Today's unavoidable costs in the base material of the business – office space – may perhaps be transmutable into tomorrow's organizational gold. This large, low-returning project may be convertible into an avoidable expense.

THE VIRTUAL ORGANIZATION

The word *virtual* has become popular in the field of *Future Work*. If something is virtual, it is said to have the effect but not the form. The expected results can be seen and experienced, yet the usual processes or structures through which they materialize have not been used. To achieve something virtually, implies the introduction of a new process or new structure. 'Virtual' is thus an excellent word to describe Future Work transformations when applied to the results that a business is achieving.

In the same way that *virtual* results can be seen, but the expected means of producing them are not actually there, so the word *transparent* means that something is there yet cannot be seen. Virtual and transparent are on opposite sides of the same coin. On the virtual side it is possible to see tangible business results, while on the transparent side people are working but cannot be seen.

In *Future Work* transforms, the traditional resources or assets seem to have vanished, or at least have become transparent. Examples include:

- **Virtual Assets** in new places of work, where fixed capital costs have been substituted for variable costs.
- **Virtual Employees**, who do not need to be physically located in a central office, and
- **Time Zone Shifting**, where the resource of time seems to expand or shrink at will.

> **The word *virtual* has become popular in the field of *Future Work*. If something is virtual, it is said to have the effect but not the form.**

The disappearance of these familiar work contexts is not magic; it is an illusion. Our astonishment stems from lack of familiarity, not from lack of substance. The power of IT has unobtrusively extended the realm of the possible beyond our current expectations. The gap is only one of perception: today's marvel will become mundane tomorrow. In the meantime we need to be able to navigate in a changing world where the perimeter seems to lie always just beyond our grasp. In order to benefit we must turn our attention away from the apparent disappearance of the familiar and look instead at the emergence of what is new. The reality of *Future Work* is to be found within the emerging boundaries of work in and around the company. We return to this in Chapter 3.

The virtual organization is the ultimate results-centred enterprise. By using *Future Work* principles, it is able to produce results that are at least equal to those of its traditional competitor but leveraged from a smaller asset base. This gives it the potential to beat the competition hands down. Its results are real and will show up in the bottom line. But if you search for the traditional means of achieving these results – the massive empires of office buildings, headcount and organizational politics; with work constrained to fixed times and locations; and the madness of large scale commuting – you will not find them, because they are not there.

Exhibit 2.3 The virtual organization

'Virtual organizations are project-focused, collaborative networks uninhibited by time and space. They are without the spatial territory and the cultural norms so important in traditional organizations. They offer the benefits of a high degree of focus on a common purpose, as well as the assembly of the right skills to accomplish that purpose precisely. Thus they offer a level of productivity unattainable in traditional organizations.

Cutting edge technology, like Lotus Notes and DEC Teamlinks, compensate for the absence of traditional workspaces. The 'fly in the ointment' is the absence of cultural and procedural norms, and the communication and affiliation that are a part of the fabric of our traditional organizations. This social vacuum creates the critical performance challenge for virtual organizations. The realization of the promise of virtual organizations is dependent upon addressing these issues head on.

Virtual organizations also present new challenges to management in areas such as role definition, clarification of boundaries, accountability and measurement of results, the unleashed power of information and impact on teams.'

HAL RICHMAN[6]
President, Productivity Solutions Inc., Halifax, Nova Scotia
Partner, PBN Private Business Networks,
both of which are run as virtual organizations

The virtual organization has innovatively and creatively used IT to restructure work. Provided that it can address the cultural challenge, it offers a flexible and highly-productive workplace. Ways of addressing the cultural dimension are covered in the chapters that follow.

The virtual organization also promises a different quality of life which has appeal to many, both in and around the organization. It offers simultaneous benefits to the business, to those who work for it, and to society at large.

It represents the structural form that will be the basis of tomorrow's competition.

The virtual office – more for less

When is an office not an office? Answer – when it is a virtual office.

In his visionary book, *The Third Wave*, the futurist Alvin Toffler[7] remarks that:

> '. . .one change is so potentially revolutionary, and so alien to our experience, it needs far more attention than it has received so far. This, of course, is the shift of work out of the office and factory and back into the home.'

More recently, in 1993, Emma Daly[8] reporting in The *Independent* has commented:

> 'Commuter hell . . . has prompted countless office workers to fantasise about working from home; the developments of computer and communications technology means such fantasies can now become reality.'

Since these comments were made we have come to realise that moving work out of the office does not necessarily mean that it must move into the home. Nor does it mean that there is a mutually exclusive choice between office and non-office working. Some of the most innovative companies using *virtual office* principles multiplex the working week, typically involving two to three days in the more traditional office. Some companies have taken this a step further and redesigned their traditional office to accommodate and maximize the benefits from this kind of working arrangement.

One such organization is the consultancy Ernst & Young who have introduced their 'hoteling' virtual office scheme which has spread from San Francisco to Chicago and New York and now operates nation-wide in the USA and is based on a system of 'hot-desking'. European introduction is planned for 1995.

Exhibit 2.4 Hoteling at Ernst & Young

E&Y checks into the virtual office

'When consultants, who often spend up to 80 per cent of their time at the client site, need to check in at E&Y for firm meetings and reviews, they preregister with the E&Y 'hoteling concierge'. The concierge allocates an office for the period required, programs a phone with the consultant's extension, and puts their name on the door. On the designated day the consultant goes back to base, plugs his/her notebook into the enterprise network, collects papers from a personal locker and is up and running within minutes.'

Management Consultancy[9]

Exhibit 2.5 Hot-desking at IBM

IBM UK £2 million saving per year from up to 7:1 'Hot-Desking' initiative

On the London South Bank, IBM UK has reported a 'hot-desking' initiative that has enabled it to reduce its office space requirement by 33 per cent. According to Michael Brooks[10], the company's property director, quoted in *Working Property* Magazine, the 90,000 square feet reduction on the original split site has enabled it to make a 'real saving of £2 million a year in space costs'. Reporting the introduction of desk-sharing ratios as high as seven to one, Brooks adds, 'The office or workstation is now an asset of the company, available to anyone who wants to use it'. IBM UK is now even looking closely at the use of its restaurant space which has until now been used for only two hours a day. Staff are now encouraged to hold informal meetings and conferences in it.

Working Property

The home is but one non-office place. There are others: the hotel, the airport lounge, even the car. A mixture of non-office work (eg to be alone to think) and traditional office work (to work face-to-face in a team) is proving to be a healthy combination for many.

This 'new breed of worker' has been described by Iain Valance[11], CEO of British Telecom as:

'. . . He is the teleworker, or telecommuter – the person who travels to work, not down the Piccadilly line but down the telephone line and who arrives at the office without actually leaving home.'

To quantify the telework potential, Francis Kinsman, a leading commentator on Teleworking has told us in a personal interview in October 1994:

'Some of the more ambitious forecasts of the past seem to have run into the ground. Some 4.6 per cent of the UK population now work from home on any one day, which is similar to the 4.8 per cent in the USA.

Meanwhile the potential is always there. A teleworking facility is available to 16 per cent of the workforce while 12 per cent do use it at some time. In addition 29 per cent of others would use it if it were available.

FRANCIS KINSMAN[12]

People who are teleworking completely meet – indeed often exceed – their work obligations. Individual targets and results are achieved, teams do in fact work together (in a more concentrated way), but physically they are not always in the traditional office place or traditional office space.

These effects are visible in the business's bottom line. The financial results can be seen and are real, yet the people who help achieve them are not physically located in the traditional office. From a traditional perspective, the office has become virtual – its effects can be seen yet it is not physically present in its expected place.

The non-office, non-home work location

Telecottages and telecentres

It is all too easy to assume that out of office means at home. Working at home can bring onerous pressures to bear on workers and their families. For the last hundred years and more we have so strongly compartmentalized our life experiences between Work, Leisure and Education that the integration into a smaller set and towards a single holistic lifestyle may not be suitable for all. This dynamic may materialize but at a slow rate, or it may put a brake on styles of *Future Work*.

> **People who are teleworking completely meet – indeed often exceed – their work obligations.**

Yet all is not lost. There exist a multiplicity of spaces which are both non-office and non-home where work may be done.

> **'Telecottage is a word taken from Sweden, where the concept was born. In its pure sense it is a community centre, equipped with modern technology such as computers, fax and photocopiers, where local people can train or work using the resources provided.'**
>
> TELECOTTAGES WALES[13]

We are seeing the emergence of a kind of local community centred workplace that is away from home yet outside the corporate office. We use the shorthand **LAWN** – Local Area Work Network – to include all such kinds of telecottage and telecentre structures. Until now, these LAWNs have been promoted to workers within a catchment community, but their ability to sell their services into the larger companies has been very limited. If they survive long enough for their major customers – the large corporations – to recognize their existence, then there will be a possibility for a vast uptake of their services.

Serviced offices

The serviced office is yet another intermediate work location. In its simplest form it provides a permanent telephone and fax point of contact to customers and suppliers of smaller businesses. In reality the owners are elsewhere – either with customers, travelling, or otherwise out of the office; perhaps even abroad.

Telephone calls are taken either by an electronic voice mailbox, or by a receptionist. Received faxes may be stored at the serviced office and then forwarded to any remote location for retrieval by any fax machine. One interesting feature of these arrangements is that even the receptionist need not be physically present at the serviced office location and may be working remotely from it. In this way some of the serviced office's employees may become virtual – the work will get done without them having to be present in the physical location of their office.

Some serviced offices actually occupy prestigious office buildings and can offer meeting facilities to their clients. When all these facilities are employed, the small businesses which use the serviced offices appear to all the world to be no different to a large established company. The trappings of the large business may be seen, but, because of the shared nature of the

Exhibit 2.6 Demographic boundaries dissolve for New York life

The insurance company, New York Life, was increasing its volume of business and needed more claims processing people to handle it. They hit a demographic snag. People who live in NY and who are at all capable with figures, could earn far more on Wall Street than any insurance company would ever pay. But, by using modern communications, the company was able to shift the work to where it could find a proficient English-speaking workforce – it went to Ireland.

The lesson for managers? Knowledge workers can work anywhere. Ideas are the most easily exported commodity in the world. That's why several large companies are having computer software written in India and some European airline reservations are administered in Barbados. They gain the benefits of highly educated and skilled people for a fraction of what they would pay in Western Europe or North America.

facility, the cost of the asset base that is being used to project them is a fraction of that for the traditional organization. The organization's office has thus become virtual – it is visible, yet the need to sink capital into it has been avoided and replaced with a variable cost.

The offshore office

Knowledge work does not need a passport in order to cross international borders.

Another new icon of the modern way of doing business is the help desk. Ring into any of the major IT software companies from the UK and your call could be put through to almost anywhere: USA, Ireland, or the Netherlands. It has now become economically viable to provide a similar 24-hour facility for any service sector running daytime UK/night-time Australasia.

The idea could be attractive, for example, to motoring organizations which have to provide a service around the clock – they simply do not need to have their control rooms fixed in the home country any more. Also direct banking accounts, open 24 hours a day, could be run worldwide from two or three centres in different time zones. In each of these examples the person you would be talking to would have instant up-to-date information such as your account details – through technology, of course.

Exhibit 2.7 British company shifts time-zones with a virtual offshore office

This company, based in Reading, England, specialises in making 35mm and similar kinds of high quality materials for conferences and sales presentations. It has now become possible for it to offer established clients a turnaround in what appears to be zero time.

Their Reading clients lodge with the company the standards to which the presentation material must comply, such as the positioning of the logo and other house-style characteristics. In some cases the client is able to present the company with a set of hand sketches at the close of one working day and collect the finished material shortly after the office opens the following morning. All that is usually necessary is to make any minor corrections and produce the physical slides. The several hours of professional layout time required to put together the presentation has not been visible to the client as this significant part of the work has actually been performed in New York.

This *Future Work* method takes advantage of the fact that daytime in NY corresponds to night-time in England. The work gets done, and to a high standard. The output is visible yet the resource that is traditionally required to produce it i.e. time seems to have shrunk dramatically. This innovative company is using *Future Work* to provide improved customer service by shrinking time.

THE DYNAMICS OF CHANGE TOWARDS FUTURE WORK

When futurists make forecasts they often identify major forces that have been growing almost imperceptibly for some time. They extend the effects into the future and talk perhaps in terms of a gradual progression or evolution towards some future envisioned state.

In contrast, we believe that the move to *Future Work* for business organizations will be more like an act of combustion. We expect a controlled explosion to occur. Our reasoning for this lies in the imperative characteristic of all business organizations – competitive pressure. In short, the more competitive the business environment, the faster and more vigorous will be the attempt to assimilate *Future Work*. This will be true not only in the highly competitive private sector; the litmus test will be how 'commercial-like' the directors and managers of the business – even a monopoly – perceive it to be.

As in all times of great change there will be leaders and followers, winners and losers. Along the path to *Future Work*, these terms apply equally to individual people, organizations, industries, societies and even nations. Who will win, who will follow, who will lead, who will lose? To consider this, we have set at centre stage a highly-stereotyped organization. Its behaviour is not particularly exciting. There are many organizations like it. The way it will behave is at the very focus of the transformation towards *Future Work*. We use the word *company* rather than *organization* to stress the competitive environment. In our stereotype, we have characterised the important lack of strategic behaviour of the company by the word *tactile*.

THE TACTILE COMPANY

'They have a mouth but cannot speak; they have eyes but cannot see; they have ears but cannot hear.'

PSALMS 115

We know of a number of organizations, notably in the retail and finance sectors where our subject is in fact towards the top of the board's strategic agenda. But many of these traditional organizations are impotent when it comes to *acting proactively* towards the opportunities on offer.

How can this be so? What is it about the large traditional organization that seems to make it ignore its best long-term interests? Surely there must be somewhere within it a sense of survival if not aspiration for a better future?

We suggest that in spite of the existence of strategy departments and strategic planners in and around the larger organizations, the very nature of the traditional corporation often gives it a tendency towards – what we shall call here – a 'Tactile Personality'. By this we mean that the organization is *not proactive*. This inertia or lack of action is sometimes described by managers as *responsive or reactive*, but the difficulty with these terms is that they can be misunderstood to mean the opposite of what we are describing. While proactive organizations will initiate action from within, the kind of organization we describe here *only* acts in response to the actions of others.

Organizational psychology

The *tactile* concept is borrowed from the field of psychology and is central to our understanding about the uptake of *Future Work*. In their book on

Neuro-Linguistic Programming – a useful collection of current thinking on the psychology of the individual – Joseph O'Connor and John Seymour introduce the idea of a preferred representational system:

> '**Visual, auditory, and kinesthetic (feeling) are the primary representation systems used in Western cultures. . . . We all use our senses externally all the time, although we will pay attention to one sense more than another depending on what we are doing. . . . What is surprising is that when we think, we tend to favour one, perhaps two, representational systems regardless of what we are thinking about.**'
>
> JOSEPH O'CONNOR AND JOHN SEYMOUR[14]

Our concept of the *tactile corporation* is based on the behaviour of the kinesthetic individual – a person who experiences the world primarily through feeling. We transport and extend this idea into the corporate plane to model this specific psychology of the organization as a whole.

Tactile behaviour

Like all other companies, the tactile company will see reports about change in the outside world. Like all other companies it cannot fail to hear stories about developments. As in other companies, it will make internal projections and forecasts based on all this evidence. Yet although it can see, hear, analyze and even understand, there is still one thing it cannot do, given these stimuli alone: *it cannot act.*

For as long as it refuses to act, it will be literally in two minds. These 'minds' may manifest themselves within different individual people, such as directors, or they may represent a generally confused, distressed and tortured organizational morale. One mind will observe the growing gap between the newly-available opportunities and the capability of the company to grasp them: this mind will want change. The other mind is actually more change-averse than it is risk-averse, unable to confront its own inadequacy. In this state, the kind of organization we are discussing both 'knows' and 'does not want to know'. It could be described, in an emotional sense, as stressed in a state of denial. However, in a business sense, it finds itself badly exposed.

What has to happen for a tactile organization to act? In order for it to act, it first has to truly and completely *believe.* In order to accept reality, any difference between theoretical supposition and hard facts must be totally eliminated. The case must be totally irrefutable, there must be no doubt.

The *only* way a tactile organization can bring itself to believe is through first-hand direct and totally unambiguous experience. It has to feel.

Companies that have neither a strong intuitive leader nor a dynamic and effective board may slip into becoming tactile. The only learning mechanism that works in this type of company, indeed the only way it progresses at all, is through the direct experience of pain. Its motto might as well be: 'I have been hurt, therefore I am'.

We stress that tactile behaviour is not 'damping'. Damping is a term we borrow from mechanics and cybernetics to indicate that an infrequent and small external stimulus should not be able to bring about a massive change in system behaviour easily. Damping is indeed quite healthy. It is a control mechanism that can set a correct and sane balance between the organization that is totally tactile at one extreme, and hysterically hyperactive at another. At the other end of the scale, large organizations always prone to overreacting to all kinds and degrees of stimuli, would quickly fail to preserve their own identity and would ultimately cease to function through disintegration. Some filtering and damping is desirable. Poor evidence must be rejected.

> The *only* way a tactile organization can bring itself to believe is through first-hand direct and totally unambiguous experience. It has to feel.

However well-designed they may be, organizations are never perfect, so that occasional deviations from the ideal may be an acceptable price to pay for an otherwise efficient and productive business system. Sometimes the exception must not be allowed to sway the rule. But obsessive and excessive damping can be an excuse for maintaining an artificial yet comfortable feeling of well-being, giving support to the belief that nothing significant is really happening around the business.

In contrast, the tactile corporation is cognisant of real opportunities and real threats. It is certainly not ignorant. Yet it is paralyzed. It cannot act until it suffers, by which time any advantage that could have been gained from its prior knowledge has been lost. A tactile company will never be a leader – it always follows. It is, of course, the ultimate follower if it survives its experience of learning. However, even if it does, it will not really prosper.

Beyond tactile

We are suggesting that as an organization is comprised of a collection of people, the effect of the group will normally tend to numb the visionary and listening senses overall. There are many factors in the traditional organization that tend to encourage this sensory dulling. The traditional exceptions appear in those organizations that are populated by some critical minimum number of specially talented people who also happen to be suitably positioned within its structure and able to affect real action.

Another and very promising *Future Work* exception is the *networked organization* which we cover in Chapter 4. This organizational form holds out for us the promise of freedom from a limited personality trait. One of its mechanisms for staying in touch with shifts in its environment lies within its ability to discuss the world as experienced through all its members. Indeed, its network of members is an important part of its environment: it almost defines itself as non-tactile. It has the opportunity to use a rich plurality of perspectives shared between people throughout the network's entire communications architecture. As these people are more in touch with, and spread out across, the real world (when compared with the more insulated traditional middle manager), network discussions may be more grounded in reality, more balanced, and more vital. The networked organization is the ultimate eclectic organizational form.

People power

Another important and promising characteristic of the networked organization is in its potential to shift the centre of gravity for strategy development away from the disembodied, somewhat artificially personified organization towards its individual members. We will touch on this theme again in Chapter 3.

First-move dynamic

Because many commercial traditional organizations tend to be tactile, theirs is a game of the 'first-move' strategy: they await the first move of others. Once the strategic leader (a non-tactile or visionary implementer) is seen as reaping significant business benefit from the change, the pack will quickly follow. The archetypal model for this is the 'price leader' whose selling price is monitored by all other suppliers in its industry, their own prices merely reflecting movements instigated by the leader. It is often a similar story for strategic change. So although we can forecast a rapid follow-the-leader response, the commercial trigger is dependent on, and waits for, the strategy leader.

Of vital importance in this first move game is that the activities of – and the benefits to – the leader must become visible, and be perceived by the competition. But many of the benefits from *Future Work* can be expected to be more hidden, as they reduce internal costs. They certainly will not be as well advertised and publicly communicated as, for example, are selling prices. Given that it is usually not in the interest of the leader to signal these benefits, very significant time-lags can be expected to build up between the first move of a leader, the public availability of competitive indicators, and the ultimate realization and analysis by a competitor. In any event, job mobility will provide a long-stop on the time it takes for a company to become aware of a competitor's first move. As individuals shift between employers, and as society ingests and adapts to the new lifestyles, so the knowledge of IT-enabled new work practices permeates commerce and industry. The implication for a company that has chosen to follow rather than to lead, is that it has to *stay alert*.

The less-commercial-like organizations also have a very significant role to play. Their motivation may well be social rather than commercial – they will not be looking over their shoulder waiting for a competitor to gain ground on them before they begin to experiment with change. We believe, therefore, that there is a profound yet submerged opportunity here for the public sector to give a lead to the practices of industry and commerce without the need for either direct intervention or contextual conditioning. Encouragement of *Future Work* by governments may come about through the use of a rarer policy instrument. In the area of the beneficial restructuring of work, the best policy may simply be best *practice*, which others will see and emulate.

MEASURING THE ORGANIZATION OF THE ORGANIZATION

As *Future Work* concepts surface within traditional organizations, the question of measurement will come up. How should a *Future Work* programme be costed, and how are the benefits to be measured? As *Future Work* has very much to do with structure, we might ask: how well is structure recognized, how well is it measured, and how is it valued in today's organization?

The manager in any large organization who has not experienced some major structural change in the last 18 months is having an easy life. It has become trite to say that the only permanent state is change. But what awesome factors are these companies struggling with, to make major structural change so commonplace and frequent?

The 'organization of the organization' – or the alternative choices behind the selective deployment of resources in performing work – is very rarely visible to shareholders. Cynically, we could say that it is often not visible to employees, either. There seems to be a tacit understanding that the structuring of work is something that is done daily by managers and, by and large, should be left to their discretion.

But organizational factors do, on occasion, surface. They sometimes appear in company accounts, being implicated in mergers, acquisitions, joint ventures and divestment activities. Occasionally we may find a 'Restructuring' charge appearing against the balance sheet. This is often a euphemism for a redundancy programme, the situation again only becoming visible when it is dire. Surely somewhere between gargantuan statistics and the simple measure of headcount (when it is reported), there must be some measure of 'organization' that would interest an outside observer? Without doubt the topic must be of interest to managers.

Accounting for structure

One of the ultimate tests of organizational effectiveness is the result on the bottom line. Two kinds of bottom-line result are of interest. One group of these only surfaces after analyzing the *composition* of the items on the Income Statement: can products be made or services be delivered at less cost? Can overheads be reduced? The second group of bottom-line benefits concern the absolute size of the bottom line itself. Can new and efficient methods of delivery be found to increase volume; can completely new service offerings be added; can new customer segments be identified; can better learning and fine-tuning inside the organization be achieved? A critical strategic question lies in the balance between these two groups. It is a question that is all too often overlooked or avoided – given that no investment is required, will the business accept or reject a structure offering higher absolute profits from lower margins at higher volume? All too many businesses answer this question by trying simply to reduce cost at the expense of making money.

The difficulty in all bottom-line comparisons of this kind is whether the important figures are in fact measurable. A key and recurring question is: 'How much does it cost to make one unit of production, a single product?'. Very often there is no single answer to this question. The traditional methods used to measure the major factors of interest to us – people and buildings – are shrouded in a mystery of accounting, even when just the *operational* aspects are concerned. The chosen method of allocation and absorption of traditional fixed costs into unit product costs can be, to say the least, problematical. The fixed costs to which we refer are those sunk within traditional buildings and traditional employment contracts. It would be shallow and almost cynical to say that no two companies will treat this problem in exactly the same way. To say that even *within the same company* different divisions will apply different treatments, is perhaps much closer to the truth. If we now are to say that we are trying to measure benefits that result from changing the *structural fabric* of the company (through the transforming effects of IT, by redeploying people and reconfiguring buildings), it is clear that precise measurement could be difficult to obtain or agree. Indeed, are traditional measurements helpful to managers?

In each area – IT, buildings and people – there are difficulties in measuring contribution and benefit. *Future Work* is at a triple focus of perplexing benefit determination; measurement is more a leap of faith than in numbers alone. But it is easier to take this leap once the overwhelming orders of magnitude of the effects are realized while maintaining an acceptable level of risk. An overwhelming and visionary business case that is robust and manages risks may provide this. If such a case can be made and is promoted by adventurous managers, then *Future Work* has a chance to become viable in the traditional organizational setting.

Management Summary

- The *era of the negative gap* has provided new structural opportunities as IT allows work to become independent of location and time.

- New structural forms are becoming possible which radically alter the asset base of the company.

- The potential to do work using fewer resources (*e.g. time*) and a lower asset base (*e.g. space*), or with less costly assets opens up opportunities for competitive advantage and improved customer service.

- The potential to move work around the world is changing the basis of international competition for knowledge-based work.

- The large traditional organization that fails to become proactive and investigate the opportunities from *Future Work* will be the most exposed.

- Introduction of *Future Work* for many traditional organizations will require a cultural shift to mirror the new work practices.

- When the shift towards IT-enabled new work practices reaches a critical mass, there will be a strong perceived need from the followers to catch up quickly.

- Organizational structure is a new competitive battlefield.

- A solid business plan that recognizes benefit and manages risks is essential to promote *Future Work*.

References

1 WILMOT, ROBB. 'Computer Integrated Management – The Next Competitive Breakthrough', Long Range Planning, 1988 **21** (6) 65–70.
2 CECIL, JOHN L. AND HALL, Eugene A. 'When IT really matters to Business Strategy', *The McKinsey Quarterly*, Autumn 1989, pp. 2–26.
3 SILVERSTONE, ROGER. Beneath the Bottom Line: Households and Information and Communications Technologies in an Age of the Consumer, The Third Charles Read Memorial Lecture, ESRC/PICT, lecture given at Imperial College, 21 May 1991.
4 LLOYD, BRUCE. 'Office Productivity – Time for a Revolution?' Long Range Planning, 1990 **23** (1) 66.
5 MILLER, ROBERT AND ASHWORTH, JON. 'NatWest Tower to rise again', *The Times*, Jan 6, 1995, p.21.
6 RICHMAN, HAL. In discussion with the authors, 1994.
7 TOFFLER, ALVIN. *The Third Wave*, Pan Books, London, 1980.
8 DALY, EMMA. 'Home is host to a new work era', The *Independent*, 12 May, 1993, p.30.
9 MANAGEMENT CONSULTANCY, 'E & Y checks into the virtual office', unattributed, September 1994.
10 BROOKS, MICHAEL. 'IBM Saves Millions in "Hot-Desking" Initiative', *Working Property*, Winter 1994, Issue 3.
11 VALANCE, IAIN. 'Tomorrow's Workplace', Queen Elizabeth Conference Centre, London, 14 September, 1988.
12 KINSMAN, FRANCIS. In telephone interview with authors, 1994.
13 TELECOTTAGES WALES. Ty'n-y-rhôs, Bwlchyddâr, Llangedwyn, nr. Oswestry SY10 9LJ.
14 O'CONNOR, JOSEPH AND SEYMOUR JOHN. 'Neuro-Linguistic Programming: Psychological Skills for Understanding and Influencing People', The Aquarian Press, e3. 1993.

Further Reading

GALBRAITH, JOHN KENNETH. 'The Theory of Countervailing Power', *American Capitalism*, Chapter IX, Boston Houghton Mifflin, Sentry Edition, 1962, pp.108–134.
HAMMER, MICHAEL & MANGURIAN, Glen E. 'The Changing Value of Communications Technology', Sloan Management Review, Winter 1987, pp.65–71.
KATZ, D. AND KAHN, R. L. *The Social Psychology of Organizations*, Wiley, 1966.

'We shape our houses and our houses shape us.'

WINSTON CHURCHILL (ATTRIBUTED)

3

THE COMPANY AND ITS EMERGING BOUNDARIES

INTRODUCTION

In this chapter our principal actors take centre stage. As we have said in our introductory remarks, we believe that the organization and the managers within it are central to the uptake of *Future Work*. We start by closely re-examining that popular organizational form – the corporation. We quickly come to appreciate the fluid nature of the corporation's present identity due to its location at the vortex of a number of powerful social trends. We prepare for our discussion by first establishing how boundaries come about, and the problems and choices that come with them. This is the taxonomy concept which will endure long after today's familiar boundaries have eroded. Every company is faced with questions of taxonomy, and we present some that are both current and pertinent to our subject.

A pervasive power shift towards *the individual* is causing familiar boundaries to come under stress both outside and within companies. We suggest that this empowerment of individuals may become an important driver towards *Future Work*. We go on to argue the general need for a wider identification of stakeholders. These are the key actors around the company, and their proper recognition becomes vital within the *Future Work* context.

We then have to consider the consequences of success. Can the new relationships and styles of *Future Work* really be sustained over time, and into the long term? If so, what demands will the emerging breed of *Future Work* organizations make on their environment, what dependencies will they create, and how can these be met? Are *Future Work* methods applicable to all organizations or only to some, and is there an optimum number of organizations that should adopt them? Will *Future Work organiza-*

> **A pervasive power shift towards *the individual* is causing familiar boundaries to come under stress both outside and within companies.**

tions rest easily within today's society, or will society itself have to change in order to accommodate them? Would such a struggle be worth the result, or will risk-aversion and apathy forever constrain us all within the confines of the traditional organizational form?

We close this chapter by examining some important boundaries and their degree of fluidity.

BOUNDARY EROSION

When we look at mature organizations in the mid-1990s, of one trend we can be certain – the assumptions and beliefs upon which they were once shaped apply less and less. The demonstrable symptom of this is 'boundary erosion'. Whether in pursuit of customer care (reorganizing distribution channels in order to get closer to the customer), outsourcing (moving whole functions out of the organization) – or pressure from employees (locating people in non-office venues), it is evident that the boundaries within and between organizations are mutating as new and unusual regroupings are already taking place.

Looking outwards, the organization is more and more having to recognize a wider community in its environment. As the long-term effects caused by depleting the world's natural resources and disseminating their processed by-products, sometimes as pollutants, become recognized, the organization is coming to be seen as an important actor in a long chain of events. 'There are some who would say that the chemicals and oil industries are special cases (the risk of noxious emissions and pollution is ever-present) and so to generalize from these particulars is inadmissible. But this is . . . to miss the point', claims Will Hutton in *Management Today*. He goes on to say:

> '**The environmental crisis is upon us here and now – and it is already impinging on business decision-making across a swathe of industries.**
>
> **No car manufacturer, for example, can be unaware that western industrialised societies are reaching saturation point with the motor car; no food retailer can ignore that it is getting harder and harder to build out-of-town superstores; no airline can be deaf to the growing opposition to airports and jet noise; and no bank can lend confidently to customers who face new, unlimited environmental liabilities. The business choice is not whether to respond to these problems but how to do so.**'
>
> WILL HUTTON[1]
> Management Today

We would say that the first step in such a response should be to identify the wider group of actors who will be affected as a result of the company's decision-making. The second step is to determine whether and how the company can distribute value and benefit to them. As companies do this, they will also become more receptive to the wider *Future Work* community that they may reach out towards. Writing in *Computing* magazine, Dom Pancucci[2] notes that UK commuters burn off 30 million gallons of fuel each day and have around 35,000 road accidents each year. The 25 per cent of additional time spent away from home adds to stress levels, and 'people who travel to work suffer from worse health and get less done than their teleworking counterparts, according to recent research gathered by BT'. When placed against the backdrop portrayed by Will Hutton, telecommuting would seem to have much to offer. The questions for decision-makers is in how to identify the actors and how to determine benefits for them and the business within their plans.

> *Future Work* will redraw boundaries that are themselves being redrawn by other organizational developments.

As organizations take on new shapes with the introduction of *Future Work*, the physical manifestation of the company becomes more devolved, apparently flatter and certainly fragmented. Thus *Future Work* will redraw boundaries that are themselves being redrawn by other organizational developments. This highlights a general need for managers to have an appreciation about the changing nature of boundaries, and the challenges they represent.

THE CREAKING CORPORATION

The corporation as the incorporated or limited company has become today's dominant stereotype of the business organization. It is the instrument through which a system of feudal ownership once gave way to one of collective private and public ownership, during an age we call the '*first power shift*' that transferred power from owners to directors representing the interests of shareholders. Many of the resulting divisions between the 'organization' and its environment have been so deeply embedded into our thinking that we have come to take these for granted.

The most important of these are:

- The corporation as a separate independent entity or legal person.
- The limitation of shareholders' liability.

The second of these encourages shareholders to pool their money so that the corporation may acquire the capital it needs to run its business. It is worth considering whether businesses that have a high proportion of knowledge-based work actually require this pooling, especially if the assets they utilize have become virtual and thus require much less capital investment. This realization, if taken together with an aspiration of workers to be more independent, may lead to a networked structure in which the work becomes outsourced. We shall return to all these topics shortly, but we shall first review the idea of 'boundary'.

In a world of changing and eroding boundaries, it is important to recognize the advantages as well as the problems that boundaries bring with them as they make divisions in and around the corporation.

Today's corporation is a familiar legal and accountable entity which works to a well-known and published set of ground rules. Indeed, it has been *defined* for just this purpose. Its 'legal personality' through the act of incorporation, has separated it from the rest of the world to make it a unique and neatly-accountable entity. At any particular time, a set of rules, such as those set by law and accounting practice, determine who or what is to be found inside the corporation (*e.g.* assets, employees and products), and what must be regarded as being outside it (*e.g.* suppliers, customers and the public at large). Within its established range of permitted powers, and together with its status and its responsibilities, the corporation knows what it is, as well as what it is not; it knows what it is empowered to do and what it must not do; it knows what it is obliged to explain to others, and what it need not disclose.

It recognizes certain individuals, other companies and groups as important and with whom it shares its destiny. Conversely, there are individuals and groups in and around the organization who claim that the organization's continuation and well-being is somehow aligned with theirs. These individuals and groups are together the stakeholders in the company (although they are not necessarily within it). Figure 3.1. shows some of the typical stakeholders that a company will recognize, being derived from relationships implied in the company's accounts. In this simple model, customers pay money to the company; suppliers are paid by the company; earnings are either retained or distributed to shareholders after interest has been paid to lenders and tax to the government. Employees also appear in the stakeholder chart, effectively as suppliers who reside within the organization's boundaries.

The corporation possesses its own identity, knows what is expected of it and what it expects from its stakeholders, and so is sure of its place in the world. It is comforted by the thought that vast numbers of other incorporated companies throughout the world share exactly the same principles that are at the foundation of its own basic structure. The corporation works and it delivers. It operates within a set of tried and tested rules. It is secure.

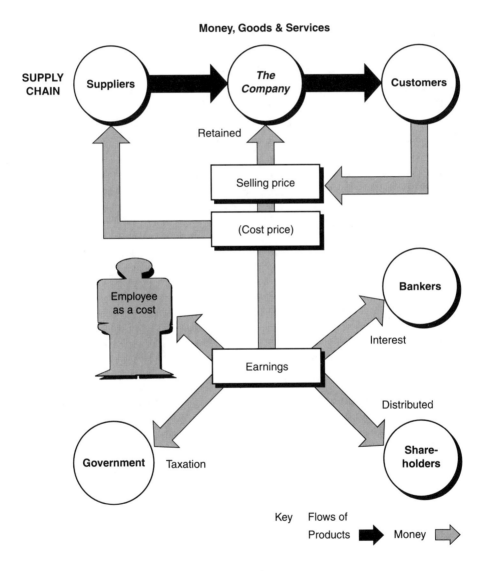

Figure 3.1 A typical traditional stakeholder chart

Or it would be secure, were it not for the *Taxonomy Dilemma, Organizational Power Shifts, Social Atomization,* and *Full-Ripple Economics;* topics we discuss in the next few pages.

The taxonomy dilemma

Taxonomy – the way we choose to classify, categorize, delineate or divide – is a very basic and important matter. It may seem so basic and so obvious that it can appear at times to ask trivial questions. But these question are far from trivial. For managers, taxonomy has to do with definition and delineation. These are questions that involve decision making and so require managers to make sound selections and exercise good judgement. Creating 'Tomorrow's Organization' requires nothing less than a radical reappraisal of some fundamental taxonomies in and around the organization. The ability to think more deeply about boundaries is the essential ingredient that is needed – not simply to transform – but to completely redefine an organization towards tomorrow.

The question of taxonomy is not only about how we divide between entities, but how we choose to group entities together. Two fundamental strategic groupings are:

- Industries as collections of suppliers, and
- Markets as collections of customers.

Both of these groupings require management decisions to determine what to include and what to exclude from the definition as it applies to a particular company. *Competitors* are other companies that the company identifies to be in the same industry as itself. The common thread that brings a specific company into the definition of *industry* could be in its ability to offer alternative products and services to currently-identified common markets. The normative behaviour of a company will be strongly connected to the choices it makes in determining who it regards to be its competitors, and who and where it perceives to be its markets and customers.

> **Creating 'Tomorrow's Organization' requires nothing less than a radical reappraisal of some fundamental taxonomies in and around the organization.**

Defining your competitors is not always straightforward. Strategic assets can help companies cross traditional industry borders. When asked what business General Motors is in, many will correctly answer that they are in the automotive business. But they have also moved into the credit card business. High-street retail stores are also in the credit card business, with their large out-of-town outlets now also competing strongly with companies such as BP in the petrol retailing business.

On the market side of the company, the question is not simply to define the market as an undifferentiated group of customers. It becomes necessary to divide the customers into meaningful groups or 'market segments'. What constitutes a meaningful grouping is of course a matter of skill and judgement. The ability to group customers into segments can make the difference between a star company and an 'also-ran'.

Exhibit 3.1 Taxonomy and competitive advantage

> The Taxonomy Dilemma results from asking the questions: *Where do I divide? How should I group?*
>
> There is more than one possible way of dividing the world to identify what the company will regard as its relevant actors and collections of actors.
>
> **This Choice through Division Involves the Judgement of Managers.** Better choices will lead to the design of better companies.

The ability to divide and group meaningfully is extremely important, but also problematical. This is the taxonomy problem. As we move towards *Future Work*, the important choices of division and grouping extend into new areas. Some of the traditional and emerging taxonomy questions are set out in Table 3.1.

Thus, there is more than one way to define a company. As we shall demonstrate later, there is more than one way to define an organization. But in the very act of definition we have chosen what to include, and what to exclude. Some choices work better than others. Some choices seem to make absolute sense at one point in time, then seem inappropriate at some later time. Definitions involve a trade-off. Herein lies the dilemma, and the risk.

Table 3.1 Some traditional and new taxonomies in and around the company

Taxonomy Questions and Decisions – How Does the Company Choose to Divide?	
QUESTION Traditional Organization	**DECISION**
SUPPLY The make *vs.* buy decision	Whether to make products in-house or buy them from an outside supplier
CUSTOMER Market segmentation	How the company chooses to target different customer groups so that its products and services can be packaged to meet their specific ranges of needs
STRATEGY – Business scope The business the company considers itself to be in (and therefore also areas that it will avoid).	The boundaries of business scope that most importantly define the products and services that the company will *not* supply

Some *Future Work* Organization Issues

OUTSOURCING The work that the company will contract out to an outside supplier	The 'core competencies' that must remain in the business and the balance of strategic risk involved in migrating work to an external market
EMPLOYMENT *Employ/contract* Who the company should employ directly	The extent of contractual terms that are necessary to protect the company whilst operating efficiently
GEOGRAPHY Where work will be done *Local/remote*	Whether the work being considered has to be performed locally, or whether it can be provided more efficiently or effectively across an electronic network
WORK LOCATION *Office/non-office* *Office/home boundary*	Whether work must be performed in an office
TIME ZONING	Prioritization and scheduling of work, e.g. whether time-zone shifting should be used to transfer work to shrink turn-around as perceived by the customer
VIRTUAL ASSETS	What assets the company has to have in tangible form (e.g. buildings, offices) as opposed to virtual form (e.g. shared satellite offices, consortia arrangements)

Some Potential Macro Issues for Companies

THE EXTENDED EMPLOYEE	The extent to which the company becomes part of its employees' extended family as the traditional boundaries between work and the home erode
CAREERS	The ability of the new *Future Work* order to sustain a supply of talented people who can populate the new structural forms. The key issue is the supply of training

The company in context

Coincidental with the dawn of the *era of the negative gap*, that we introduced in Chapter 2, there has been a growing concern about some fundamental definitions, taxonomies and boundaries as applied to the company. As long ago as 1989 Tom Peters was asking:

> 'What is an organization? What is a product? What is a market? What is a customer?
>
> I used to think I knew the answers. I don't now. Is an organization a pyramid, a network, a network of organizations? Where are its boundaries? Is the idea of boundaries even helpful? . . .
>
> . . . And what is a customer? An adversary? A partner?
>
> . . . Our so-recently tried-and-true (yet still recent) management tools are, arguably, worthless, many downright dangerous.'
>
> TOM PETERS[3]
> in *The Economist*, 4 March, 1989

These questions go to the very heart of the *taxonomy dilemma*, challenging all our familiar boundary definitions that we have until now taken for granted. They leave little doubt that these definitions have been stressed to the point at which the traditional organization has become a *creaking company*. When we look in a wider context, we also find that there are questions being asked about the fundamental taxonomy that divides the company from society at the macro level. Consider this comment made in 1988 in relation to Britain, but which is equally applicable elsewhere:

> 'I believe that Britain is suffering and has suffered badly in the past 20 years because of a failure by businessmen and politicians to clarify the role of business in society. This has caused governments and industrial leaders to make bad decisions and it has caused employees all over the country to feel less than satisfied with their working lives.'
>
> ANDREW CAMPBELL[4]
> Director, Ashridge Strategic Management

When we talk about transforming today's organization, it is important to recognize the problems and choices that are implicity behind our definitions of its key elements. Also, there appear to be more dimensions to the role of business than have been generally recognized until now. There seems to be a need for a better ability to determine who the relevant actors should be. This vital realization comes at a time when there is a resurgence of interest in systems theory. Managers are today rediscovering and reinterpreting much of the systems thinking that seems to have been forgotten over the last three decades. This resurgence is to be welcomed and encouraged.

Systems theory offers an extremely powerful approach in addressing management problems. Its application has tended to be directed towards the determination of *relationships* between a given set of actors. This bias towards activities and processes has been extremely useful in designing business transforms, but it does to an extent presuppose who the actors involved in those transforms will be.

Our discussion of the taxonomy dilemma seems to demand that even before the process relationships are considered, some initial work is needed in determining the relevant actors, as well as their meaningful segmentation and grouping from the organization's perspective.

This staking out of territories, and the seeking out of the wider meaningful audiences and actors is an important exercise for all of today's organizations, even prior to their consideration of any *Future Work* dimension. To succeed, managers will need to be able to deal with issues of scope and classification, taxonomy and collection. These are the tools of hierarchy theory (which system theory lays claim to as one of its branches) that need to be applied at the very start of any organizational transformation to create the organization of tomorrow.

Once we come to recognize problems in the current taxonomy, there are basically two ways forward. One way is to give up on the ideas of definition and taxonomy altogether. This would present us with a view of the world as a chaotic, almost unknowable mass which presents frequent transient short-term opportunities for entrepreneurial players. The alternative approach, and the one that is clearly needed to progress into the world of *Future Work*, is to have a fresh look at the taxonomy. Technically speaking, the introduction of a new taxonomy in any subject is normally hailed to be the start of a new paradigm. Indeed, in the *era of the negative gap* and in the advance towards *Future Work* we believe that *nothing less than a new management paradigm is required*. Its challenge is to introduce a sufficiently broad degree of abstraction in our thinking, so we may manage the problems of definition (taxonomy) and scope (extended stakeholders) that we have found in our subject area. It must enable managers to work through the taxonomy dilemma as they set their organization within an *appropriate context*.

New organizational power shifts

The *first power shift* we have mentioned, separated owners, in the form of individuals and families, from the directors and managers who came to manage the business. The increasing number of knowledge-workers, may perhaps herald a new power shift. This time, the power will travel one step further along the line by empowering individuals and encouraging them to manage themselves. The question of 'ownership' by the company of the individual, in the form of the popular employment contract thus comes under question, if not under threat.

It is interesting to note that this question of ownership has been changing in recent years. It was Goethe[5] who long ago said: *'What we do not understand we do not possess'*. The modern corporation has rephrased this to: *What we do not possess we do not control*. As recently as 1975, Neil Kinnock[6], who was later to become British Labour party leader, accurately reflected in the *Tribune* the then current thinking when he said: *'We cannot remove the evils of capitalism without taking its source of power: ownership'*. But the decade that was to follow saw the implementation of a pervasive and sustained *divestment* of ownership under the banner of *privatization*. Ownership and power were being pulled apart. Power was shifting towards investors in the form of the new shareholders. To the extent that these shareholders were individual people, it could be said that power was shifting from collective monopoly ownership towards consumers and individual ownership.

Similarly, at the corporate level, it used to be thought that people had to be 'owned' by the company through a permanent employment contract so as to foster loyalty and, in some cases, to protect confidentiality. The emerging question is one of extent. Do *all* people have to be employed in this way?

SOCIAL ATOMIZATION – GETTING TO THE INDIVIDUAL

On another side of the business is the consumer. The ability to pinpoint and communicate directly with an individual prospect who has been narrowly-targeted and accurately qualified has long been the dream of those who run marketing campaigns. Now it is no longer necessary to swamp an entire hemisphere with advertising material in order to obtain a desired volume of sales at a pitiful conversion rate in the sub-one-percent region. Marketers are beginning to use database and communication technologies intelligently to prospect individuals who are already likely to need their products and stand a much greater chance of becoming customers.

The individual is becoming more visible and more accessible. No longer is it necessary to always treat the world as an enormous, undifferentiated mass. Today broadly-defined groups are being replaced with individual people. For instance, national radio now runs in parallel with a multiplicity of local radio stations addressing highly specialized and segmented audiences. The Internet – the worldwide 'information super-highway' – provides each of its tens of millions of individuals with a highly-defined address space in the form of interest groups, and can also reach out to individual forum members.

And along this conduit of communication, power is steadily shifting from a small number of massive institutions towards the massive number of individual people.

This second shift of power towards the individual is not simply confined to companies; it appears to be a symptom of an even more fundamental and underlying shift in society:

> **'The cultural revolution of the later 20th century can thus best be understood as the triumph of the individual over society, or rather, the breaking of the threads which in the past have woven human beings into social textures.'**
>
> ERIC HOBSBAWM[7]
> *The Age of Extremes*

Again, one of the key factors behind the shift is the emergence of the new technologies that make possible global markets and global trading. These same technologies also allow more accessibility to those who govern. They also promise the opportunity to overcome some of the problems of operating a democracy with large numbers of people. The individual voter could be polled for views on a variety of subjects at far lower cost and more frequently than, say, the four- or five-year cycles of general elections. In the UK, Anne Campbell, Member of Parliament for Cambridge, has taken a lead and now runs regular constituency surgeries on the Internet. She is in good company. The White House and HM Treasury also offer Internet access, as do the US Government, the CIA, the Prime Minister of Japan, and the UN Development Programme.

Electronic democracy

For many countries a referendum is a costly and thus infrequent mechanism for measuring popular opinion. The day may be fast approaching when a plebiscite may be a viable possibility. This would require a voting system that guaranteed individual voters free access to the technology that would be required in order to cast their vote: enfranchisement must not be dependent on the ownership of technology. Just such a system may become possible. The UK National Lottery, set up rapidly in 1994, is based on a network that links thousands of highly-accessible retail outlets to a central validation computer, possibly with spare capacity. Television stations already run opinion polls using regular broadcasts, teletext and prime-rate telephone lines. Naturally the possibilities of a national voting system based on technologies such as these raises serious questions of confidentiality and validity. Techniques that have been pioneered on the Internet are already able to address some of these fears. Through its Anonymous Posting Service, the Internet currently provides a mechanism through which untraceable messages cannot only be received – but also responded to – without compromising individual confidentiality. The same facility has a serious business use, too. Large companies could request help and receive advice, for example on dealing with a damaging computer virus, on a completely anonymous basis without alerting or alarming shareholders of the problem's existence.

The prospect of a cost-effective, readily-available and thus frequent plebiscite offers another conduit of power. By this means power may one day shift from representation of the many by the few, to the representation of all by themselves.

The consumerization of work

At the same time that accessibility and power have been shifting towards individuals, and as new possibilities open up, so people's expectations have been rising. This is typified by the growing consumer movement. As consumers, we have come to expect superior service and excellent products, and, most importantly, we are more willing to question and challenge suppliers who dash our expectations. Looking towards the business as an employer, individual workers are beginning to question today's current assumptions about how work is to be done. Indeed managers have been encouraging them to do so. The quality movement, in stressing the paramount importance of the business purpose, has endorsed a variety of innovative work practices, by encouraging more lateral thinking on the part of workers who, in turn, should now feel that they have become more empowered. The seeds of a trend towards a more self-managed organizational form, such as the *networked organization* that we will describe later in some detail, have been sown.

Flexible-working time has recently been gaining popularity but the idea has been constrained by the need for people to work together. Until now this has made convergence at a single physical location – usually the office – inevitable. Now that it is possible to work independently of location as

> **As consumers, we have come to expect superior service and excellent products, and, most importantly, we are more willing to question and challenge suppliers who dash our expectations.**

well as time, much greater real flexibility becomes possible. To the extent that this new flexibility can enable people to better synchronize and share their time between work and non-work activities, we believe there to be a latent build-up of new expectations that the 'work organizations' will be under considerable pressure to satisfy.

Convergence on the home

From the individual's point of view, other interesting and important structural events are taking place. Technology seems to be bringing about a new climate of convergence in which life spheres that we have in the past regarded as occupying totally different environments share a new common platform. Bringing together the hitherto highly-compartmentalized worlds of home, leisure, learning and recreation, these trends bring with them the new tools of the trade of *Future Work*. We show this in Figure 3.2.

Drawing these threads together leads us to believe that today's employees may soon have the aspiration, motivation and methods for *Future Work* at their disposal, *independently* of the actions of companies in their role as employers. Referring back to Figure 1.1, we observe that in a climate of technological opportunity, businesses are challenged to inform and modify their strategies, possibly in the light of pressure applied by employees and the needs of workers. Businesses must be prepared.

Full-ripple economics

One area that is in need of renovation as a result of *social atomization* is economics. As power shifts away from the institution towards the individual, and as the wider consequences of what once seemed to be simple production and exchange become deeper and more visible, so the ability of traditional economics to explain total value distribution comes under considerable strain.

Very simply, our perception of the context within which we are now to regard the company has broadened. At face value, companies process raw

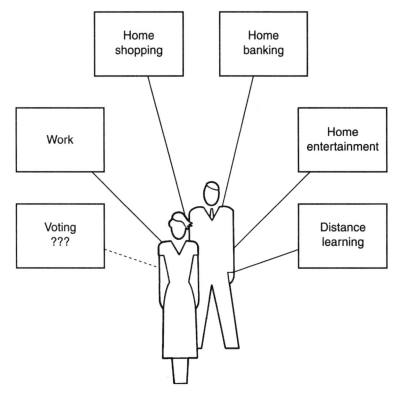

Figure 3.2 New technologies converging on the home and individual

materials and other inputs, add value, and sell products and services for a profit. This has been the traditional micro-view of the company. The exercise, for example, of setting prices at which products will be traded, although not altogether trivial, has been feasible and manageable using the current tools of economics. But the exchange of money between two parties is proving to be an inadequate token for measuring value in a way that society will endorse.

As alert consumers, we have become more interested in how the raw materials were obtained and at what cost. We have come to be concerned not simply with the trading cost but the *full-ripple* cost to society, e.g. to the environment. The ethical investment movement has been built on concerns such as these.

In the down-stream direction, we are becoming interested about how and where the product will be used, and again at what real *total social* cost.

We are becoming interested in not just the obvious consumer, but those in and around the consumer's environment. Interest is steadily shifting on the *ultimate consumer* who may represent people in future generations whose life quality and opportunity may be adversely affected by the production and consumption of today's products.

We are all now coming to suspect that the artificial division between the company and its environment has been too rigid and too constraining. It seems we have cut off too much of the richness of reality which is now left abandoned and forgotten somewhere outside the negotiated perimeter of the organization.

Consequently, there is today a pervasive and growing demand to expand and widen our concept and recognition of stakeholders. Figure 3.3 includes *extended stakeholders* and is more representative of the requirements of a modern perspective than that of Figure 3.1.

For some aspects of *Future Work* it is essential to include some newly-recognized extended stakeholders into our thinking in the form of the families of individuals adopting the new lifestyles that come about by shifting work out of the office. Professional groups become extremely relevant when considering *Future Work*, or indeed any transformation of a business process that crosses functional (professional) boundaries.

We see *Future Work* towards the leading edge of a more general trend that demands recognition of a wider circle of stakeholders within and around the company. As new networked structures emerge in selling, shopping, learning and working, so the wider circle of stakeholders around the company will become more involved in negotiating and regulating it (*see* Figure 3.4).

The boundary-less company?

However we choose to restructure work, it does not seem very meaningful to talk of the 'boundary-less organization'. Boundaries are inevitable. What we can say, though, is that one taxonomy may replace another as new lines are drawn to replace the old. While the changeover is taking place the world may appear to have become virtual, as some things no longer appear in familiar places. The key to making it real again is to grasp the nature of the new taxonomy that is driving the change of boundary.

In declaring that 'the traditional organizational map describes a world that no longer exists', Larry Hirschhorn and Thomas Gilmore observe:

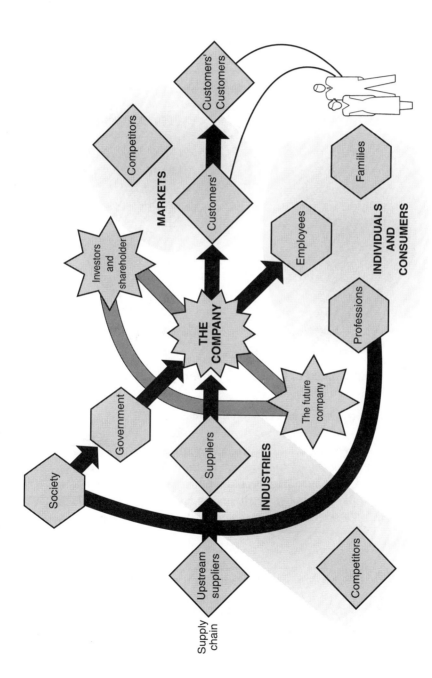

Figure 3.3 A simplified modern stakeholder chart for the extended company

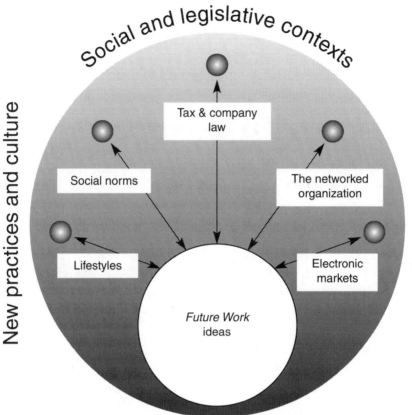

Figure 3.4 The rich context of the *Future Work* organization

> 'Managers are right to break down the boundaries that make organi-
> zations rigid and unresponsive. But they are wrong if they think that
> doing so eliminates the need for boundaries altogether. Indeed, once
> traditional boundaries of hierarchy, function and geography dis-
> appear, a new set of boundaries becomes important. . .
>
> Yet knowing how to recognize these new boundaries and use them
> productively is the essence of management in the flexible organization.'
>
> LARRY HIRSCHHORN AND THOMAS GILMORE[8]
> *Harvard Business Review*

In whatever form the redrawn boundaries may appear, we should not become
overly concerned with the traditional labels we use to describe the actors that
appear within their perimeters. An organization that was once a customer

may now appear to be a partner. Yesterday's partner may become a competitor. Indeed, it frequently occurs that a particular organization may be a customer, competitor and partner at the same time. Such a realization of apparent ambiguity can be a source of confusion. But it is simply explained, understood and managed, through a taxonomy that focuses on roles that are defined within a specific

> **The project perspective concentrates our attention on the meaningful *results* of projects, rather than on generic formal labels that once simplified, yet now have become simplistic.**

business activity. Such as taxonomy will regard a business as a collection of separate projects. Within this it becomes easy to accept that any actor can play a multiplicity of roles at the same time. By removing the requirement for every actor to maintain one specific role over all time, the apparent role ambiguity is removed. The project perspective concentrates our attention on the meaningful *results* of projects, rather than on generic formal labels that once simplified, yet now have become simplistic.

The twin concepts of (a) atomization into a set of projects, and, (b) the focus of attention on *results* rather than the means to achieve them, are fundamental also to *Future Work*. It is for this reason that *virtual teams* may be constructed, and indeed may produce excellent performance, yet – on a traditional basis – the roles that might be expected to construct them will be absent. These highly-effective teams may be comprised of individuals who are employed by apparently competing companies. For virtual teams, the speed of assembling and regrouping is so fast that a formal traditional model such as a joint venture would be too cumbersome to operate. It is the project taxonomy that enables us to comprehend and navigate a *virtual world of Future Work* in which results always claim the top priority.

For the manager, the challenge may be to introduce a recognition of *full-ripple economics* in a measured and appropriate way into the mission and strategy of the business. It is no longer a certainty that the more distant a stakeholder is along the chain, the less important they will be. For instance it is not impossible for some businesses to be brought to their knees by an environmental lobbying group. On the other hand *Future Work* may have much to offer 'remote' stakeholders, when issues such as traffic congestion and pollution are accounted for. A framework for accommodating the linkage between stakeholders and the business mission and social responsibility charter is to be found in Chapter 8.

CAREERS IN THE FUTURE WORK ORGANIZATION

We plant a seed in the company called *Future Work*. What shall we find when the spring comes? Will it flower? Will it survive? Will our plant find nourishment, will it propagate and take over our garden, or survive for just a single season and die? If we believe that it will survive, then who will tend the garden? The key questions are shown in Table 3.2.

Table 3.2 Questions of seeding and sustaining

Question	Issue
Seeding	Can *Future Work* prototypes be built within today's organization?
Sustainability	Will environmental mechanisms emerge that are needed in order to support the *sustained viability* of the *Future Work* organizations?

Given the growing wealth of case studies, there is now no question that seeding has already taken place. It is the second question that is of vital importance. Managers need to know what environmental assumptions are being planted into their business strategies as *Future Work* practices gain momentum. In adopting *Future Work* within their individual organizations, managers are in effect making demands and expecting responses at a wider macro level. Both managers and those in government will need to know whether these expectations can be met. We suggest that there are two determinants of sustainability. It is interesting again to note that both these constraints on *Future Work* feasibility involve individuals. They are:

- The extent of adoption of *Future Work* across organizations within an area prescribed by individual mobility.
- The feasibility of individual careers.

The critical question is whether it will be possible to populate *Future Work* organizations with people having the appropriate knowledge, competencies and skills that are required in order to work for them or with them. This is the 'Population Problem'. It quite simply asks:

- How many organizations will demand that people work in new ways?
- Will a sufficient number of trained and skilled people be available to work in the newly-emerging organizational forms, and
- If so, is it possible to demonstrate this by describing a typical career of such an individual?

The extent of adoption

The *Future Work* idea proclaims that tomorrow not all work will be of the traditional kind. The *population problem* questions how many *organizations* are able to adopt *Future Work* practices in order for the *practices* to remain viable over time.

Figure 3.5 suggests that only some work lends itself to *Future Work* implementation, and leads us to suggest that there is an optimum population of

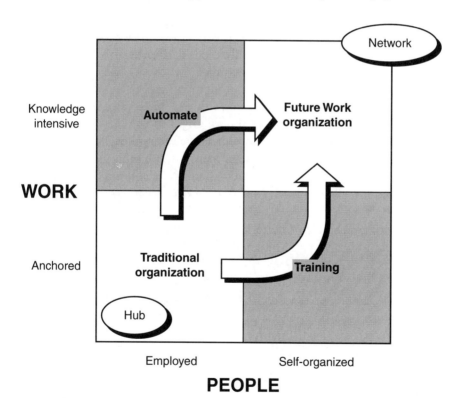

Figure 3.5 Routes to *Future Work* on the people-work matrix

The full migration to *Future Work* requires knowledge-intensive work to be carried out by self-organized people.

organizations, or divisions within a traditional organization, that adopt new practices. Below some number, a critical mass will not be achieved and the learning that is needed between adopting organizations will not easily flow. If a certain higher population number is exceeded, then the training and development of staff and the matching of people to work may become difficult. The association with a profession, although in some cases less relevant tomorrow, may demand a flow of people between the traditional and emerging organizational forms. The outsourced *Future Work* organization would seem to suffer the most exposure, offering less access for the individual to training and development, unless new ways can be found to deliver and acquire the required skills.

Automation

It is not especially difficult to imagine the migration of office-based work to a *Future Work* style. But are there certain types of work that can never become separated from a specific location nor be performed other than at a fixed time? We will briefly discuss the extent to which work may lend itself to a *Future Work* treatment.

Work that involves heavy capital equipment (e.g. in building construction or car manufacturing) may seem at first sight to offer little scope for adapting to a *Future Work* style. So, too, might direct work in the extraction sector. Let us take as an extreme example the physical mining of coal. Management history has a lot to say about, quite literally, working at the coal face. It may be surprising to discover here an early prototype of an effective and extremely efficient *networked organization.*

In their discussion about the 'element of choice and the mutual influence of technology and the social system', F. E. Emery and E. L. Trist[9] in *Socio-Technical Systems* overview more than a decade of early studies in the British coal mining industry. They contrast the difference between a conventional organization of work – in which there is a complex formal structure with simple work roles (the 'traditional hierarchy') – against a 'composite' system based on a simple formal structure and complex work roles ('team network'). Miners in the conventional group share no sense of belongingness and recognize no responsibility for the consequences of their actions to those outside their own *task* group. On the other hand, the relationships are quite different for those miners working in the composite system where there is strong commitment to the whole *group* task. These miners will be 'drawn into a variety of tasks in co-operation with different members of the total group . . . and . . . may be drawn into any task on the coal-face with any member of the total group'.

Writing as long ago as 1960, Emery and Trist establish an important vignette that relates technology (in its sense of how work is done) to human organizations, basing their discussion on an actual organizational change. Some allowance must be made for the special nature of the work location: the coal mine is a dangerous place and any supporting social context is sure to engender

> *Virtual reality* **can conjure up assets in unexpected places.**

some additional sense of safety in its workers. Nonetheless, when translated into the modern idiom, as individuals become more empowered, the networked form wins impressively over the traditional organization at the coal face. Analyzing data from E. L. Trist and H. Murray[10], the conclusion is that the 'networked' system produces 22 per cent more coal from each daily cut, requires almost no ancillary work, no additional labour, and it is extremely dependable in its flow of output.

Of course, it may appear that there is some limit in the extent to which *Future Work* could be able to reach out into these manufacturing and extraction industries, simply because of the physical nature of the work. But this, too, is changing. *Virtual reality* can conjure up assets in unexpected places. The possibility of *virtual surgery* is today being seriously discussed. One day, patients may not travel abroad to visit a specialist surgeon. They may instead be able to have the surgeon operate on them via an electronic network instead. It is not too difficult to see how, in a world of driver-less trains and autopilots, this idea could be applied to a coal mine using robots. Naturally, the work of these miners would be *virtual*. Their efforts would be visible at the mine, but they would be located elsewhere. The possibility we have described is in the separation of skill from physical labour and location (*see the 'Automate' arrow in Figure 3.5*).

Our new ability to distil human skill from work and exclude ourselves from the tasks of physical labour by delegating it to a machine is only to be expected. Has it not been a long-time aim of humanity to climb forever upwards on Maslow's[11] triangle, and have we not adopted technology as our tool to help us in achieving this? Surely, *Future Work* is nothing less than an inevitable consequence of our own aspirations? But in unleashing technology we have found that, left untamed, it possesses a force and a drive of its own. *Artificial intelligence* is a technology that offers to take the remaining human skills, distil them even further and then migrate them also into the province of the robot. If this were to happen, then what of work itself?

As automation offers the opportunity, and the choice, to migrate work to a *Future Work* style we have found an apparently unchallenged force that is attempting to draw new boundaries. Behind this force lies an unfettered power taxonomy. As assets become virtual and as human labour becomes less relevant in the performance of work, so the traditional Marxist divisions and dynamics between the ownership of capital and the provision labour erode. Economics has become stressed with the advent of social atomization; we consider politics to be under similar stress from *Future Work*.

Training

As *Future Work* requires people to be more self-organized, it will suit some more than others. 'Self-organized' will mean the ability to work in a temporary project style, in a more flexible way, and may in some cases require people to dissolve some of their established boundaries between home and work with which they have become comfortable. It may be possible to develop some of the required skills through training, together with competence development through an appraisal system acting as a lever of organizational change.

Future Work therefore requires a coincidence of certain kinds of work and certain kinds of people. It is not applicable to all. *Future Work* may depend on the existence of the traditional organization from where the training and development of its people may have to take place. As *Future Work* grasps a greater share of all work, the limitation on its uptake may be in the mobility of individuals to migrate between its structure and the traditional organization. A very large organization may have an advantage in being able to adopt both styles of work within itself. We show in Figure 3.5 how the 'network' and 'hub' arrangement that we describe in Chapter 4 can involve mixed styles within such an organization.

TODAY'S BOUNDARIES

The structural changes that are needed to create tomorrow's organization out of today's imply a redrawing of boundaries. We have already touched on some social and political areas within and around which boundaries are already shifting.

It is important to identify which boundaries may need to shift and how moveable they may be. We are also interested in important boundaries already in motion.

Within the supply chain, Larry Hirschhorn and Thomas Gilmore cite four *psychological boundaries* that they see as important in a shift towards flexible work. These are:

- Authority boundary – *Who is in charge of what?*
- Task boundary – *Who does what?*
- Political boundary – *What's in it for us?*
- Identity boundary – *Who is, and isn't, 'us'?*

In addition to these boundaries, we now describe the effects of some other important taxonomies that are redrawing boundaries in the wider setting of the company.

A taxonomy of professions

One fundamental taxonomy inside the traditional organization is expressed in how it chooses to divide labour. This is normally mirrored on the organization chart. Historically we fit the organization into a broad framework to include finance, operations, personnel and marketing and so on. The IT function has recently become added to this list, and/or is to be found under Finance or Operations.

Professional careers create and maintain their own 'boundaries' within the organization which reinforce 'functional' divisions. Professional careers permeate and spread their boundaries across and throughout whole industries. The demise of the 'job-for-life' expectation of workers, and some *Future Work* ideas challenge these traditional boundaries. So, too, do process-based organizational transforms, especially those that demand generalists rather than specialists, as they cut right across these boundaries.

The organization has shaped the professions, and the professions have imprinted their shape onto the traditional organization. To the extent that professions recognize archetypical career paths, the expectations of their members have reinforced traditional functional boundaries. The recent popularity for professional bodies to supplement examination proficiency at a point in time with Continuing Professional Development (CPD) has extended their reach to embrace a longer span of time in the individual's working life. It is hard to see how, with only the exception of a few extremely talented individuals, this arrangement will encourage and support multiprofessional careers.

Single-profession, or 'boilerplate' careers have already come under pressure in a changed business environment. Career structures are already starting to respond and adapt to some extent. In arguing for a 'career-resilient workforce' in which a current employer takes some responsibility for the future career of an employee after they have left the company, Waterman *et. al.* explain:

> 'People mourn its passing: the long time covenant between employee and employer. We remember fondly the days when IBM could offer lifetime employment. . . most of us understood that respectable companies would offer at least a measure of job security in exchange for adequate performance and some exhibition of loyalty. No longer. . . . most people and most companies now hardened by down-sizings, de-layerings, right-sizings, layoffs, and restructurings, have concluded that the old covenant is null. . .
>
> The usual view of a career path must change. In the old days it pretty much meant sticking with one company and rising in one speciality area. These days, both companies and employees are healthier if employees have multiple skills, if they can move easily across functional boundaries . . . and if they feel comfortable moving on when the right fit within the company can no longer be found. . .
>
> The switch from career dependence to career resilience is not only important but also inevitable.'
>
> ROBERT WATERMAN, JUDITH WATERMAN AND BETSY COLLARD[12]
> *Harvard Business Review*

We argue that the traditional specialist single-profession career structure is less important and less relevant within the modern organization due to several pressures, not least of which is the demand made on individuals and organizations to have a greater 'all-round' or even an holistic perspective. Any move away from a specialist single-profession career path may tend to relax constraints that otherwise might impede a shift towards the uptake of *Future Work*.

The outsourcing taxonomy

Outsourcing – the outside placement of work that had been performed within the organization – is often explained in terms of the need for businesses to concentrate on their core activities. In this view, the purpose of outsourcing is to concentrate added-value by retaining and developing the core business while buying in the non-core services. The idea is attractive if these newly-created markets of outsourced suppliers are large enough, and therefore sufficiently cost competitive, to offer an overall net gain once the redistribution of

> **Outsourcing is also becoming a vital ingredient in organizational development and restructuring.**

risk together with the loss of control that is attached to buying-in rather than owning outright, are calculated. One problem with the 'core' idea is that very often businesses will not know what the elements of their core business actually are, and more importantly what it may one day *become* within a newly-developing strategy. In some cases, today's non-core activity may be tomorrow's crown jewels. As in statistical theory there are two kinds of error that can be made: keeping what is not needed, and disposing of that which should have been kept. The *risk of divestment* starts to become apparent once the organization has already outsourced its garden maintenance, staff restaurant and security facilities.

Outsourcing is also becoming a vital ingredient in organizational development and restructuring. During any major change the established organization must at the same time:

- Plan change.
- Introduce change.
- Continue to manage the business profitably.

Such an organization will be very stretched. Perhaps the most stretched resource will be its managers. Outsourcing offers a way of concentrating scarce management effort into making progress in the important priority activities of change whilst retaining the momentum of the business.

For the employee, outsourcing represents a structural unfreezing. The opportunity to gain more knowledge or learn new skills may provide an opportunity to part company with a rigid professional career path. The new outsource industry may be more receptive to flexible work ideas. The individual may decide to become self-employed (*see* Figure 3.6), working on a fixed-term contract basis, and the *Future Work* knowledge-worker may become *self-organized*. The steps from self-employed to self-managed and self-organized forms of work become possible for the very same reasons that organizations may now become virtual. Virtual assets enable a self-employed individual to compete with a traditional organization.

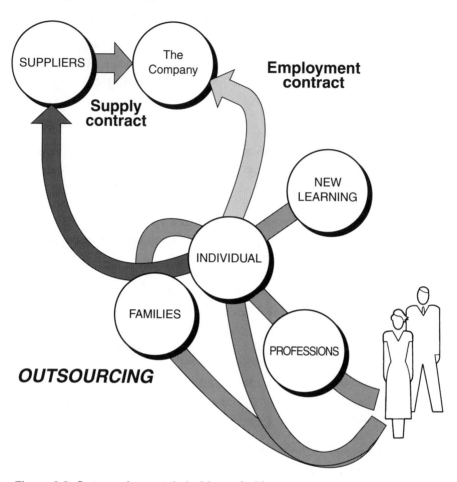

Figure 3.6 Outsourcing – stakeholder switching

The dissolving national taxonomy

'There are no longer Japanese companies or American companies or German companies. We all compete in a single global market. Japanese executives carry American Express cards. Hondas are built in the US. British Airways flies tourists to Spain. Italian banks finance Canadian paper companies.

People, products, technologies, money and ideas know no national boundaries.'

TOMMASOS ZANZOTTO[13]
Chairman and Chief Executive
Hilton International

The ability for work to travel unhindered across national borders (*the Offshore Office in Chapter 2*), is not new. In this endeavour it has been big business not technology that has been paving the way. As long ago as the 1970s, the multinationals as described

> **Language has already become the new taxonomy for the location of knowledge-work.**

by Tugendhat[14] were able to draw their boundaries across national frontiers and transfer assets without much hindrance from national governments, even the home government. Big businesses have already imprinted their own taxonomy on their world, replacing the familiar lines of 'political geography' that are found in textbooks. The difference today is one of enfranchisement. Within a context of a power shift towards the individual and the pervasiveness and affordability of IT, the door is beginning to open for the smaller operator. Virtual assets are able not only to make an individual appear to be a company (*the Virtual Corporation concept*). If they so wish, a network of individuals can appear as a multinational company – *The Virtual Multinational*.

The axis of language

Language has already become the new taxonomy for the location of knowledge-work. One new axis of work spans New York, Barbados, Co. Kerry, The Highlands and Islands of Scotland, Bombay, Singapore and beyond. Another, places Martinique, Guadeloupe and Paris within the same domain. In the emerging global world of *Future Work*, it is *language* rather than national boundary that defines where work is done.

Training for national advantage

The territory we enter is truly uncharted. What appears to be emerging is a supranational economic system that can act independently of any strongly recognizable political or legislative framework. In terms of the allocation of work, there really do appear to be no apparent political boundaries in evidence. The implications for national competitive advantage seem clear. The challenge at the national level – to the extent that this is still a valid concept – is to identify unique differentiators within the native-language segment of its market. The simple truth seems to be that national advantage in an era of *Future Work* will come about through an innovative and skilled pool of resident knowledge-workers linked by a common culture and language.

Management summary

- There is a growing need to expand our concept of *the company*. One challenge is to identify and include extended stakeholders.

- We are witnessing the disappearance of some old boundaries as new ones are being drawn.

- The company has found itself at the focus of both historic as well as newly-emerging taxonomies and needs a way to navigate these.

- By using virtual assets, and as part of a wider shift of power, the knowledge-based self-organized individual emerges as a competitor to the traditional corporation.

- There are issues surrounding the long-term viability of *Future Work*. We have identified the extent of adoption and the sustainability of individual careers to be key factors in determining this.

- Technology is beginning to relocate work along axes of language and competence regardless of national frontiers of boundaries.

References

1 HUTTON, WILL. 'Red alert on green concerns', *Management Today*, Jan. 1995, pp.28–30.
2 PANCUCCI, DOM. 'Teleworking study focuses on health', *Computing*, 20 October 1994, p.43.
3 PETERS, TOM *quoted in* The Economist, 4 March, 1989.
4 CAMPBELL, ANDREW. 'What is business for?', *Strategic Society Planning News*, November 1988, p.7
5 GOETHE, JOHANN WOLFGANG VON, attributed to him.
6 KINNOCK, NEIL. *Tribune*, 1975.
7 HOBSBAWM, ERIC. *The Age of Extremes: the short 20th. century 1914–1991*, Michael Joseph, 1994.
8 HIRSCHHORN, LARRY AND GILMORE, THOMAS. 'The New Boundaries of the "Boundaryless" Company', *Harvard Business Review*, May–June 1992, pp.104–115.
9 EMERY, F. E. AND TRIST, E. L. 'Socio-Technical Systems', in *Emery 1969*. Also *in* Churchman, C. W. and Verhulst, M. (eds.), *Management Science, Models and Techniques*, vol.2, Pergamon,1960, pp.83-97.
10 TRIST, E. L. AND MURRAY, H. 'Work organization at the coal face: a comparative study of mining systems', Tavistock Institute of Human Relations, doc. no. 506, 1948.
11 MASLOW, A. H. *Motivation and Personality*, Harper and Row, New York, 1954.
12 WATERMAN, ROBERT H., WATERMAN, JUDITH A., AND COLLARD, BETSY A. 'Towards a Career-Resilient Workforce', Harvard Business Review, July–August 1994, p.87–95.
13 ZANZOTTO, TOMMASOS, in correspondence with the authors, 1995.
14 TUGENDHAT, CHRISTOPHER. *The Multinationals*, Penguin, 1971.

Further Reading

CHECKLAND, PETER. Systems Thinking, Systems Practice, Wiley, 1984.

CHURCHMAN, C. WEST. The Design of Enquiring Systems: Basic Concepts of System and Organization, Basic Books, New York, 1971.

CHURCHMAN, C. WEST. *The Systems Approach*, Delacorte Press, 1968.

ELDRIDGE, J. E. T. AND CROMBIE, A. D. *A Sociology of Organisations*, Studies in Sociology, George Allen & Unwin, London, 1974, Chapter 2, 'Defining and Labelling Organisations', pp.21–36.

EMERY, F. E. AND TRIST, E. L. 'The causal texture of organizational environments', *Human Relations*, 1965.

HAMPDEN-TURNER, CHARLES, PETERS, TOM AND JAIKUMAR, JAY. 'The Boundaries of Business: Commentaries from the Experts', *Harvard Business Review*, Sept–Oct 1991, pp.93–103.

KUHN, T. *Structure of Scientific Revolutions*, University of Chicago Press, 1962.

LEWIN, KURT. Field Theory in Social Science: Selected Theoretical Papers, Tavistock, 1952.

SIMON, HERBERT A. 'The Organization of Complex Systems', *Hierarchy Theory: The Challenge of Complex Systems*, H. H. Pattee (ed.), New York, G. Braziller, 1973.

'The predominant form of organization in the Industrial Economy, the divisionalized functional hierarchy , is characterized by a set of management principles centred around the notion of an hierarchy: chain of command, span of control, paper-based memo communications, and so forth. This organizational structure is slowly giving way to an alternative structure, termed the "network" structure, characterized by an alternative set of management principles: point-to-point electronic-based communication, teams, and strategic alliances. The network structure is more appropriate for leveraging information technology.'

P. BRADLEY, J. A. HAUSMAN AND R. L. NOLAN

Globalization, Technology and Competition – The Fusion of Computers and Telecommunications in the 1990s, Harvard Business School Press, Boston, Massachusetts, 1993.

4

NETWORKING: THE FUTURE ORGANIZATION FORM

INTRODUCTION

As organizations, responding to increasing global competition, strive to become fast, flat, flexible and open, the concept of the networked organization has taken hold. Whether to create new business opportunities, improve overall effectiveness or just to provide business intelligence, networking is a concept reborn in the 1990s.

In this chapter we will examine the impact that technology is having on the emerging networked organization; we will look at the various forms that can be found and the part each can play in enhancing organizational performance. We will also

Networking is not in fact a new phenomenon but rather an age-old concept.

examine the organization design issues to be considered in transforming the value chains of business in this way.

Our aim in this chapter is to brief the reader on developments in organizational transformation to the networked form. It leads us to present an indication of organization readiness to move to an alternative form.

NETWORKING OPPORTUNITIES

Networking is not in fact a new phenomenon but rather an age-old concept. It has been present for many years in the English language in expressions such as 'the old school tie' and in a business context through organizations such as professional institutes, craft guilds and trade associations. We can all identify networks of personal contacts which we use to support organizational as well as personal needs. Personal networks within and outside the organization provide information, give support, are used to progress career and serve many other purposes. Some are formal such as professional associations. But much networking is not in any way formalized and inside the organization the complex web of networks form what would usually be referred to as the *informal organization*. There has always been a tension, even in the most highly bureaucratized organizations, between the 'formal' and 'informal' organization. It is widely recognized that without its informal networks the organization would not be able to function. Also, it has long been recognized that for executive management the existence of strong informal networks across the organization can have advantages when trying to push through decisions as well as presenting them with hurdles to be overcome.

At the level of the organization, businesses have always maintained networks of suppliers and customers. In many economies these business relations have traditionally been strong and lasting. It is only in relatively recent times that purchasing decisions have been put on a more 'objective' basis and been dominated by price competition and only then in certain cultural settings. Traditionally much business was done between companies based on a high level of trust and co-operation and little in the way of legal formality between them. The intensification of competition was a major factor leading companies in many western countries to focus on the savings to be gained by squeezing suppliers and increasing the level of competition between them. Relations between points in the supply chain have tended to become adversarial as the legislative framework for controlling relationships has been developed and at the same time purchasers have sought to squeeze costs out of the system thereby maximizing short-term gain. Despite this tendency some well-known examples exist of companies that have maintained strong relationships with key suppliers and worked with them in *partnership,* improving overall performance within their supply chain. Most notable amongst these is Marks and Spencer Plc in the UK.

However, over the last few years we have seen dramatic changes in the opportunities available for people to network for their own personal benefit as well as that of their organizations. Networking has been promoted by governments and trade bodies at both a national and international level as a means for aiding economic development and the well-being of business. As an example of thinking at the policy level, effective networking between companies is seen as essential in getting the rapid transfer, deployment and exploitation of technology. Governments have provided seed corn in the way of grants to stimulate networking e.g. the EU's programmes such as SPRINT. Business is encouraged to be more outward looking; to become more aware of developments and opportunities as well as its own competitive position. Governments look to networks to provide input into policy-making by representing the collective voice and opinion of various constituent bodies.

Technology supporting networking

It is highly probable that the factor having greatest impact on the scale of networking, taking place at all levels in organizations, is the use of electronic communications which, once widely accessible, enable the creation and maintenance of networks with great ease and at low cost. The communications technology available and being used to facilitate inter- and intra-organization networking is in many forms, and designed to meet many different purposes. For example, Internet which gives users access to a worldwide network of information and mail services is said to be growing at 1 million users per month (*Financial Times*[1], 25 November, 1994) and at such a rate that if maintained everyone on the planet would be connected by the year 2003 (*Sunday Times*[2], 20 November, 1994). However no one actually knows the rate of growth because it is impossible to monitor. Advanced software is now available to make this worldwide interaction ever easier and more sophisticated. New services are emerging which give cheap access to Internet for business and other purposes. These open up at the press of a button the opportunity for information retrieval direct from most universities and research establishments as well as access to a worldwide web of expertise and interests. Even more advanced applications are now feasible based on combinations of voice mail, video conferencing and data transmission, including applications such as remote surgery using video conferencing and remote sensing devices which simulate for the surgeon the performance of the actual surgical instruments even though many miles distant.

> **Electronic Data Interchange (EDI) is revolutionizing the way of operating between businesses.**

Electronic Data Interchange (EDI) is revolutionizing the way of operating between businesses. Transmitting orders between business in support of just-in-time delivery is just one of many low level applications on systems which allow sophisticated logistics management systems to be implemented. Tracking of goods through the supply chain is now feasible for any organization at a relatively low cost and companies such as Federal Express depend upon such systems to track each individual packet as it progresses through the worldwide delivery network.

This capability to manage the interface better between businesses in what has been described as the supply chain, but perhaps more accurately seen as the value network or constellation, has enabled some businesses to gain significant competitive advantage. There are examples of businesses that have successfully stolen a march over competitors and even new companies that have emerged to challenge large corporations in their core markets.

Many organizations are taking the opportunity to review what actual business they wish to be in, focus on core activity and manage those elements which are non-core by contracting work to a network of suppliers, both first and second tier. This process is made more practical in many situations by powerful communications links. It also leads to the development of a complex web of relationships which can be described as the *networked organization*.

THE NETWORKED ORGANIZATION

Towards a definition

The networked organization was described by R. E. Miles and C. C. Snow[3] as a cluster of firms, specialist units or individuals co-ordinated by market mechanisms rather than chains of command. H. Bahrami[4] describes it as 'more akin to a federation or a constellation of business units that are typically interdependent, relying on one another for critical expertise and know-how and having a peer relationship with the centre'. He then sees the role of the centre as the orchestration of broad strategic vision, provision of a shared organizational and administrative infrastructure and ensuring a unity of mission and purpose. However, each business will see itself as the centre of its own unique network within its own value chain.

The networked organization was depicted as in Figure 4.1 by Gareth Morgan[5] in his book *Creative Organization Theory*. Model 6 contrasts sharply with the notion of a traditional hierarchy. It also contrasts sharply with the concept of the vertically integrated supply chain which many organizations have striven to achieve as its strategy for reducing uncertainty in the supply market. The latter strategy is based on financial domination and control of key elements in the supply chain. Conversely, the form depicted by Gareth Morgan is a much more fluid set of arrangements between companies within a network of trading arrangements. The hub company may well at any time be competing with a particular company in some areas while at the same time co-operating in others. Some suppliers will be closely tied into the network but others will be on the fringe with much looser relationships with the hub. Included within these suppliers will be the peripheral workforce referred to by C. Handy[6] in his book *The Future of Work*. This may well include former full-time employees whose skills, whilst still of value to the organization, are no longer so essential that they need to reside within the core.

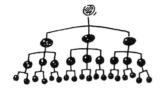

Model 1: The rigid bureaucracy

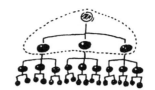

Model 2: The bureaucracy with
a senior 'management' team

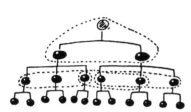

Model 3: The bureaucracy with
project teams and
task forces.

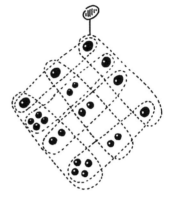

Model 4: The matrix organization

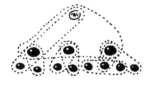

Model 5: The project
organization

Model 6: The loosely-coupled
organic network

Figure 4.1 The emerging networked organization

The network will be in a constant state of flux, adjusting to the changing
needs of the hub as it services its dynamic customer base. In this model,
however, customers themselves are also viewed as part of the network. Flows
of information between elements of the network are vital for effective strategic direction at the hub and this information system and the data it holds
may well be seen as one of the principal assets arising from this network.

This unique network of relationships may well be the basis of a company's competitive advantage. It certainly is of sufficient value to the business for it to need to understand its operation and potential for development and exploitation.

Electronic communication is making possible speedy dialogue across the network in any direction as well as facilitating broadcast messages from any point to all members, opening up the possibility of interactions between all actors within the network. As we saw earlier, this is fast becoming a reality as the result of a number of converging forces – the confluence of two economic trends, the declining cost of computing and of long-distance communications, further compounded by the intensification of global competition and the desire for greater employee empowerment. The hub, even if it ever did have the ability, certainly can no longer control the lines of communication tightly within the network. Furthermore, the orderly network shown in Figure 4.1 may be extended to give a more complete picture as shown in Figure 4.2, where it is depicted as something that looks like a tangled spider's web. This new networking capability poses some very interesting questions for managers within organizations.

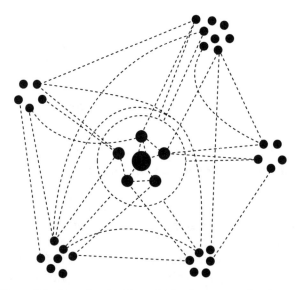

Figure 4.2 The spider's web of networks in the networked organizations

Network configurations

The consequences of the type of development just described are already observable. Applications based on the transmission across networks of routine business transactions such as printing pay cheques, writing invoices, bill payment and making reservations were among the first to be economic to automate. In early phases of IT adoption the emphasis in many organizations has been on automating existing routine operations. But of greater significance, those businesses that have become leaders rather than followers in applying technology in high-value applications have been successful in gaining short-term competitive advantage by developing innovatively electronic networks in close support of their business goals. Many examples are cited in the popular press. One of the best known and early examples is American Airline's booking system, Sabre, which is now worth more than the airline that first developed it. This on-line booking service is available in travel agencies which are connected electronically. A key feature of such a system is the opportunity created to sell bookings on the parent airline. These type of systems have been developed further by companies that have set out to adopt Electronic Data Interchange (EDI) with their key suppliers and in consequence looked closely at their purchasing policy – with a view to identifying those key suppliers with whom they wish to work more closely – and adopt a co-operative model of strategic partnering to govern their relationships. However this is just one form of what might be seen as the networked organization; one in which new ways of doing business have been developed but technology has been adopted essentially in support of traditional approaches to managing organizations.

Another observable form of networking is seen in organizations that have set about using free-text applications to develop electronic communities crossing time and space boundaries. These systems may have facilities such as e-mail, bulletin boards, structured electronic conferencing and workflow management systems. However, they are embarking on a route which is likely to lead to fundamental questioning of the assumptions underlying their structure and working practices.

A further distinct form is apparent in organizations which have taken a deliberate decision to focus on core activities and set about using electronic networks to manage the outsourcing of those aspects of their work which are non-core. These organizations are taking the advice of 'sticking to the knitting' by contracting out a range of activities which are not central to their business and in areas where there are more effective providers than their own in-house operations. By contracting out in this way they would often be seeking to release capital for areas of business development where they are aiming to be 'best-in-class', or setting out to provide competition for internally provided services as a means of testing the internal efficiency. Most excitingly, in some instances, those engaged in setting up new enterprises are adopting this form in its extreme, involving the minimum of personnel in the core and creating the ultimate networked organization which is then defined as the *virtual corporation*. These organizations are challenging many of our basic assumptions about how best to conduct business and manage the wealth creating activities within our societies.

The basis of the networked organization – people and technology

The networked organization then can be seen as having two distinct components. The first is the technology infrastructure which allows the transfer of packets of electronic information and enables the speedy transfer of information between pre-defined points on the network. The second component of the networked organization is the social aspect, the people on the network and how they use it to interact.

The application of networks is described by Lee Sproull and Sara Kiesler[7] in their book *Connections – New Ways of Working in the Networked Organization*, shown in Figure 4.3. An important point to make about many of these electronic communications systems is that just like traditional mail services the communications, unlike the traditional telephone, can be accessed by the participants at their own convenience – many of these systems are 'store and forward', i.e. ('asynchronous') as opposed to 'real time' (synchronous). However, unlike the telephone where discussions are instantaneous and ephemeral, there is a record of the communication stored for as long as either of the parties wish it to be so. Importantly this is the basis of *memory* for the virtual corporation. and has the potential for easy and quick access by the workforce so as to enhance their own performance and that of the overall operation.

The networked organization then can be seen as having two distinct components. The first is the technology infrastructure which allows the transfer of packets of electronic information and enables the speedy trans-

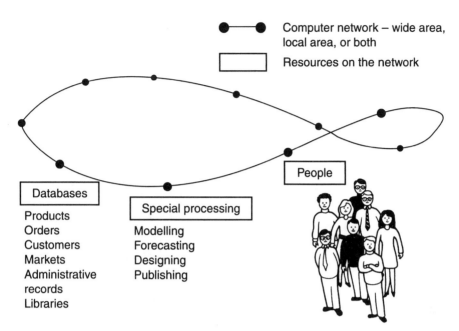

Figure 4.3 The electronic network

fer of information between pre-defined points on the network. The second component of the networked organization is the social aspect, the people on the network and how they use it to interact. Figure 4.3 shows how both databased and idea-based communication can be supported by one technological network. However, it cannot be overemphasized that the form of networking activity in the organization and beyond will be determined, not by the technology, but by people, whether decision-makers or users. Those responsible for overall design and operations management will have a major impact on how the network develops and the extent to which it is supportive of the long-term business intent; those having access to it as users will determine how it gets used within the constraints imposed by the designers.

EXAMPLES OF THE NETWORKED ORGANIZATION

Type 1 – JIT communications in the stable network

The first category described above of technology application in the networked organization is its use to transmit formatted information between

Exhibit 4.1 EDI in the supermarket chain

Case Study 1: Electronic Data Interchange in supermarket chain

Background:
- Tesco – at the time was one of the largest food retailer in the UK.
- Over 400 stores with more than 8 million customers served weekly.
- Over 25,000 weekly orders.
- A highly competitive industry where cutting lead times and just-in-time delivery could improve competitive edge.

EDI introduction:
- 1980s saw the rationalization of distribution routes with the development of central distribution depots.
- Early 1980s saw adoption of magnetic tapes for receipt of store invoices from major suppliers resulting in reduction in number of queries and reduced administration costs for all parties.
- 1984 introduced transmission of orders direct to suppliers via leased lines which resulted in reduced lead times from suppliers and reduced stock levels in stores.
- Joined TRADANET – a third party value-added network – to supply EDI.
- A pilot in 1988 involved five suppliers. This grew to 1000 by 1992 and included suppliers in many parts of the EU.
- Data exchange included:
  - pricing information
  - the supply of historical and forecast demand data
  - provisional and final orders
- Planned data exchange
  - proof of delivery and any refusal delivery notification
  - invoicing
  - payment.
- E-mail facilitated communications.

Business impact:
- Reduced administrative costs through automation.
- Reduced error rates and speedier handling of queries.
- Prompt and consistent payment of suppliers.
- Improved relations with suppliers as those directly involved have contact.
- Joint working improved supply chain performance.

Issues in setting up EDI:
- High level management commitment behind the development.
- Communications at all levels during the development.
- Sound project management was put in place.
- Supplier understanding through communications.
- Support for suppliers particularly sme's without the in-house resources to introduce EDI themselves.
- An effective audit trail had to be in place.
- The project itself generated considerable duplicated effort and additional work which had to be resourced.
- Trust had to be developed in the accuracy of system-generated information.
- Costs and benefits needed to be monitored.

Exhibit 4.2 Networking supporting international engineering design

Case Study 2: Creating an international design capability

Background:
- John Brown Engineering Ltd is part of Trafalgar House Plc, a large and diverse organization including property, hotels, shipping and engineering interests.
- John Brown has over 150 sites in over 30 countries where it is involved in designing, constructing and commissioning engineering plant.

Systems:
- It has developed its own high capacity telecommunications network, JOIN.
- It has developed ENGINES, an Oracle based database, that provides the necessary infrastructure for CAD systems to relate to each other.
- The network supports voice, facsimile, electronic mail and video conferencing across country offices and construction sites.
- JOIN now facilitates the concurrent engineering of projects from anywhere in the world.
- The redefinition of computer aided engineering by creating rules-based CAD systems on relational databases as well as project management systems has introduced 'best-of-breed' applications to run over the open infrastructure.
- There are now 8,000 PCs, 600 workstations and 150 UNIX servers on the network.

Outcomes:
- Virtual teams can be created for projects comprising people located throughout the world.
- The impact of workload peaks and troughs on the labour force can now be reduced by distributing work throughout offices worldwide.
- Work can be distributed to the most cost-efficient part of the organization.
- Clients can be offered a 'total capability' with confidence from the local office even though it might in itself be small – 'creating scale without mass'.
- The company can interoperate with the client's own systems and data.
- Projects can be progressed 24 hours in each day by moving work between locations.
- Considerable cost savings have been achieved.

Additional benefits:
- Clients have adopted John Brown's systems for their own business. This has improved *partnering* possibilities and increased the likelihood of additional project work.
- The systems have led to, and supported the development of, consistent best practice throughout the John Brown design offices, not by imposition but rather by encouraging conformity and the use of 'expert systems' to ensure consistency in quality.

points in the network. We suggested that this type of network can be developed to pass information about sales, invoicing, inventory, accounting and other routine data between nodes on the network. The first case study described here gives an example of the application of Electronic Data Interchange (EDI).

In the supermarket case study we see an example of a company that has used technology to connect its suppliers, its distribution function and its stores. Operating in a highly competitive industry, one area where cost savings can be made is in the lead time between order and delivery to the customer. EDI is seen as a tool which enables managers to be proactive and make pre-emptive decisions to minimize the problems associated with controlling the flow of goods through the supply chain. Notable reductions in delivery lead times have been achieved from supplier to store – seven days to under 24 hours for many products.

Electronic mail was not a major feature in this first case study although it has an important role to play in sharing information and ideas in problem solving. EDI permits the transfer of routine data; electronic mail supports the application by enabling queries to be raised and discussions to take place in arriving at solutions – the non-routine activities.

The second case introduces an international design and construction organization which has set out to gain competitive advantage by being able to offer clients a *local office worldwide* which gives access to the total organization's capability around the world without the local office having to bear the overhead associated with having the people present locally. By moving design around the globe the organization can smooth out the work demands more effectively, obtain ready access for clients needing top level expertise, introduce more standardization in working methods and generally offer the client a more efficient and effective service.

Type 2 – the connected community forming the dynamic network

The capability to send free text messages over networks makes possible electronic mail and a range of other applications often referred to as computer-based or computer-mediated communications. These not only include mail which is essentially one-to-one but also one-to-group systems such as bulletin boards and electronic conferencing. These systems use computer text processing tools and computer networks to provide high speed message processing and exchange. Unlike data processing applications that typically manipulate fixed-format numerical data, electronic mail lets people use free-format natural language in their messages to one another. These systems have now been further developed into a new generation of Windows-based *groupware* products designed to enable groups to function more effectively.

The third and fourth case studies illustrate the development of the networked organization based on the creation of a groupware infrastructure which gives those within the network easy access to good networking technology and information services.

The third case is based on a community of academics and students. During the first phase of network development, there has been no compulsion on students or academics to join and use the network. It is available to support learners but they have to bear the costs of establishing links and on-going communications. It is also available to course managers to enable them to engage new faculty in teaching by giving access to the system from wherever they are based. The benefits have to be sold by the provider of the educational programmes and the system is managed centrally to provide services related to the personal development of participants. The strategy adopted is one of persuasion based on the perception of added-value created by membership of the network. The real benefits of the system will only be realized when it has been integrated into both programme design and delivery. This requires a thorough understanding of pedagogy such that design can take full advantage of the technology in order to provide solutions meeting learner needs.

The fourth case demonstrates a rather different application. The system has been put in place by the senior management to support clear business objectives. However, it has been implemented into a culture where traditionally much work has been done independently by consultants who do not normally willingly share information about clients and specific projects – their reward system tends to mitigate against such sharing. However, changing competitive pressures are forcing them to develop new co-operative ways of working. Use of the system is again left to the individual consultants. By channelling important communications through the network rather than using more traditional means management will encourage use; clear adoption by the senior partners can also promote the new style of working.

Both case examples show how technology can be used to support major change in the way of doing business which would have a major impact on traditional organization and practice. In both cases the technological infrastructure is in place and users are being encouraged to develop its innovative uses to enhance business opportunities.

Exhibit 4.3 Networking in a training community

Case Study 3: Developing a distributed international training network

Background:
- Henley Management College is a provider of management programmes leading to MBAs offered through distance learning.
- It offers programmes worldwide and works with partners in over 20 countries.
- It aims to provide an internationally based MBA using inputs from around the world in the design and delivery of programmes.
- Students need not only distance learning materials but also support to help them develop their understanding and ability to apply their learning.

Groupware implementation:
- A computer mediated communications system was introduced in 1988 to provide electronic tutor support, tutorials and information services – the electronic business school.
- A major review of activities in 1993 led to the adoption of a Windows-based groupware system – *LotusNotes*.
- Students, administrative support and tutors are connected into the system.
- Access is available 24 hours each day from home via modem or from the office via modem or through internal electronic networks (LANs connected to an X25 link).
- Workshops, help lines, electronic mail, conferences and information services are available.
- Tutors have the opportunity to discuss the development of the programme and course materials.
- The network of partners have facilities to assist in the management of the programme and its development.

Outcomes:
- A wide range of level of take-up is apparent between, on the one hand the enthusiasts, then the 'lurkers' (those who observe discussion and don't join in) and finally the non-participants who never connect.
- Considerable use is made of informal forums, e.g. coffee rooms for wide-ranging discussions of a serious and less serious nature.
- Opportunities for adding new facilities such as access to searching remote databases, group problem-solving applications, design of management databases have been identified by users as they have become familiar with the system and spotted opportunities.

Exhibit 4.4 Networking in management consultancy

> ### Case Study 4: Re-engineering a consultancy by supportive networking
>
> **Background:**
> - Price Waterhouse with as many as 50,000 employees in over 450 offices in 113 countries.
> - Accounting/finance and general business consulting.
> - Aims to provide multifunctional service in operational consulting and related implementation.
> - Relationship building with clients is important.
> - Consultants need latest information on changing regulations and interpretation.
> - Skills dispersed around the world but need to combine for specific assignments.
> - Need to re-engineer the proposal stage of projects to meet reducing client deadlines.
> - Need to access earlier projects to understand methodologies and see outcomes.
> - Client contact lists need to be accessible to a range of people.
>
> **Groupware introduction:**
> - Championed by a senior executive with the vision.
> - 1989 decision to raise the technology to *state of the art*.
> - All consultants are linked using groupware including a client tracking system.
>
> **Business impact:**
> - Success in obtaining new work under short deadlines.
> - Information overload avoided by careful management of the system – keeping databases well organized and clear of confusing and irrelevant material.
> - Best practice is now accessible to all consultants wherever based.

The fifth case is rather different. It demonstrates how a young business based on knowledge work is using technology to develop an organization which could be described as a *virtual organization*. It is focusing on using its intellectual skills rather than creating a service organization to deliver and support its software products. It is using the networking to link its suppliers and its customers. It is able to remain dynamic and flexible by maintaining a very small core but having access through its network to highly-skilled resources to support its business moves.

Exhibit 4.5 A dynamic software company at the hub of its service delivery

---

Case Study 5: The small company challenging the giants

Background:
- *Common Knowledge* is a specialist software company based near Stanford University in Palo Alto, Northern California.
- Its main product is a system called *Arrange* which is sold to businesses of all sizes and all around the globe.

Management philosophy:
- To maintain as small and tight an infrastructure as possible so as to concentrate on 'staying alive'.

The organization:
- It has an office which on any one day probably has no more than four staff present.
- It outsources everything that it considers is not essential to its core business:
  - distribution and package manufacture is outsourced
  - technical support for its product is outsourced.
- High-level programming is carried out by people working from home.

The use of technology in managing the business:
- Telephone queries into the office are rerouted by the switchboard to the right person wherever based.
- Demonstration copies of the software are distributed through Internet and Compuserve so that users can trial before they purchase.
- The company has its own space on Internet where it handles user queries and provides tips, updates and new versions at low distribution costs.
- Its programmers are linked electronically.

Outcomes:
- The company successfully sells and supports its products worldwide.
- It maintains low fixed costs and can compete with suppliers with much greater resource backing.

Type 3 – managing non-core activities, the internal network

The sixth and final case study in this section describes a utility company which is developing itself as a knowledge-based organization. It is contracting out all activities which are not essential to undertake internally and

Exhibit 4.6 Internal networks in a privatized utility

Case Study 6: The developing organization of a utility company

Background:
- Yorkshire Water is a recently privatized UK organization which for many years had been in public ownership.
- Its customer base is the many individual households as well as commercial and industrial premises which are in its region of operation.
- Within its territory it has a monopoly although its pricing is under the control of a national regulator.
- Its business is the provision of clean and waste water services.

The networked organization:
- The need to cut costs to meet the targets set by the regulator has led to a major strategic review of the business.
- The organization is striving to become flexible in order to be proactive in facing its changing economic environment.
- Its core activities have been identified as:
  - dealing with the customer and managing the customer interface
  - process management and the management of functionality
  - the management of the economic regulation of the industry.
- In the field of technology the emphasis is upon planning implementation of change rather than the development of the technology *per se*.
- The operation of plant and its maintenance are not seen as core activity and therefore are subjected to market testing. If the internal provider proves less costly than outside contractors the contract is awarded internally.
- The region covered is in three discrete areas. Market testing in one area establishes performance indicators for the other two.
- The decision-making process involved line management in examining key operational activities and assessing risk. Initial candidates for outsourcing were seen as among the most potentially difficult areas. The primary difficulty was the lack of experience amongst contractors in the field.
- Partnership with contractors is seen as vital for long-term success.

Outcomes:
- Outsourcing is a response to a hard-nosed business analysis and will remain so.
- The long-term strategies are essentially based around the increasing application of technology.
- Partnering with suppliers is essential if technological advances are to be realized in business benefits.
- Cost reductions have been achieved.

cannot be done more cost effectively in-house. It sees itself as a provider of customer service with core competencies in strategic technology management and the management of service delivery. Technology is providing an important infrastructure for the management of the provision of services to both business and domestic clients. The network is based on forming a constellation of suppliers and customers. The suppliers of contracted out services are *in partnership* with the utility company, working closely together to improve performance in meeting the needs of the customer. However, work which has been contracted out in one geographical area is not automatically contracted out in the other two remaining areas. This approach creates competition for in-house services with the intention of achieving the most cost-effective delivery arrangements. Where services are contracted out, the benefits in performance improvement beyond those required by the industry regulator are shared between the contractor and the utility company. The internal service providers are expected to achieve similar levels of improvement. The hub of the network is that part of the utility company which forms the knowledge-based enterprise.

EFFICIENCY IMPROVEMENT OR TRANSFORMATION?

We have presented rather contrasting case studies to illustrate three moves in the direction of a networked organization. In the first type, the introduction of EDI has focused primarily on improving efficiency and making possible a much reduced lead time between identification of need and delivery of goods. The emphasis was upon developing a much more responsive system than was in place before the application of technology. EDI, with its regularized flow of information between defined points in the supply chain, has enabled the development of successful just-in-time operations. It has enabled management to get a much better control over its operations. Also, in many cases of the application of EDI, the business has been able to redesign internal operations and thereby significantly reduce manpower needs. Such changes go well beyond the search for efficiency improvement and have often enabled organizations to do new things in different ways. They have brought about a transformation in processes and organization.

This form of networked organization can be described as a ***stable network organization*** – a core firm linked forwards and backwards to a limited number of carefully selected partners. R. E. Miles and C. C. Snow suggest that this type of network has its roots in the structure and operating logic of the functional organization. Rather than seeking to become vertically integrated through ownership it seeks to form a stable set of relationships within the supply chain. However each component is required to remain competitive by supplying other companies as well as often competing with other supply partners for business. They point out that upstream networks linking suppliers to a core firm are commonplace in the automotive industry, whereas downstream relationships are often found with computer hardware manufacturers and their value-added retailers.

The second type of case, as illustrated in Cases 3 and 4, has focused more on using the technology to introduce new ways of working which will involve a change in a deep-seated organization culture and work practices. Even if the organization did not intend it to be such, the development of an electronic network leads to new and different ways of doing things. However, in the short term, this will not necessarily result in added-value for the organization. In one of the cases presented the organization is attempting to move to a higher level of co-operative work as it strives to leverage the contribution of senior consultants in a marketplace where fee income is under pressure. By information sharing its goal is to increase the ability of all consultants to deliver service to the client. Through the use of collaborative technologies it aims to enable the lead time from enquiry to bid to be significantly compressed by allowing 'time and place', independent team members to be involved in preparing the tender documents. By having consultants able to access information about projects, methodologies and its client base it seeks to increase effectiveness in obtaining and managing work. By networking it aims generally to increase the capability of both individuals and the organization to respond to changing business opportunities. It is attempting to use technology as one means for transforming itself to a more responsive and innovative organization. R. E. Miles and C. C. Snow identify this form as the *dynamic network*. Task-focused teams made up of both internal and external resources form and disband at frequent intervals and the organization seems to be in a constant state of flux. Probably the ultimate form of dynamic network is the virtual organization based on a loosely-connected network of providers whose resources are brought together for specific projects then disbanded only to be reconfigured for later projects as they arise. The fifth case illustrates this form in the young business which has not set out to emulate well-established businesses in its market, but rather to organize itself differently so as to be flexible and responsive.

The utility case study represents a third form described by R. E. Miles and C. C. Snow as the *internal network*. The emphasis in such examples is on creating market benefits by having the various departments or divisions within the firm buy and sell outside the firm as well as within.

For organizations operating in a marketplace where there are long lead times before predictable changes in these markets, suppliers or customers, take place, the maintenance of a stable organization with a focus on continuous efficiency improvement is usually appropriate. In such situations partnering with others in the supply chain is one strategy to try to reduce the impact of changes in the business environment by gaining greater control over the market in which the business operates and reducing peaks and troughs in the business cycle. It also allows for risk sharing on innovative projects with no one organization in the supply chain taking all the risks when all will benefit if successful. However, fewer and fewer organizations are operating under conditions where this approach is feasible. The more that the environment is turbulent and unpredictable the more that the organization needs to be structured in a way that enables it to respond dynamically. Speedy and accurate information between nodes in the supply network, transmitting information about changing customer needs to decision-points, is fast becoming a prerequisite for business in the global economy. Organizations are having to transform themselves to achieve this state.

> **The more that the environment is turbulent and unpredictable the more that the organization needs to be structured in a way that enables it to respond dynamically.**

For organizations operating in a labour market where skills and expertise are plentiful there is less pressure to implement the networked organization. However, where skills are in short supply those that the organization has access to must be leveraged. The capability to gain access to skills electronically can offer significant benefits as we saw in several of the cases described. Under such conditions the development of a networked organization has direct relevance.

Network organizations are characterized by R. E. Miles and C. C. Snow as having:

1 A preference to use the collective assets of several firms in the value chain rather than become vertically integrated.
2 A reliance more on market mechanisms than administrative processes to manage resource flows.
3 A recognition by constituent parts of the network of their interdependence and sharing of information, co-operation and customization of products and services to maintain their positions.

4 Participants who play a more proactive role than in traditional buyer-supplier relationships.
5 Closer relationships based on trust and the sharing of benefits from joint improvement.

Whatever the pressures for, and aspirations of, the move towards a greater degree of networking, it is vital to recognize the rationale and aims and translate them into a design philosophy to underpin the chosen desired form. This design philosophy might be seen as the practical manifestation of the culture sought in the transformed organization. But so often those working on the development of the networking infrastructure have not thought through the underlying assumptions governing their work and have little perception of the likely secondary impact of their actions.

Designing the infrastructure

In referring to the design of the networked organization based on person-to-person communications, Lee Sproull and Sara Kiesler identify four principles:

1 *Everyone communicates via the network* – there is no longer a group of users and non-users – and it therefore follows that everyone must have ready access to the network.
2 *There should be open access to people and information* – this is based on the assumption that every employee has something relevant to contribute and to gain from participation.
3 *The provision of forums through which people can work together* – here there is the assumption that a degree of facilitation is necessary.
4 *Policies and incentives to encourage information exchange* – this may be seen as the support infrastructure for the development of a networking culture.

These guiding principles are put forward here to promote discussion and certainly they lead to the raising of issues which need thorough airing and debate. For example, to what extent is it necessary and desirable to provide such open access to information and accept the challenges which will result for senior management? To what extent is it desirable for staff in all parts of the world to discuss sensitive issues openly? What impact will such openness have on the authority of management and its role? Won't too much discussion lead to a lack of decisiveness and result in management looking weak? Can electronic communications adequately support the form of communication necessary to do business and add value to that business?

There appear to be two opposite ideas of staff empowerment. At the one extreme, the system is designed to allow management to exercise maximum control with staff empowered within clearly defined and delineated boundaries. At the other end, the system allows complete openness with the workforce benefiting from access to a wide range of information and support to enable them to respond flexibly in meeting the client's needs. In the stable network the information flows might be strictly controlled and, as we saw earlier, be based on high levels of automated transaction processing. In sharp contrast for the dynamic network, the open access of the system is normally seen as of vital importance in developing the new ways of working being sought. In practice, systems are probably not designed at either extreme. Additionally, such systems do not replace more conventional means of communicating, they offer an alternative. Whatever the basis of system design adopted, much interaction will still take place using earlier, well-tried and tested means with which all staff are familiar. It may well be that key strategic decisions will continue to be made in more traditional face-to-face settings and the more sensitive issues discussed in private. However those organizations that are seeking to transform themselves into a highly responsive knowledge-based enterprise based on electronic networking move in a direction with no defined end point – they embark on a journey of exploration.

In the next section we look at some of the possible outcomes resulting from measures to establish the network infrastructure within organizations.

THE IMPACT OF NETWORKING ON ORGANIZATIONS

Possible impact of communications technology

Electronic networks undoubtedly accelerate the rate of information flow. This in part is because the asynchronous nature of the operations allows users – by accessing the stored data – to deal with messages wherever they are located and at whatever time suits them. But it is also a consequence of the capability, not only to communicate one-to-one but also to broadcast simultaneously to many people both within and outside the organization. This capability to have groups of people remote from each other tied into an effective communication system can have clear organization benefits in terms of productivity

> **Electronic networks undoubtedly accelerate the rate of information flow.**

gains. Once the system is in place the direct cost of communications can be drastically reduced. Group working can be made more effective also both within the organization and across organization boundaries. A greater degree of integration within the organization is practical. These potential gains are reasonably apparent. They relate very much to the efficiency type of gain possible from such systems.

However, it is clear from the case studies that many companies are not focusing on benefits in terms of savings, such as on communications costs, but rather looking to get greater benefits to be achieved by transforming the organization to a new state. They are attempting to bring about fundamental changes in how people work. They are not just seeking to provide a new medium of communications to enable people 'to do more of the same', but rather 'to find new things to do'. They are seeking, at all levels, to unleash the untapped skills of people capable of meeting the challenges of rapidly changing marketplace conditions by developing the dynamic form of network.

> **Power in organizations is based on what and who people know. Access to information is vital to those responsible for managing business operations. Electronic systems make it possible to distribute that information widely, cheaply and quickly.**

An important aspect of this is that they are setting out on an adventure into the unknown. The outcomes are far from certain. Not all the consequences of introducing comprehensive networks are predictable. One certainty is that some companies will build their success on finding new applications for their skills by utilizing the potential of such systems. They will strive consciously to maximize learning at all levels from the individual to the team and the very organization itself. This capacity for organizational learning will be a major source of competitive advantage.

However there is sufficient experience and research into these systems for us to be aware of many of the hurdles to be overcome.

A shift in power and influence

Power in organizations is based on what and who people know. Access to information is vital to those responsible for managing business operations. Electronic systems make it possible to distribute that information widely, cheaply and quickly. They can lead to much unsupervised information sharing. Network-based communications allow people to bypass traditional information gate-keepers and access information sources directly. These systems ignore traditional hierarchical levels by giving equal status to messages from all participants. Employees, through networking with others, may well be able to piece together more about the company than management would see as desirable. Moreover, according to S. Zuboff[8] in her book *The Age of the Smart Machine* influence in these systems is based more on the quality of ideas, the quality of written expression and the ability to respond sensitively to others rather than intimidation or style. Changes therefore take place in the relative power of the people involved in transacting. This is likely to be very uncomfortable for many traditional executives and managers as well as the entrenched workforce.

Traditionally resource allocation in organizations has been the domain of executives and specific decisions have generally remained relatively unchallenged. A new, more open style of organization, makes it much easier for all employees to be aware of the relative merits of each business case and to question the decision-making processes. Management interest and attention in promoting various causes will also be more apparent.

The impact on managerial work

We have already seen the dramatic effects on the need for middle management of the capacity of information management systems to collect and process data and present it to decision-makers. The empowerment of employees has also impacted by changing the role more to that of a facilitator rather than supervisor. Network-based communications will impact further on the role of line management, but more significantly it will require executive management to also change behaviour if the full benefits are to be realized. But these systems not only pose a threat, they also offer an opportunity. Executives can use these systems to become more visible in their organizations and increase the effectiveness of their own communications. However many executives will have to develop and refine their skills in this area. It is also more feasible to delegate responsibility widely throughout the dispersed organization and at the same time monitor and control operations more effectively.

One of the main concerns of executives when their organizations become electronically networked is that they anticipate information overload. Certainly, electronic communications do allow people to send not only irrelevant and inaccurate information, but also trivia. Whilst the direct costs of communications can be reduced dramatically at the same time the actual communications costs can also rise dramatically. The ability to broadcast trivia has costs attached. Even serious messages e.g. requests for information which are generally broadcast have costs which are unlikely to be borne by the author. It is possible to estimate read time, reply time and the value of responses to electronic messages and establish a feel for the actual communication costs. Studies of traditional management practices have shown that considerable energy is put into communications, much of it spoken, and that it is a major part of the managerial job. In the electronic environment, managers need to develop new strategies for managing communications. Systems are being developed to assist in this task by sifting and categorizing electronic messages. Clear organization rules about what to put where on systems can also assist, and simple discipline such as the use of well-worded headings to messages can aid this process.

Secretaries have traditionally screened messages to their managers to ensure that executives do not receive irrelevant or unnecessary information and requests. Electronic systems can lead to the bypassing of these traditional filtering mechanisms. Also messages which are intended as confidential to the recipient can easily be modified and forwarded to others thus possibly making the sender vulnerable. The bypassing of authority structures can also result in a loss of accountability and personal responsibility. The managerial style as organizations move from the hierarchical to the networked is characterized by informality and equality, lateral, diagonal and bottom-up communications.

> **The managerial style as organizations move from the hierarchical to the networked is characterized by informality and equality, lateral, diagonal and bottom-up communications.**

However, it is inevitable that electronic communications will replace some face-to-face communications and also that it will be difficult ultimately for the executives to avoid working directly on such systems and adjusting their style to take advantage of the wider choice of communications medium.

Coping electronically

Another concern expressed about electronic networking is that it cannot fully replicate the characteristics of face-to-face meetings. The form of electronic communication most widely used at present, being based on plain text, does not allow for the 'personalness' or richness of communication that is normal between people who can see and hear each other. Messages are not put into the context which is much more easily established in situations with face-to-face contact. All the nuances present when groups of people interact are missed. Many recipients of electronic messages feel threatened by this lack of contextual information. Much 'reading between the lines' takes place and in consequence messages are easily misunderstood or misinterpreted. There is also evidence to suggest that senders tend to overlook the audience and make little effort to compensate for the lack of information about the broader context.

In practice people are often less inhibited when using electronic communications. People tend to be less constrained by conventional norms and rules guiding behaviour and more open in expressing their views. They often feel less committed to what they write and are less concerned about the social reception they will receive. Also, because most mail systems do not include cues about the status of the sender, the recipient is often unclear what sort of status messages might have within the organizational context. So again replies often then do not follow normal convention. People also tend to forget that messages once cleared from their own screen have not been destroyed and may reside for long periods in the storage of other people's systems. This, of course, can form the basis of *organizational memory*, referred to earlier. Even so, based on their own experiments, L. S. Sproull and S. Keisler suggested that people are more comfortable with self-disclosure to the computer than they are with face-to-face interviews – they feel safe from surveillance and criticism and find it easier to disagree with, confront and take exception to the opinions of others.

So there is clear evidence that people behave differently when using electronic systems than in the more familiar face-to-face situation. In consequence these systems require personal adjustment on the part of all users if they are to be effectively deployed.

Managing electronic meetings

Managers who are skilled at chairing conventional meetings are faced with the need to develop new skills when leading electronic meetings. In addition to sensitivity to the points made earlier, the manager has to recognize alternative approaches for managing different types of meeting and membership and learn how to apply them appropriately. One tendency, since communication is asynchronous, is for the inexperienced manager to respond to each comment made by other participants and take on an 'expert role'. This can easily give the impression of a desire to demonstrate superior knowledge. Managers inexperienced in electronic meetings also often overestimate the capability of participants to contribute effectively to electronic meetings. For example, complex issues which are usually best dealt with in other media get introduced to meetings at an early stage when participants are unfamiliar with the format. New chairing skills are needed to identify how best to present information for discussion and how to organize discussion so that participants feel that they have had sufficient opportunity to seek information, express views, contribute suggestions and join in decision-making. Given the lack of normal cues, even simple ones such as silences, the manager has to develop new strategies for achieving the task outcomes sought from electronic meetings and at the same time having participants feel that it has also met their own needs. Many of these problems are present in all business meetings; however we are familiar with approaches for conventional settings, but totally unfamiliar with how to interact within the new media.

Electronic meetings give people the opportunity to contribute in their own time. They have the chance to reflect and compose their inputs. Those who feel inhibited in a conventional meeting may well not be so in the electronic arena. One consequence is that often there are more inputs than would be possible within the conventional setting. The lack of inhibition also leads to livelier discussion. Consequently, agreement may be more difficult for the chair to achieve. There is some evidence that more disagreement occurs than in conventional settings, particularly conflict over policies and practices. This is likely to have an impact on group dynamics and presents a new set of challenges for management.

Skills in projecting leadership qualities through electronic networks will be difficult to develop given the nature and limitations of the medium and current understanding of how people can have impact through its use. Even where video conferencing is in place the skills needed are much different from those in face-to-face situations. However, whilst more distributed leadership functions are sometimes observed in distributed groups, it seems that strong leadership is necessary for decision efficiency. The latter is often perceived as more so electronically than in face-to-face meetings where contributors have to queue to make contributions which often then go unnoticed.

> **Electronic meetings give people the opportunity to contribute in their own time.**

The internal security of information and the system itself, authority to act on behalf of the employer, the right to privacy and compliance with data protection legislation are all issues that need to be dealt with. Also in some circumstances intellectual property rights will be an issue.

Whichever form the networked organization takes, stable, dynamic or internal, managers will need to be able to demonstrate general commercial skills particularly in service specification and contracting, negotiation and brokerage. They will be required to work extensively in, and with, teams and they will be required to show leadership as they will no longer be in a position to refer to higher levels in the hierarchy. They will often feel less well-informed than those reporting to them, less necessary and less in control. There will be less of a requirement to be responsible for directing employees and more for encouraging the development and effective use of networks and for measuring and rewarding results. With the removal of layers of middle management in many organizations, those managers remaining in the system as well as those they manage are being expected to be more proactive. They will have to spend more time listening to diverse groups with different aims from the relationship and then influencing them to commit to project goals. The networked organization will clearly need good networkers to maintain it. Managers within networked organizations will also have to be good at managing the termination of relationships with partners. The act of marriage is always much simpler than the act of divorce. The latter usually takes up considerable management effort and skill!

Careers in the networked organization

Career management is a key issue for the networked organization. The flattening of structures which has gone alongside much of the development of the networked organization has removed the layers of management which used to form the route for steady progress up the organization's hierarchy. In many companies this route has all but disappeared. Companies will have to find other means for developing the senior executive of the future. Individuals are already recognizing that organizations are putting the onus on them personally to take responsibility for their own career development. Changing loyalties are resulting from the recognition that companies are no longer recruiting for life but rather only for as long as the individual has competencies useful to that employer. New routes for development will include means such as experience of a diversity of projects, periods in different functions within the organization, secondment to suppliers and customers, periods of special assignment working closely with directors. Movement of personnel between partners in the network will help reinforce the network as well as strengthen the individual's capability to manage within it. Assisting personnel with their own development is becoming a key task of line management.

> **Career management is a key issue for the networked organization.**

MAINTAINING THE NETWORKED ORGANIZATION

Potential for failure

R. E. Miles and C. C. Snow make some important observations about the causes of failure of the networked organization. They suggest that just as the functional, divisionalized and matrix forms in their turn have all found favour, they have also been misapplied and failed in many cases and as a result fallen out of favour. Executives have been over eager to adopt new forms even when the logic for doing so is not apparent. Also they have been prepared to extend any one form beyond its appropriateness. They cite the example of vertical integration as stretching the model of functional organization too far and eventually creating problems. They see these problems as the result of the resources needed to co-ordinate efforts and to keep an extensive chain of resources highly loaded at a balanced level and the problems of establishing the relative costs and contribution of each element. However, the functional form is ideal for the delivery of a limited number of products where demand can be forecast and production runs scheduled. Companies who find their market no longer fits need to look at other forms but often management hold on too long.

There are many causes of failure. The main ones are:

1 The stable network

As stated earlier the stable network has its roots in the functional organization and is designed (or has evolved) to serve a mostly predictable market by linking together independently-owned specialized assets in the product or service chain. Earlier we learned that these companies in the value chain are encouraged to supply other customers so that the core firm benefits both from technology transfer and the constant competitive challenge. Companies are contractually tied within the chain.

A major cause of failure is a tendency to allow suppliers to concentrate too much on supplying the core firm and losing the competitive edge that comes from supplying many businesses. This may be the result of customization of the product or service to meet the core firm's requirements such that there is no other business to be supplied. It may result when there is rapid expansion of the core firm's business and the supplier becomes dedicated as a result of capacity limitations in the short term. Another cause of failure occurs when the core firm's management becomes heavily involved in supporting the supplier and starts to erode the supplier's own capability to manage its own operations.

Additional causes of failure include the failure to 'live up to expectations'. In forming partnerships with suppliers, core firms will indicate the benefits of partnering relations. The parties are both selling themselves and the core firm the advantages of a partnering arrangement. Often the benefits are oversold and false expectations created. When it becomes clear that expectations are not going to be fulfilled management will become disillusioned and divert its attention to other more promising opportunities, whether seeking alternative suppliers or chasing other business possibilities.

Many of these partnerships depend upon a few key personnel and their continuing support. When there are personnel changes there is often a rethink of management philosophy and at such times the partnering arrangements are under threat. Economic cycles also have an impact. When the economy is buoyant, companies will favour partnering with key suppliers to ensure supply and maintain lower costs. However when the economy is weak these same purchasers will often revert to a more traditional purchasing policy and more adversarial relations with suppliers.

2 *The dynamic network*

We saw earlier that this form shares its logic with the divisionalized form of organization. It has strong central evaluation with local operating autonomy in order that it can respond to changing market conditions in each of the areas in which it operates. For it to be successful it must have access to a pool of adequate potential suppliers. It must also have core skills which these suppliers are not themselves able to replicate easily. In order to maintain its position there is the danger that it will become secretive, use contractual clauses to protect itself and search for preferential treatment from particular partners. All of this can lead to a lack of dynamism and result in a failure to achieve the full potential of the network.

Where the dynamic network has an infrastructure based on electronic communications there is the potential for failure to achieve the objectives if the technology fails to provide an adequate system to support the planned development. Also if the implementation process is weak, executive management unwilling to support and drive through the changes and if partners cannot also be brought into the scope of the facilities, success will be difficult to achieve. Having got the network up and running is itself not a guarantee of success. Effort has to be put into maintaining the network as a business and social entity and the continuous improvement of service for the customer.

Culture clashes often become apparent some time after the initiation of the relationship and the inability of management to cope with diversity can be another source of failure. Often networks just become over-stretched and start to fail to meet the needs of any of the parties.

3 The internal network

This form of network is based on the principle that an internal market is established within the firm. Its main purpose is to gain competitive advantage through shared utilization of scarce resources and the continuing development and exchange of managerial and technological know-how. R. E. Miles and C. C. Snow suggest that this form can fail because if it is successful it will attempt to move from its core into ever riskier ventures which will stretch its management capability. They further suggest that it is also prone to corporate intervention in distorting price mechanisms or the flow of resources, seemingly to achieve long-term benefits but with short-term consequences. These exceptions can become regular features.

> **Complacency is probably one of the most significant sources of the failure of networks.**

Other risks include a failure to maintain competition by adopting one supplier and then getting 'locked in', weak contractual arrangements which give the opportunity for the supplier to raise prices above those budgeted for, failure to benefit from the relationship to upgrade the core business's personnel and technological capability.

It is apparent that networked organizations are complex to set up and manage. Only if individuals are constantly learning how to set up relationships and manage them better and then transfer this new competence into organizational competence will the networked organization be successful. Several points which are particularly clear are: the need for clarity of objective understood throughout the organization; the appropriate choice of network given the nature of the market, the industry and its competition; and the appropriate choice of network given the form of the existing organization and the capability of its personnel. Another important element in success is the constant attention to continuous improvement of operations. Complacency is probably one of the most significant sources of the failure of networks.

The importance of human resource strategy

The business's Human Resource (HR) strategy must support the strategic direction of the business, ensuring an adequate and timely supply of a competent and well-motivated management and workforce. In the networked organization the HR strategy cannot afford to be inward looking and based exclusively on the notion of a full-time employed workforce. It has to embrace the wider network and accommodate flexible ways as business demand changes.

The new style HR strategy is well illustrated in the computer company ICL that has developed a *total resource model for the flexed organization* as described by D. Sillitoe[9]. This has been designed recognizing a number of key challenges facing the core organization including the following specific needs:

1 To communicate strategy and direction throughout the network.
2 To maintain a corporate culture throughout the network.
3 To build cohesion and continuity.
4 For internal communications to task teams.
5 For flexible compensation and benefits packages to meet the demands of a flexed workforce.
6 To provide career development for members of the flexed workforce.

The relative costs of different means for engaging the workforce (including full-time and part-time employees, revenue earning contractors, freelance staff, home-workers, home-based staff and associates) need to be constantly monitored. A key to success in gaining new business is the ability to form project teams from across the flexed organization. Therefore, as a priority, personnel records need to be up to date, reliable and easily accessible for those putting together project teams.

MAKING THE RIGHT MOVES – READINESS TO BECOME THE NETWORKED ORGANIZATION

We have looked at many aspects of three forms of networked organization. In this concluding section we summarize those key aspects in deciding where each form fits in and assessing the readiness of the organization to move in that direction.

Management summary

1 The Stable Network
- Competition based on constant and ruthless price cutting.
- Mature industry.

- Significant improvements possible from just-in-time delivery in the supply chain.
- Competitors already partnering with the market's most efficient suppliers.
- Speedy response times required in the marketplace.
- The necessity of becoming more customer focused.
- Technological advance only feasible through partnerships with suppliers and customers.

2 The Dynamic Network

- Competition based on capability to deliver innovative solutions.
- Rapidly changing market demands.
- Scarcity of knowledge-based resources.
- Compressed lead times for projects.
- Demands and pressure from staff for empowerment.

3 The Internal Network

- Hidden costs of operation.
- Cost inefficiencies from internal sourcing.
- Priority need to release capital and other resources for development of core activities.
- Overfunctionalization and specialization.
- Need to change the culture to a customer focus.
- Problems in recruiting and retaining specialist skills.
- Inability to keep up with technological developments.

References

1 'Calling in the Web' London, *Financial Times*, 25 November, 1994, p16.
2 'Internet casts its spell on 1m people' London, *Sunday Times*, 20 November, 1994, p2.11.
3 MILES R. E., SNOW C. C. *'Causes of Failure in Network Organizations'*, *California Management Review*, Summer, 1992, pp 53–72.
4 BAHRAMI H. *'The Emerging Flexible Organization: Perspectives from Silicon Valley'*, *California Management Review*, Summer, 1992, pp 33–51.
5 MORGAN G. *'Creative Organization Theory'*, Newbury Park, California, Sage Publications, 1989.
6 HANDY C. *'The Future of Work'*, Oxford, Basil Blackwell, 1984.
7 SPROULL L. S., KIESLER S. 'Connections: New Ways of Working in the Networked Organization', Cambridge, Massachusetts, MIT Press, 1991.
8 ZUBOFF S. *'In the Age of the Smart Machine'*, New York, Basic Books, 1988.
9 SILLITOE D. 'Implementing the Flexible Organization' in Rassam C. (Ed) *'Managing Flexible Employees'*, Henley-on-Thames, Future Work Forum, Henley Management College, 1995.

'The Information Society – new ways of living and working together . . . It is a revolution based on information, itself the expression of human knowledge. Technological progress now enables us to process, store, retrieve and communicate information in whatever form it may take – oral, written or visual – unconstrained by distance, time and volume. This revolution adds huge capacities to human intelligence and constitutes a resource which changes the way we work together and the way we live together.'

M BANGEMANN

'Europe and the global information society – Recommendations to the European Council', Brussels, 1994. Ref CD–84–94–290–EN–C.

5

MAXIMIZING PRODUCTIVITY IN THE INFORMATION AGE

Moving to the Mobile Workforce

INTRODUCTION

For much of the productive work carried out in organizations, information and communications technology has made it possible to disconnect the place and time of work from the point at which the output is needed. But most of our institutions, rather than embracing the new opportunities, are built around outmoded concepts derived from the Industrial Revolution and based on the principles of the subdivision of work and the control of the worker. However, the information age offers us the opportunity to adopt a radically different set of underlying assumptions on which to base the design of work. Our organizations are having to become increasingly capable of rapid response to changes in market conditions, but most have yet to unlock the potential offered by using technology to free up the workforce and enable it to deliver the flexible response being sought.

While many of the principles for designing new style organizations to suit the information age have been discussed over many years the widespread application of the concepts has yet to take place. Even though technology offers the opportunity to create a productive mobile workforce, so far few organizations have been successful in adopting these new forms. However it is becoming clear from a growing body of evidence that the new organization based on a mobile workforce can be a reality, but, more importantly, those bold enough to take this route can gain business advantages over those still basing their organizations on concepts passed on from earlier phases of industrialization.

In this chapter we give the reader an understanding of trends, alternative models for organization by reference to case studies, guidance on how to progress to new forms of working and new concepts for the office. We finish with some key pointers.

THE INCREASINGLY MOBILE WORKFORCE

Since the subdivision of labour led to such developments as sales teams to visit customers' premises and sell the products of manufacturing industry, organizations have had 'mobile employees'. But mobile employees now include:

1 Those for whom the primary task is carried out on customer premises e.g. service/maintenance engineers, meter readers, inspectors (such as buildings and health and safety), information systems designers, auditors and social workers.
2 Those moving people or goods between two points, e.g. lorry, train and bus drivers.
3 Those who work increasingly at home or on third-party premises such as multiservice telecentres.

The options available to the company as we have seen in one of our case examples, John Brown Plc, include the mobility of the work rather than the worker. Work can be moved around the world, crossing time zones in ways which make 24-hour continuous working possible without people working antisocial hours, but also in centres where the cost of labour offers competitive advantage. In the case reported, work from home is unfeasible being uneconomic because of the sophistication of equipment and systems needed to support the high level design activity.

So why is the mobile workforce and movement of work of particular interest at this time?

As reported in Chapter 2, developments in technology are increasing the extent to which work in organizations is location- and time-independent. As we have discussed earlier the laptop PC, modem and telecommunication links have made it economically viable and practically feasible for many more employees in many parts of the world to carry out their work away from a fixed location; the office. Freeing up employees in this way makes them more mobile in that they can move their work to the place which best suits the client's needs, the organization's needs and their own personal needs. It also makes possible the effective transfer by organizations of low value labour-intensive clerical work and more routine work to any location worldwide. Such working practices are described variously as *teleworking, the mobile office* and *flexible working* and take place from *home, the business's satellite offices, telecentres/telecottages, customer premises, hotels* and *cars*. The actual terminology is not as relevant as the principal which is one of time and place independence for the carrying out of the tasks which make up work.

The main reason for the current interest is that organizations, individual employees and the community at large can benefit from the adoption of more flexible working practices. The potential benefits to the organization include savings through more effective use of office space and usually overall reductions in space needs. Also savings can result from increased call rates from mobile staff. In the case of teleworkers no longer required to commute at fixed times each day, organizations are finding benefits in productivity levels. Customer satisfaction improvements may well also be achieved by more effective organizational responses. In the case of teleworkers themselves, reduced commuting and greater control over the use of their time can have personal benefits and lead to improved quality of life. Communities can benefit from reductions in traffic pollution and a regeneration of rural communities and dormitory suburbs normally only sparsely inhabited during working hours.

Teleworking

Probably the most widely used expression to describe 'time and space independent' working is *teleworking*. Teleworking in its many forms has received much attention in the media and has been talked about for many years. Possibly the level of interest shown has arisen because the lifestyle has particular appeal to journalists and writers. However take-up of the concept during the 1980s was much slower than many of the predictions. Looking at the reasons for slow progress during that decade we can see that while the initial concept of teleworking as working away from the office was sound in itself, early practice had severe limitations due in large measure to the limitations of the technology in offering acceptable substitutes for many of the preferred aspects of traditional working practice, in particular the social contact, and also its basic assumption of transferring working from office to home. It also had limitations in its ability to support the required way of working of many people in organizations. Much work is based on teams and early software solutions were just not designed to support group processes. So one might conclude that in early stages of the concept's development it met neither the business need to justify the investment required nor the needs of

> **Probably the most widely used expression to describe 'time and space independent' working is *teleworking*.**

the individual teleworker. But the 1990s has seen a major change and take-up in both the US and the UK seems to have reached the point where a rapid and real increase is apparent.

This rapid increase in the take-up of teleworking is reflected in a number of recent surveys. For example, U. Huws[1] in a 1993 study for UK's

Employment Dept found that 113 out of 1,003 companies reported employing some staff who worked at home more than 50 per cent of their time. Of these, 58 were employing teleworkers, i.e. those using information and communications technology. The companies were most commonly based in London and the South East, followed by East Anglia and the North West. Many occupations were reported as teleworking. Staff were predominantly women except for consultants, computer professionals or working on accounts/financial services. A Wall Street Journal[2] article in 1993 reported that company employees in the US working at home for at least part of the time rose 15 per cent in 1992 to 7.6 million. Not all employees, however prefer this option; 33 per cent of the 280 participants in a one-year study in Washington's Puget Sound region stopped working at home at the end of the period. N. Hodson[3] studying the UK reported as many as 1.2m working as teleworkers by 1994 and B. Murray[4], in the same year, based on a Henley Management College/NCC survey found that 36 per cent of responding companies were using teleworkers and that this is expected to rise by 1996 to over 60 per cent. This compares with an earlier survey in 1991 where 13 per cent of organizations were using teleworkers and 16 per cent actively considering introducing schemes.

There are also major projects under way – particularly in the US – but in countries as diverse as the West Indies, India and the Philippines. For example, following the last earthquake, rapid changes have taken place in the Los Angeles area to disperse work back to local communities for both business and social reasons. In the New York area distributed office projects are being sponsored by the Federal Government. In Europe support for large demonstration projects in peripheral areas has come from the European Commission. Some remote areas such as the Grampian Region in Scotland have put in place a technological infrastructure to support such developments. In some countries, such as Barbados in the West Indies, it has become government policy to attract work from higher wage economies by developing the concept of an electronic island with tele-centres offering business competitively priced off-shore work.

In Phoenix, Arizona, the state authorities have gone as far as regulating that any company with over 100 employees has to have teleworking at least 5 per cent of the time and for companies in the 50 to 100 group this figure is 10 per cent.

So what has changed that is leading to this move towards the mobile workforce? Is it just a passing fad? Is it being promoted by equipment and service providers with a vested interest or does it really provide the business benefits reported? Or is it the politicians who want to be seen to be tackling unemployment problems or trying to redress the decline of rural communities or the impact of traffic pollution in major conurbations?

THE FACTORS INFLUENCING CHANGE

Efficiency vs. effectiveness

For organizations to adopt the concept of a mobile workforce there has to be some major business driver. In many cases the change is driven by the desire to cut overheads such as the cost of premises, the cost of travel time between office and customer and the cost of a full-time workforce unlikely to be fully utilized due to variable and unpredictable workloads. Cutting such costs is attractive, particularly if the benefits show directly on the bottom line and are on-going or if the business realizes assets which can be better deployed on developing its core activities. Investment can be justified in measurable terms and additional second-order benefits may be anticipated when people release the potential of the IT to which they have access. In some cases small additional investment may even be seen as a way of unlocking the unfulfilled benefits from earlier IT investment.

However not all organizations are moving in this direction for efficiency motives. Some are seeking to rethink the way they do business given the changing demands of the customer, the changing economics of doing business and the changing expectations and aspirations of their employees. These companies are seeking a much more radical change in the way the business operates and seeking strategic gains through making such dramatic change. They are transforming their operations by re-engineering their processes to take advantage of the available and emerging possibilities.

Often these more radical changes are driven by attempts to create advantage by offering a higher level of service to customers. This can be seen in organizations such as the UK telecomms giant, BT, where not long ago a faulty domestic telephone would remain unusable for a considerable time awaiting the arrival of an engineer and British Gas where – unless there was immediate danger – a call would go into a long queue. These organizations have made use of mobile telephony and a degree of process re-engineering to improve their response times greatly. This in turn creates new expectations on the part of customers. If one provider can do it why can't another? This is the *First-Move Dynamic* we referred to in Chapter 2.

Outsourcing for flexibility

The radical rethink may well be within a strategic review of core vs. non-core business and how best to manage the non-core activities. Because of technological developments non-core activities can be outsourced in ways not possible ten or even five years ago. This implies a new possibility for the *Taxonomy of the Organization* which we discussed in Chapter 3. Businesses can and are contracting out work of many types. But areas such as administration, systems design and engineering design can be transferred (internally) or outsourced (externally) to any part of the world and managed effectively from the centre using the technology now available. Some companies are seizing the opportunities to rethink their organization in order to concentrate their efforts on the high added-value work in their supply chain. Also they are creating organizations which can respond more flexibly to changing marketplace conditions by concentrating on core business and buying-in services to meet specific demands as needed. With so much scope many businesses are having difficulty deciding what to keep and what to divest, particularly as it can have such a major impact on what is then defined as the core of the business and its long-term capability for development.

The developing skills marketplace

Reduced economic activity and organizational delayering has resulted in an extended pool of talented and experienced people available to meet the specialist needs of business. Many are beginning to appreciate the possibility that electronic networking offers for creating business opportunities, assembling teams to work on assignments and for personal updating. As staff in organizations become more familiar with facilities such as electronic mail there is a new market developing for consultants who use such facilities and hence are readily accessible for advice wherever they are located. Many of these liberated managers are developing niches for their consultancy which will lead them to question whether or not they would wish ever to return full-time to the corporate umbrella.

Another pressure is coming from employees themselves as they redraw the boundaries around the location and time of work. Early teleworkers were described by Jack Nilles[5], the Californian guru on telecommuting as 'teleguerillas' – the employee who had a computer at home and started sneaking work home to complete assignments outside office hours. When talking to managers, one often finds examples of teleworking in organizations which are also outside the recognized policies and practices of their organization. Managers seeking to retain the skills of particular individuals will make special arrangements for these staff to work away from the office. This may be despite a lack of overall company agreement on important issues about terms and conditions of employment, health and safety, equipment security etc. and may be purely an ad hoc arrangement.

What we are seeing is changing demands from employees who are expecting their employer to be more flexible in allowing people to work at times and places that better suit their needs so long as it does not reduce their overall performance. So we have new expectations and pressures from employees as well as the business imperative. Certainly in areas of skills shortage, this is an important factor influencing the development of mobility for those staff who are more aware of the possibilities offered by the emerging technologies.

The reasons for introducing flexible working include those summarized by Chris Ridgewell[6] of Mercury Communications Plc in Figure 5.1.

Operational:
- to move closer to the customer
- to improve the quality of service
- to improve productivity
- to manage change, e.g. flatten the hierarchy.

Financial:
- to reduce overhead costs
- to reduce space needs.

Human Resource:
- to retain or enlarge skills base
- to meet employee demands
- to reduce staff turnover
- to extend geographical recruiting areas
- to redeploy (redundant) staff
- to recruit disadvantaged people.

Figure 5.1 Reasons for adopting flexible working

A survey carried out in the UK by Ovum[7] identified the main drivers towards more use of mobile communications as *the improvement of productivity*, followed by *more responsiveness to customers* and *to improve sales effectiveness*.

TYPES OF MOBILE EMPLOYEES

Some illustrations of the various forms of work carried out by mobile staff and methods of organizing it are illustrated in Figure 5.2

Travelling staff

- IBM and Digital have implemented 'hot-desking' for their consultants providing them with mobile equipment and having perhaps only desk space for 40 per cent of their staff in their office building.
- Oxfordshire County Council in the UK has equipped *social workers* and *weights and measures inspectors* with mobile technology to support their operations.
- The British Post Office has equipped *consultants* to work from home and other sites.
- Price Waterhouse has adopted groupware so that their *consultants* can share data worldwide from wherever located.

Home-based staff

- In the US the Blue Cross Insurance Co has *'cottage keyers'* to key in insurance claims from their homes.
- In Scotland an Argyll-based company uses 30 teleworkers to compile a medical database for a Dutch publisher.
- BT ran a well-publicized experiment with *directory enquiries clerks* in the Scottish Highlands and Islands working from home.
- Another well-publicized scheme in the UK was the ICL off-shoot CPS which employed *software planners* and *analysts* who work from home.
- The Housing Executive in Northern Ireland has introduced homeworking for maternity and family carers and female middle management.
- An accounting manager for Hewlett-Packard in the US.
- A transcriptionist for a Madison, Wisconsin, hospital.
- The US law firm Gray, Carey Ware and Friedenrich has teleworkers writing and editing legal documents.

Telecottage/telecentre based staff

- 15,000 of the City of Los Angeles' 40,000 employees work from tele-centres.
- Gwynedd County Council in North Wales – *inspectors of education* and *architects* have a neighbourhood office offering links to HQ.
- A Glasgow estate agency uses an Argyll-based bureau to carry out *administration*.

Figure 5.2 Examples of mobile employees

These examples serve to illustrate the wide range of tasks successfully performed away from the conventional office environment.

Forms of mobile working

We have categorized these working patterns into three broad areas:

1 Truly mobile workers who are constantly travelling. They are likely to spend time travelling by road, rail or air. They are also likely to spend considerable time on the premises of client organizations. These personnel are increasingly being supplied with a range of equipment to improve their effectiveness, e.g. laptop PC, mobile phone or pager, groupware or other communications platform software.
2 Staff who spend varying proportions of their working week based at home but perhaps making some use of the employer's conventional office. These staff may have a laptop or be equipped with a more permanent home office. Companies are now emerging which specialize in supplying services to these homeworkers.
3 Staff who spend all or part of their working week based in a telecottage or similar but may spend some time also in a conventional office. These telecottages are likely to be provided by a third party and may be hired on a permanent basis or as required. Many of these telecentres have been provided under initiatives supported by local or central government.

A further categorization would relate to the basis of employment:

1 Directly employed staff on the same basic contract as other employees of the organization.
2 Self-employed staff engaged directly by the organization. These may include former employees or staff engaged specifically as mobile workers. They may be engaged on a long-term basis or for specific projects.
3 Staff employed by a third party. Again work may be subcontracted over the long term or the contract just cover a defined project.

The location-independent workforce

Various types of alternatives to the conventional office have emerged. The initial teleworking concept was based on the home. However as well as advantages there are many disadvantages in working from home and for many people it is just not a viable prospect.

Alternative organizational arrangements have emerged. For example, telecottages are centres provided by third parties at which mobile staff or their employers can purchase space. They would normally offer a range of technology to support the mobile employee including electronic links for data transmission and perhaps teleconferencing. They may also offer a telephone answering or call divert system. Secretarial support and other back-up facilities could also be available. The neighbourhood office is a variation on the telecottage offering a 'home' for mobile workers whose territory is some way from the head office and whose employer does not wish to carry the overhead of a fixed office. Such employees can hire facilities as and when needed. Space can be hired on a long-term arrangement with the group of employees then perhaps 'hot-desking' – the total space being greater than the average demand level but insufficient to meet the needs if all employees wanted to use it at the same time. Or it can be booked when required. Some companies have set up their own satellite offices built close to clusters of residences of existing or potential employees.

Many of these centres, in addition to office accommodation, offer a wide range of services including training facilities. Some telecentres have actually grown out of training centres, particularly in rural areas where there is a shortage of both easily accessible training and work. Having carried out training for the unemployed these centres have progressed naturally to trying to find gainful employment and in doing so diversified into becoming a telecentre. They may also offer shared childcare or nursery provision and information services to help the self-employed. Some are multiservice centres offering other business services such as translation and multilingual information services/kiosks.

The developing strategy

It is suggested by C. Ridgewell that the various forms of teleworking are suitable at different levels of activity as illustrated in Figure 5.3. This tends to assume that an organization wishes to avoid directly managing many dispersed teleworkers based from home. However, examples such as FI, the UK computer software company established on the basis of home-working, demonstrate that this is both feasible and successful. Also software development is making this ever more practical.

Mobile employees – adding value for the customer

We looked earlier at the reasons for adopting a more flexible way of working by offering the workforce the opportunity to be more mobile. One key question that has to be addressed is 'how will such arrangements add value for the customer?' A second and vital question for consideration is 'how will such a development fit into the long-term strategy of the business?'

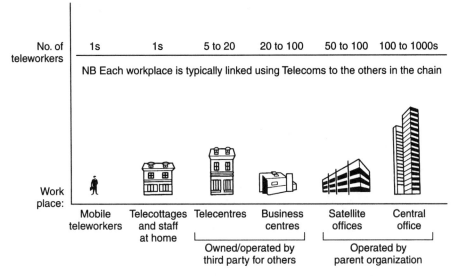

No. of teleworkers	1s	1s	5 to 20	20 to 100	50 to 100	100 to 1000s

NB Each workplace is typically linked using Telecoms to the others in the chain

Work place:	Mobile teleworkers	Telecottages and staff at home	Telecentres	Business centres	Satellite offices	Central office

Owned/operated by third party for others — Operated by parent organization

Figure 5.3 Different forms of teleworking and scale of operation

In practice there are many ways in which flexible working may increase the added-value for clients and customers. Obvious ways include: if the staff member is more readily accessible to the customer; if the provider can reduce the lapsed time between customer call and effective response; if the costs of servicing the customer need are reduced and savings passed on in part or whole to the customer.

However there are also risks of failure in implementation. Many managers are unhappy about a loss of control when staff are not physically in their sight. There is often an unspoken assumption that work is valuable only to the extent that it can be observed by a manager. This concern about the trustworthiness of remote employees in some cases will be justified. Not all staff will respond positively when given the responsibility for managing their own time without direct supervision. Nor will they be able to cope effectively with a change from performance measurement being based on the physical observation of their work to measurement based on the quality and quantity of the outcomes of their efforts. However the electronic systems can be designed such that managers receive more detailed and timely information about employee performance than was previously the case. This may well serve to allay the concerns of management about the potential for loss of control, however it may also result in resentment on the part of the staff involved. There is an interesting paradox in that on the one hand many organizations are talking about empowering staff but at the same time they are

> **Training and development have an important role to play in successful mobile employee implementation. Counselling may also be necessary in early stages of implementation.**

imposing stricter monitoring and control systems via the use of technology. Such changes do not go unnoticed by staff who will recognize such features in the trade-offs being made as they move to new ways of working. Some will of course find ways of bypassing this type of system just as they would any other management system that tries to introduce control of staff activity and performance. Also, as employees take greater responsibility for scheduling their own work they will find that work crosses a boundary and comes to intrude more into their social and family life if the technology is in the home and gives clients and managers ready access. Training and development have an important role to play in successful mobile employee implementation. Counselling may also be necessary in early stages of implementation.

Exhibit 5.1 Supporting the mobile maintenance workforce

Case Study 1: Maintenance workers

Reasons for change:
- At Rank Xerox, UK – to gain improved customer satisfaction.
- To improve employee motivation.
- To improve business results.
- To improve productivity.

Features of the new arrangements:
- Self-managing work teams.
- Empowerment of teams.
- Team-based reward system introduced.
- Information systems designed to deliver information needed for team decision-making.
- Training given to support new role.
- Engineer Customer Call-based Handling Operation (ECCHO) system implemented.

Benefits achieved:
- Teams gradually taking responsibility for operational decision-making.
- Improved staff/manager ratio.
- Improved customer satisfaction and improved productivity.

The first case study presented in this section illustrates how one company, Rank Xerox, improved the overall performance of its UK service teams responsible for repairing and maintaining equipment installed in customer premises. Rank were suffering particularly from Japanese competition and set out to improve considerably the level of service offered to their customers. This was part of a corporate initiative to improve the quality of overall operations.

The second case study deals with sales teams based at the Basingstoke office of the Digital Corporation in the UK. Again the organization was experiencing severe turbulence in its marketplace. The core of the business was experiencing rapid change in customer demand. To meet these changing needs Digital had to become much less technology-led and much more focused on responding to customer needs. They needed to be able to

Exhibit 5.2 Freeing up knowledge-based staff

Case Study 2: Professional staff in a computer company

Reasons for change:
- An internal study revealed that on average an office utilization factor of 12 to 14 per cent was all that was being achieved at Digital in the UK.
- Current informal home working was studied and productivity gains appeared significant.
- The European organization of business units at times made relocation to the centre of the activity impractical for all employees involved.
- The sales force need to spend much of their time on clients' premises.

Features of the new arrangements:
- Teams of consultants hot-desk.
- Investment in technology to support the new way of working.
- Flexible office space planning to facilitate flexible team work.
- Integrated IT infrastructure including computer integrated telephony, electronic office technology, voice and fax.
- Personal telephone numbers which follow staff wherever they are.
- Empowered secretaries moving into an operations management role.

Outcomes:
- Considerable real estate savings.
- A breakdown of traditional hierarchies.
- A new management style.
- A more flexible way of working which allows an effective response to customer needs.

respond by rapidly bringing together project teams able to bid for work and then carrying it out to time, specification and budget. In rethinking their approach they have introduced more flexible ways of working for teams which have included a reduction in office space and hence overhead. These moves are part of Digital's strategic response to their rapidly changing market conditions.

The third case describes a project within UK local government. The motives for the project are only partially business related. It forms part of the development of its personnel policy and is part of a range of options to improve access to work and equality of opportunity. The flexiplace project

Exhibit 5.3 Teleworking for public sector staff

Case Study 3: Flexible working in a UK local authority

Reasons for change:
- To achieve equal opportunities, to improve recruitment and retention of staff at Oxfordshire County Council.
- To improve efficiency and quality of service.
- To reduce unnecessary car utilization.

Features of new arrangements:
- Working both at an office base and at home. Agreed core hours have to be worked:
  1. In the office, or
  2. Working from home as a base but going to meet clients or visit sites, or
  3. Working mainly at home.
- The schemes are part of a wider programme of flexible arrangements and other support, e.g. workplace nurseries.
- There is no compulsion and staff agree arrangements directly with the manager.
- Initial project was in Trading Standards department but extended to Social Services and Leisure and Arts.

Outcomes:
- Lower reported work-related stress.
- Reduction of business travel.
- Effective systems of communication and monitoring have been developed.
- Minimal set up costs with little demand for highly sophisticated equipment for home use.

complements initiatives aimed at reducing time dependence. The council considers that this way of working would not be suitable for all its jobs but also that it is unlikely that a high proportion of staff would prefer to work in this mode. Their estimate is that no more than 10 per cent of its staff complement would take up the option at any time.

The fourth case describes a pilot project within a different UK local authority. This is not part of a major corporate initiative but rather a project within particular departments to look at how best to organize both the architects' department and social workers. The county is sparsely populated and the county offices are not easily accessible from many parts of the administrative area. However, again we see the drive coming from an effort to improve customer service levels and at the same time getting higher value-added from staff. The fifth case describes another example of the use of a neighbourhood office provided by a third party as a satellite office for a government department.

The mobile workforce – achieving benefits for the organization

Earlier we identified some of the motives organizations might have for introducing flexible working through creating a more mobile workforce. We also saw that there is evidence that such changes are taking place in many organizations rather more as a local response to particular pressures than as a concerted rethink of how best to do business.

In looking for guiding principles for the rethink we turn to Stan Davis[8], the futurologist, who identifies a number of tips for better performance in the information age:

> '. . . capture and use information at each point of contact with the customer . . . configure the business to run any time and in real time . . . configure the business to run in any place.'

Clearly before starting any major rethink of how to deploy IT more effectively to support the creation of a more mobile workforce the organization has to be clear in terms of its mission and strategy. However the mission and strategy have to be informed by what is practical or likely to be so over the planning time scale. The new roles for HR and IT executives and the linkage between work processes and mission is further discussed in Chapter 8.

If one adopts the principle advocated by Stan Davis when designing work organization, the underlying questions when deciding what equipment and software to supply to mobile employees are:

Exhibit 5.4 Neighbourhood office development

Case Study 4: Architects' Department in rural area in North Wales

Reasons for change:
- Travelling time between projects and Head Office (HO) was excessive for staff of *Gwynedd County Council.*
- Greater utilization of staff could be achieved by having easier local access to HO support services.
- Queries could be handled quicker.

Features of new arrangements:
- Staff have access to a neighbourhood office within the community which they serve.
- The office is equipped with video conferencing and other high level communications facilities to HO.
- There is local secretarial back-up available.
- Diaries and appointments are still organized from HO.
- Project records are maintained at HO.

Exhibit 5.5 A local base for office bound staff

Case Study 5: The Statistical Department of a Regional Government Administration in Austria

Reasons for change:
- To allow flexible use of staff, increase productivity and improve competitiveness of the organization.
- To overcome geographical barriers and reduce commuting with attendant environmental benefits.
- To help employees manage their time more effectively.
- To help the organization get closer to its customers.

Features of new arrangements:
- A group of staff has been offered the possibility of split-site working spending 2–3 days from home and having the option to get support services from a neighbourhood office on demand. They work the rest of the week from their traditional office.
- Electronic links to the head office have not been instigated because of the sensitivity of the data and the volumes involved.
- Great care has been paid to the identification of suitable work, appropriate staff, defining new working arrangements and methods for evaluation of the organization.

Outcomes:
- A pilot group of staff now have flexible working and the management co-ordination necessary has increased considerably.
- Reduced travel time for staff.

1 How quickly do we need information centrally which is captured at the point of contact with customers?
2 How will we use that information to add value for the customer by improving the service offered?
3 How important is it that the person dealing with the customer has direct access to the latest information on products, services and customers including the particular customer being dealt with at the time?
4 What is the pay-back period for the organization on the investment required?
5 What long-term benefits could be achieved as a result of the investment?

If we look back at the case studies described earlier we can see that:

1 In the case of Xerox, the service engineers were able to pick up information about call-outs from Head Office, they had information on their PC about the previous maintenance record of the machine being attended to and they were able to record and transmit information about the nature of the problem and actions taken to the central database. Such information has a number of potential uses. If a particular pattern of faults is emerging, speedy action can be taken to locate and correct the problem whether in design, manufacture, installation or maintenance. Information on usage and breakdown rates are indicators of the potential for replacement sales. Spare parts management can be considerably improved in many similar situations.
2 At Digital, the sales team might be working on different projects but they were able to access other members of the team and a wider network to assist in solving problems. Within a guaranteed time period customers were able to get a response from a member of the team wherever they were working. The potential also exists for management to be better informed about output from the various teams. Quality standards can be made more consistent if data is shared and made common.
3 The architects were better able to resolve queries with HO and get a response more quickly to contractors and the communities being served. Information could also be relayed to HO more quickly and then accessed by others for purposes such as invoice and claims settlement. If sharing of data between architects was to be introduced they would be better able to act consistently in passing judgements. Environmental benefits are reported.

The long-term benefits which the organizations might look for include greater co-operation through team-based working at Xerox, increased flexibility and customer responsiveness at Digital and higher productivity and the ability to meet the Citizens' Charter in Local Government. The long-term benefits sought are very much in line with the provision of higher levels of customer service in order to at least match, if not better, the competition.

Being aware of the hurdles

Clearly for these long-term benefits to be gained any project has to fit closely to strategic objectives, be carefully planned and implemented and finally follow-up action instigated to ensure that the new form of organization keeps progressing in the desired direction. But before putting plans in place it is important to be aware of the hurdles that have to be overcome for it to be a success.

Culture

As is the case with any major organizational change it is likely that there will have to be a major cultural change to make it work effectively. Not only will such change be necessary but as a result of implementing such change there will be secondary cultural changes not necessarily predicted at the outset. Probably the most significant is in the attitude and behaviour of managers. This is the group which in many ways has the most to lose. The move to increased staff mobility might well be part of a broader move to bring about employee empowerment. Even if it is not an intended outcome, or is not made explicit in the planning phase, it may well arise as a consequence of the changes but in a rather more painful way. If the aim is to improve the performance of staff when dealing with customers, whether external or internal, by providing greater access to information on which decisions are based the employee is better able to make those decisions personally. Effectiveness in this process will result, among other factors, from proper authority and appropriate training. If the organization is not prepared to work in this way and is currently very hierarchical and bureaucratic it may well not be ready for such moves and perhaps should not embark on such projects at this stage.

Involvement

Another key component in introducing the change will be how the staff including the management are involved in the processes of design and implementation. As we will see later, a participative approach to designing change offers an opportunity to involve staff in planning the changes and gaining their commitment to them.

We saw from the Rank Xerox case the emphasis placed upon training to develop the new competencies required for effective working under the new work organization. Training will not only cover competence with the new technology but also the development of the all important skills of interacting effectively with others at a distance.

From this same case we saw the development of an infrastructure to support teamworking. The reward systems were brought into line with the new organizational form. Individual incentives were replaced by team-based rewards. First line managers were also encouraged to take on more of a support role encouraging the team to develop the skills and confidence to take on more responsibility. At Digital, managers have become *coaches*, reflecting the nature of the changed role demanded of them in relation to the team.

Operational infrastructure

Clearly great care has to be taken to bring in line a number of key factors which will support the new ways of working and if not aligned will hinder and inhibit development. These are represented in Figure 5.4.

It is essential that mobile employees are clear about the organization's requirements. These need to be specified in output terms rather than input, i.e. what is to be achieved rather than the specifics of how it is to be done. It is also essential that the employee understands not only what the organi-

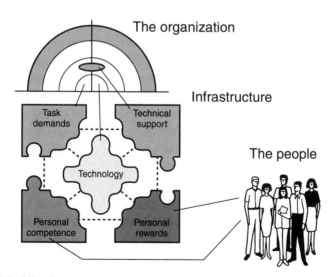

Figure 5.4 Aligning conditions for effective mobile working

> **It is essential that mobile employees are clear about the organization's requirements.**

zation expects but also what can be expected from the organization in the way of support and supervision. If the individual does not possess the competencies needed to perform at a satisfactory level compared to the traditional office arrangement the organization will experience difficulty, because close monitoring is not practical for much work which is now being done away from the office and out of management's sight. The organization has to establish appropriate methods for selection, training and development, work allocation, and performance monitoring and review. The role of management has to be clarified and working procedures and practices established.

The organization's technological capability

Probably one of the greatest barriers to successful implementation is the lack of technological capability within the organization. Where organizations do not already possess the technological infrastructure based on successful local area networks, and employ internally at least those technologies essential for effective remote, or out of office working, the learning curve will be very steep and perhaps too much to contemplate. Ideally, not only those employees who are to become the mobile workforce will have had considerable exposure to the basic systems which they will now employ, but more importantly the technical understanding and competence within the organization generally will be able to match the needs of the move to new ways of working. The level of understanding required is normally accumulated over time but even in the most capable of organizations it is likely to be necessary to call upon additional expertise in the form of consultancy whether independent or from a supplier.

So a useful early step before committing to implementation is a technical audit of the capability of the Information Systems Department and those operational departments which are to be involved. Strategies for implementation may well then include considerable provision for training and development, outsourcing of facilities management and even the work itself.

Adequacy of technology and technical support for mobile working

There are some obvious golden rules about technical support for mobile employees which are often not adhered to by technologists specifying and developing systems. Simplicity is one of the first golden rules. Staff working remote from a central office are likely to get more frustrated and more quickly if they are unable to cope or experience technical difficulties with hardware and software. Help is not as easily to hand as in the conventional office. Electronic mail also allows people to readily share their frustrations even though not perhaps meeting regularly, so dissatisfaction can be spread very quickly around the network. Systems can soon lose credibility and the whole concept be put at risk. Standardization of systems is a second golden rule. Some users will inevitably have specific requirements not shared by others but, in the main, systems should be standard so that employees can help each other rather than always depending upon a central service. However, a system of high-quality technical support must be put in place and aligned with the needs of the mobile employee. All too often the support services in organizations are geared up to serving those staff in the building and for those without easy access it is often difficult to get priority service over local internal customers.

Technical support needs to go well beyond the provision and support of appropriate hardware and software. There are many issues associated with home-based working which the organization has to understand and provide for. In many areas it will need to assist staff to understand new requirements and also make appropriate provision. Amongst these are health and safety, third party and personal liability insurance, implications for tax of a home-based office, provision and ownership of equipment, restrictions on use of and access to employer-owned equipment and data security. We will go on to look at these in more detail later in this chapter.

Helping staff cope

It is widely recognized that there is a range of problems experienced by those who move from traditional office employment to some form of more mobile or flexible working. Where much of the work is home-based it raises concerns about isolation, tensions between domestic and work life, intrusion into the home, psychological attachment to the employing organization, access to training and career opportunities. Organizations implementing such change are looking for business benefits but a balance has to be struck such that the individual also feels that the personal benefits out-weigh the costs both short and long term. Care is needed in the planning phase and negotiations with employee representatives are likely to be delicate and difficult. The organization needs to give careful consideration to how it is going to keep its mobile workforce informed and involved. It also needs to consider how it is going to maintain a sense of identity, shared values and culture and what these are now to be.

One key issue for the prospective mobile employee is that of career development. Generally in organizations there is an assumption that careers develop in a linear progression over the employee's working life. Flexible working and absence from the office may well jeopardize career prospects and even in practice, if not the case, the concerns individuals have about this can be a barrier to implementation.

In a recent article entitled *The Flexible Workplace: What Have We Learned?*, Charles Rodgers[9], from his own observations of the introduction of flexible working, suggests the following conditions as important for successful implementation:

1 Strong support from the top of the organization and a clearly communicated business case.
2 The support of individual managers who are competent and whose behaviour reflects that support.
3 A good relationship between manager and employee and a willingness on both sides to work together to implement change.

Implementation at IBM in Germany followed agreement by the Supervisory Board and resulted in the identification of the following good practice statement for teleworking initiatives:

1 The scheme should be voluntary.
2 There should be no change in the employment contact.
3 Schemes should not be purely home-working but involve one or two days per week in the traditional office.
4 Employees should be compensated for their use of their home and all equipment should be provided.

It may well prove difficult to achieve these where a major rethink of ways of working is being sought.

We have then identified a number of areas of concern and conditions which have to be aligned in order to make the move to the mobile office both attractive and workable. Not all will be applicable in every situation. Additional issues will arise if transborder work is involved. One key management task, however, is contingency planning. What if it all goes wrong or just doesn't seem to be working. How will management know? What metrics will be used to monitor implementation? How sound are plans for dealing with possible negative experiences?

Tackling the practical issues

There are a number of potential practical difficulties to investigate before introducing teleworking. In Figure 5.5 we have highlighted many of these.

Clearly they will not all apply to each of the forms of teleworking, nevertheless we present it here as a check-list to guide investigations by those whose concern is with implementation of teleworking. These matters are dealt with in detail in the various handbooks and guidelines which are now available and through associations of teleworkers and telecottages etc.

Problems arise because of differences in laws at local, national and also community level in the case of the European Union. Any legislation which covers work in the home is difficult to police and regulate. Again in this area further difficulties arise when the work is carried out transborder. Whose regulations apply to what in such circumstances?

Figure 5.5 A checklist of issues to be considered when implementing teleworking

- The employment status of teleworkers – direct employees vs. self-employed.
- The contract of employment including termination rights.
- Insurance for homeworking.
- Health and Safety Legislation and homeworking.
- The definition of industrial injury when people are home-based.
- Conditions resulting from collective agreements with the unions vs. the law.
- Privacy rights and data protection.
- Data security at home and in transmission.
- Equality of career opportunities compared to the traditional workforce.
- Legality of electronic documents created outside the office.
- Adequacy of physical facilities at home.
- Equipment and furniture provision by the employer for the home.
- Costs of telephone and postage.
- Restrictions imposed on use of leasehold domestic property.
- Legalities of planning legislation and homeworking.
- Liability for business rate rather than council tax for the home when used as a business location.
- Responsibility of employee for third-party damages when home-based.
- Income tax and payments for use of home as office.
- Benefit-in-kind of access to employer-provided technology for use in home.
- Tax allowances for use of home as office.
- Capital gains liability where home is also used for business.

In formulating agreements with trades unions a review of agreements forged by other companies with their trade unions will assist. A recent collective agreement between BT, a major UK employer, and the National Telecommunications Union has clauses under the following headings:

1 **Application and selection procedures** – no employee has the right to be allowed to telework.
2 Issues to be addressed when considering teleworking:
   – *job related requirements* – preventing isolation, autonomy of the jobholder, management by deliverables, job satisfaction, existing job-related travel requirements, career development, individual nature of existing job.
   – *personal requirements* – personal qualities, domestic circumstances.
   – *industrial relations* – informing the local union branch of arrangements.
3 **Terms and conditions** – contractual hours remain the same unless agreed by the individual concerned; attendance requirements at the office must be notified well in advance; pay, annual leave, superannuation and other contractual entitlements remain unaltered; London weightings remain for those living in the area; travel and subsistence is to be paid to homeworkers from the home location; employee communications to be maintained; individual contracts to be amended before teleworking commences.
4 **Health and Safety at Work** – covered by the legislation to include work at home.
5 **Local by-laws** – the company will assist employees in checking that they are not in breach of by-laws by working at home and other pertinent matters.
6 **Insurance cover** – any additional premiums for the use of home as an office will be paid by the company.
7 **Security** – protection of company confidential information; provision for safe disposal of privacy marked waste; equipment security provisions.
8 **Provision of equipment** – explains inland revenue rules regarding personal use; allowances for additional costs of using home as an office.
9 **Capital Gains Tax** – regulations explained.
10 **Termination of Teleworking Agreement** – annual review of arrangements.
11 **Management and Supervision:**
   – *career development*
   – *day-to-day supervision* – including home visits
   – *use of technology* – by managers for supervising teleworkers
   – *group work* – provision for teleworkers to be team members
   – *new employees* – not normally to be recruited as teleworkers

Equal opportunities features in a personnel manual prepared for use in introducing teleworking into the UK government's Benefits Agency. It recommends:

> '. . . in view of the particular nature of homeworking, draw the line manager's attention to
> 1. Equal Opportunities Policy Statement.
> 2. Equal Opportunities Code of Practice.
>
> Acts of discrimination and disregard of Equal Opportunities Policies are treated as disciplinary offences.'

Having reviewed some of the practical aspects of teleworking which need to be considered and agreed before embarking on any major activity we now go on to look at the office itself. In order to maximize outcomes any planning to increase the mobility of the workforce should be accompanied by a fundamental look at the office and its use.

NEW CONCEPTS IN SPACE PLANNING

Questioning the concept of the office

Clearly one of the reasons for introducing mobile/flexible working is the desire to reduce fixed overheads including those arising from operating offices. However office accommodation is something very dear to the hearts of many employees. It is a measure of status and standing within the organization. For many employees it is their own personal territory. Making changes often creates major problems for organizations and decisions are often taken at levels which appear to the outsider more senior than should be necessary.

According to Andrew Laing[10] of the planning consultants DEGW much commercial office development has been driven by property developers rather than by an understanding of the needs of the end-user. As a consequence the space created has failed to address issues such as

1 The quality of life at work.
2 Expectations as to where work will take place.
3 Green issues and the healthy work place.
4 A responsive environment.

But a more *damning* criticism is that workspaces are just not designed to support the ways of working being encouraged as a response to intensified competition and the need for organizational innovativeness and flexibility.

One company which is seen as leading the way in office design to support a new culture is Scandinavian Airlines (SAS) in their office building near Stockholm. The architect, Niels Torp, examined the need for employee mobility and translated this into a workspace designed to meet human and organizational needs. His inspiration is said to have come from walking around the narrow streets of the old part of Stockholm. The result is a HO building which is a series of connected buildings along either side of a glass-covered, tree-lined avenue which is used for impromptu meetings and staff refreshment at pavement-style cafés. The office areas comprise narrow rooms dissolving into broad deep rooms so as to achieve a human scale in areas which are actually quite large. This creates a feeling of intimacy for staff who appear to be working alongside no more than 30 others. Separate offices are of different shapes. Corridors, or rather walkways, cut across each area diagonally rather than splitting the space down the middle. All of this is designed to create a sense of community and encourage the free exchange of ideas between teams.

A more immediate driver for change is the search for overhead cost savings. If we look first at office utilization it would surprise some executives if they became aware of the redundancy present in much of their office space. Before introducing their 'hot-desking' scheme, according to Neil Harris[11], Digital found that at most they were only achieving 22 per cent utilization of their UK office space and that 50 per cent of desks were empty at any one time. They calculated that they were in fact achieving a 12 to 14 per cent utilization factor.

New approaches to space planning

Given the increase in mobility afforded employees many companies have recognized that there can be considerable cost savings to be gained by rethinking office utilization. *Hot-desking* describes an approach which provides workspace for only a limited number of staff at any one time and with staff having no fixed desk or office location. *Floating offices* also describe the situation where staff are equipped to work at the most appropriate location and again do not have a fixed facility in their home office. Computer companies such as Digital in Sweden and Finland as well as the UK and IBM in the UK have been at the forefront in implementing hot-desking and also redesigning office space to suit the new ways of working and organizational form they seek to encourage. But it is not just computer vendors who are making these changes; another example given here is based on Andersen Consultant's, London HQ.

The principles underlying the new design concepts as articulated by Laing are:

1 Design to support the business process.
2 Design to support the management of space over time.
3 Design to facilitate building and energy management over time.

The following comment by F. Duffy (in F. Donnelly[12]), also of DEGW, seems to sum up the view being taken by some companies.

> **'The idea of an office with thousands of desks is an old fashioned concept. The office should be thought of as a place where people meet, interact and create – a sort of old-fashioned club.'**

The move to new office designs ought to be viewed not just as a means for reducing desk-space and costs but rather as a means for developing the new working practices being sought to meet the challenges faced by business. As each business is in a unique position it will seek its own bespoke solutions to the design of its workspace. The consequences of moving to more open use of space go beyond the cost savings. The relationships between staff change; the role of the manager changes; the expectations for involvement and influence change. Companies such as DEC see this form of working supporting their corporate aim of becoming a learning organization, so they are looking for a lot more than mere cost savings from the changes which are being introduced.

> **The move to new office designs ought to be viewed not just as a means for reducing desk-space and costs but rather as a means for developing the new working practices being sought to meet the challenges faced by business.**

Cases for illustration

Exhibit 5.6 A new concept in offices

> ### *Case Study 6: A computer company's head office in Sweden*
>
> **Background:**
> - Digital's headquarters building housed approximately 450 people including sales account and customer services groups. DEC-Site, a team specializing in planning, designing and managing the physical environment along with the country management team was located in a nearby building.

Exhibit 5.6 (cont.) A new concept in offices

Problem:
- DEC-site occupied glass-fronted offices each containing one or two employees and arranged in rows. Breaks at 10.00 and 15.00 enabled staff to meet informally but, despite this, communications generally were seen to be poor. The team was situated some way away from key contacts in the sales groups. Also there was too much paper in circulation and being stored unnecessarily.

Changes:
- The DEC-site was to be housed in the main building. Four members of the 16 strong team were responsible for establishing the new office accommodation.

  The design proposed built on four themes – an archipelago, the beach, the garden and the golf course all of which were depicted in the natural office.

  On the floor a central green island is enclosed by a brown beach with blue water at its edges. Ramps cross the blue water to raised floor areas, on one side to the bridge of a ship and on the other to a quiet room. Informal meetings and light breakfast in the morning are encouraged on the ship where round tables and chairs provide the working arrangements. The quiet room is glass-fronted but with soft furnishings so that eight people can meet round the central irregular and angular table. One wall has along it a putting course for relaxation.

  A large indoor tree is a centre piece of the office. It has pieces of fruit suspended which if gently pressed release a computer workstation from the ceiling. The working level is adjustable and chairs of different design are available to offer different working postures.

  Each staff member has a personal, mobile workdesk with mounted bookcase and drawers. When not in use they are stored in a nearby room but then brought to the workspace when needed. Additionally each person has a limited shelf space.

  Much of the wall covering is in slatted wooden panelling in the style of Swedish archipelago and providing a noise absorbing covering. The natural lighting is supplemented by automatically controlled interior lighting.

  Cordless telephones enable staff to walk around the office whilst making calls. The system also allows them to keep in touch with the switchboard when outside the office.

Outcomes:
- A 50 per cent saving in office space; 20 per cent increase in productivity; improved communications; 70 per cent reduction in paperwork; 70 per cent reduction in energy and lighting costs; reduction in other operating costs; noise reduction.

Exhibit 5.7 Hot-desking in a bank

Case Study 7: A Canadian Bank

Background:
- The Bank of Montreal in Toronto was seeking to reduce its leased floor-space and to improve its internal customer service. One of the first groups to move to the concept of the floating office was project managers from the Business Systems Group. This group of 25 staff used to spend as much as 90 per cent of their time in branch offices at site meetings.

Changes:
- Staff have been equipped with a range of technology. All have portable PCs, modems and pagers. Some were also equipped with cellular phones. The software for communications has been designed to support their work and give access to a wide range of applications which reside on the home office computer. Staff are required to respond swiftly to calls and this is assessed as part of their performance review. They are also required to file regular performance reports via e-mail. There are now eight desks at HQ for the 25 staff.

Outcomes:
- Real estate leasing and office support costs reduced by over 30 per cent. Positive staff responses to their greater freedom to organize their own schedule and work where most suitable. They practise 'time-shifting' to reduce time wasted commuting during rush-hours.

Designing for empowerment and self-reliance

As we have seen, maximizing the benefits from facilitating the mobility of the workforce requires a radical rethink. Much of this centres around the creation of both a physical and emotional environment in which the individual will seek to maximize his/her contribution. It requires the organization to embrace the notion and practice of *empowerment*. But through empowerment one is also seeking self-reliance and independent working. The organizational infrastructure has to support what for many is a radical shift in behaviour.

But maximizing the return also requires a thorough review of work processes and a critical review of their contribution to added-value for the customer. It requires more than the view that the same employee will maintain a virtual presence within an apparently unaltered organization. It requires a design approach which returns to basics.

Exhibit 5.8 Space saving by a consultancy

Case Study 8: A Consultancy's UK Headquarters Building

Background:
- Andersen Consulting was enjoying a considerable growth rate during the early 1990s. Its HQ building had a further ten years to run on its lease and Andersen did not want to move particularly given its convenient location. So they were seeking ways for improving their office utilization.

Changes:
- One floor of the building was redesigned to accommodate 160 staff but with only 55 workstations. A floor administrator using a personal PC books desk space for consultants wishing to use the office. No one has a particular desk but everyone has a large filing drawer which contains portable boxes of work. A floor steward takes the work boxes to the allocated workspace before the consultant arrives. Each desk has a networked PC with standard software and there is access to LotusNotes groupware.

  The long narrow floor layout which had a central corridor has been redesigned into sections to create an atmosphere of small group work areas. Some of these have been designed for small teams or individuals to spread themselves, others with less space for short-term tasks. There is also an area with easy chairs for less formal activity. This area is particularly important because it is intended to promote interchange and networking.

  The most senior staff still have their own permanent offices and the secretaries have permanent work areas with two located together to serve a group of consultants. If senior managers are not using their office others can do so.

Outcomes:
- The capacity of the accommodation has been doubled. Desk occupancy is about 33 per cent. Staff have responded positively.

Organizations may wish to start on this route in a tentative manner, implementing one or two trials so as to promote understanding and develop appropriate skills. Many organizations will implement more widespread schemes but limited in scope in order to satisfy short-term organizational demands. Being limited in approach these schemes are unlikely to result in the competitive advantages that are possible from incorporating these changes into a more major review of organizational operations within the value chain such as advocated by proponents of business process re-engineering.

A major limiting factor for many large organizations will be the 'baggage which they already carry'. The cost of moving swiftly to a new form of organization may just not be feasible. For example, Hans-Olaf Henkel, a former Chairman of the Board of IBM World Trade Europe/Middle East/Africa Corporation, has indicated that IBM in Germany could only afford to set up 100 of its staff as teleworkers despite much greater interest and what appears to be strong market positioning reasons behind the move. Commitments to existing office leases and property investment, the capital costs of providing access to the facilities needed and the prospect of major organizational disruption all lead those of faint heart to decide against such moves. But right behind these tentatively moving organizations are those new niche players in the market which are using the technology to create virtual corporations and in this way creating global networks which can out-compete the large and slow-moving corporations.

RETHINKING THE ORGANIZATION OF WORK

In this section we summarize the key points arising out of this chapter.

Management summary

- Technology can be used to enable time and space independence for much productive effort.
- Many different organizational models have been established for the effective distribution of work.
- Drivers for change to a more mobile workforce go beyond organizational aims and purposes to include personal aspirations and *societal* pressures.
- For implementation to be successful the intention of added-value for the customer must be the focus of attention in the design phase.
- Significant productivity improvements have been claimed by many organizations which have implemented more flexible work practices.
- Practical problems need thorough consideration prior to implementation. Prototyping should be used to assist in subsequent wider implementation.
- Adequate technological capability is an essential for successful implementation.
- A radical rethink of the use of office space has the possibility for major overhead reduction but cost savings will not always fund the investment needed for moving to new work forms.
- A strategic approach bringing together and integrating the business need, IT developments and HR issues will result in the greatest pay-off.

References

1 HUWS U. 'Teleworking in Britain', Sheffield, England, Employment Department, 1993.
2 SHELLENBARGER S. '*Some Thrive, but Many Wilt Working at Home*', *Wall Street Journal*, Tuesday, 14 December, 1993, pp B1.
3 HODSON N. '*The Business Case for Telematics*' in Henley Future Work Forum (Ed), '*The Real Business Benefits of Telecommunications*', Henley-on-Thames, England, Henley Management College, April 1994.
4 MURRAY B. '*The National Telecommunications Survey*' in Henley Future Work Forum (Ed), '*The Real Business Benefits of Telecommunications*', Henley-on-Thames, England, Henley Management College, April 1994.
5 FROST Y., BIRCHALL D. W. 'In Discussion with Jack Nilles', Henley-on-Thames, England, Henley Management College, 1993.
6 RIDGEWELL C. '*The Mercury Experience*' in Frost Y. (Ed) '*The Flexible Workplace*', Henley-on-Thames, England, The Henley Future Work Forum, 1993, pp 25–36.
7 Ovum 'Flexible Working with Information Technology: The Business Opportunity', 1, Mortimer Street, London, June 1993.
8 DAVIS S. 'Twenty tips for developing 20/20 vision for businesses', *Journal of Management Development*, Volume 12, Issue 6, 1993, pp15–20.
9 RODGERS C. S. '*The Flexible Workplace: What Have We Learned?*', *Human Resource Management*, Volume 31, Issue 3, Fall 1992, pp183–199.
10 LAING A. '*The Changing Workplace*' in Frost Y. (Ed) '*The Flexible Workplace*', The Henley Future Work Forum, 1993, pp 6–12.
11 HARRIS N. '*The Digital Experience*' in Frost Y. (Ed) '*The Flexible Workplace*', Henley-on-Thames, UK, The Henley Future Work Forum, 1993, pp 13–24.
12 DONNELLY F. '*Space Oddities*', *Computing*, 3 September, 1992, pp 30–31.

'Too often when we begin a piece of knowledge work with a team we assume that all members of the team are comfortable working together, that we all know how to behave appropriately in team meetings, that we understand each other's point of view, that we care more about the success of the team than our individual accomplishments, that we understand and agree upon the role the team leader is to play, how we are going to make decisions, what information we need to collect or develop to answer the questions we are asking, how we will get that information, and what we will know when we have finished our work.'

WILLIAM A. PASMORE

Creating Strategic Change – Designing the Flexible High Performing Organization, John Wiley, New York, 1994.

6

HIGH-PERFORMANCE DISTRIBUTED TEAMS

INTRODUCTION

One of the most exciting challenges facing organizations is that of using technology to support high-performing teams when working in distributed mode. Those organizations that are successful in developing skills in forming, managing and terminating distributed project teams comprising people from around the globe will be the winners in the late 1990s. Why would the authors make such a bold claim?

Imagine a situation where a new product is to be developed and launched into a highly-competitive marketplace. The most capable expertise for this process no longer resides within the boundaries of the organization. It is located all over the world, employed by traditional organizations as well as operating as independent contractors. Traditionally the project executive would have sought to either bring the resources together under one roof for the project's duration or, if this should not be possible, accept the high direct and opportunity cost of having people travel regularly to attend working meetings. The lapsed time from exploratory discussions to project realization would be considerable. This is no longer feasible because of the rate at which competition can develop such new products. Some organizations have already realized the potential of technology to transform ways of working in such circumstances. Not only has technology the capability to cut down on costs both direct and indirect but more significantly it enables business to concertina activities, adopting fast-track methods or simultaneous engineering to significantly reduce development times.

In this chapter we first examine the concept of teamworking in the modern organization, looking at design, development and management issues. We then look in detail at how technology can be deployed to support teams. Finally we look at how organizations can move to these new ways of working and the factors to be considered so as to ensure high performance from distributed teams. Our aim is to give both background principles and practical solutions.

TEAMS IN ORGANIZATIONS

Teams rather than groups?

It is commonplace to hear executives describe their organization with such expressions as 'we have excellent teamwork here', 'we all pull together as a team', 'we have a high level of team morale'. But what does this mean? Why has it become fashionable to talk about organizations in such terms and why the interest placed on 'leadership' qualities perhaps even at the expense of managerial competencies?

One of the key reasons for this change is that former management hierarchies are no longer able to cope with the pace of change needed in organizations. The need for swift action in areas such as getting new products into the marketplace, the implementation of new systems of working, responding to customer demands and capitalizing on business opportunities, make it just not possible for managers within functionally-based organizations to operate effectively. If they are to beat off competition there is no longer sufficient time for them if they follow the practices which still abound in many traditional functionally-based organizations. To meet the new challenges, staff are having to be deployed differently, coming together into task forces to achieve defined needs. Increasingly work in organizations is of a project nature with clearly defined end goals, operational procedures and resource allocation. Time pressures and skills needed force organizations to adopt a team-based approach and hence the increasing need for teams of people to come together to share the responsibility for achieving the task demands.

Following on from this move towards team-based project work there is also an interest in how best to manage such teams. Team leadership has become a key skill in the new organizational paradigm.

As we have is already observed, the expression *team* is used in many contexts. For our purposes here is a working definition is taken from a recent book, *The Wisdom of Teams* by Jon Katzenbach and Douglas Smith[1]:

> 'A team is a small number of people with complementary skills who are committed to a common purpose, performance goals, and approach for which they hold themselves mutually accountable.'

Applying this definition, it is immediately apparent that many of the bold statements made by executives about teamwork in their organization, rather than being explanations of how work is organized, really deal with a feeling of shared destiny that they hope employees experience and a shared sense of commitment to the organization's goals which they are encouraging. Also, at the operational level we hear many managers referring to 'my team' when really they are referring to a group of people within their area of responsibility over whom they have authority, for whose output they are responsible and who they see as having some common interest based on their own administrative unit. In such circumstances the work carried out by one member of staff does not necessarily require interaction with other members of the work unit. Tasks are not necessarily interdependent. These staff are put together rather more for administrative and managerial purposes than with the aim of fostering team-based working. In many such cases there is considerable lost potential resulting from a failure to make effective use of teamworking.

Having applied this definition to make distinctions about organizational arrangements which are not based on 'teams', we can now proceed to look in more detail at how to make teams effective.

One key feature of our definition is that team members share a common goal. But our definition requires more than this – it requires members of the team to recognize and accept joint responsibility for the team's output. In order to achieve this the team obviously has to have access to all those resources necessary for its successful task achievement.

So the skills needed for the team to be effective go well beyond those required for success on the technical aspects of their task. In addition to technical or functional skills, team members also need to have group problem-solving and decision-making as well as interpersonal skills.

DESIGNING TEAMS

Meeting the need

As we saw earlier, teams can have different purposes. The team may be working on implementation of a defined project, it may have been set up to solve problems whether loosely or closely defined, it may be responsible for formulating strategic direction. The team may have a short life with tight deadlines, alternatively, it may have no intended termination point when created. Members of the team may well be working on several projects simultaneously and have membership of multiple teams, overlapping or otherwise. The team may be one of many within a matrix organization structure or it may be drawn from a more traditional functionally-based and hierarchical structure and be seen as self-contained and rather unusual.

In establishing teams organizations are working on the assumption that the performance of the team will be greater than that possible by any one or several individuals working independently. For example, by bringing together complementary skills and perspectives to problem-solving the team has the potential to achieve superior solutions. There is also often the assumption that, when faced with the need for rapid change, teams will be able to respond more quickly than individual employees in their normal hierarchical positions within the organization. Diversity amongst team members is also seen as a strength, bringing as it does many different perspectives and a tension between conflicting views which can often lead to creative solutions. Further, there is a widely held belief that working in teams can offer higher levels of personal development and, following on from this, higher satisfaction for members.

Each team is unique, not only in purpose and the context in which the task is to be carried out, but also in structural features such as size and composition and in the personality mix and experience of co-operative work of members. In consequence, each team has its own development path, some achieving far more than expected, others failing despite high expectations at the outset.

Sources of failure

Failure of teams to perform are identified by Nicola Phillips[2] in her book, *Managing International Teams* as including:

1 Not enough variety in members' backgrounds and experience.
2 Too much variety.
3 Failure to use, or inappropriate use of, the skills and experiences of group members.
4 Too large a group to encourage participation.
5 The group structure does not enable members to contribute effectively.
6 Lack of focus or direction.
7 Time wasted due to lack of controls or appropriate information.
8 Individuals working to their own agenda rather than that of the group as a whole.

Added to this may be the failure of the group to devote energy and time to activities which develop and maintain effective group functioning.

Design for success

Joseph McGrath[3], who along with Andrea Hollingshead has produced an excellent summary of research into groups interacting with technology, in earlier work developed a model for the study of groups. According to this model, or framework, the essential feature of a group is the interaction of its members in some recognized relation to one another. They suggest four major forces that fashion the group's behaviour:

1 The characteristics of the group's task.
2 The pattern of relationships among group members prior to interaction.
3 The environment in which the group assembles – physical, socio-cultural and technological.
4 The individual properties of group members which include their psychological state and their social abilities.

Hackman and Morris[4], in their writings in the mid-1970s, went beyond this and suggested that both performance on the task and other positive outcomes as far as the group is concerned, was not only the result of inputs such as those brought to the group by individuals (e.g. skills, attitudes and personality), the characteristics of the group (e.g. structure, size and cohesiveness), and environment-level factors (e.g. task characteristics, reward structure and stress levels), but importantly performance is strongly influenced by the group interaction process. This model suggests that the quality of this interaction process will have a major influence on the outcomes regardless of the quality of the inputs. It will influence the effort brought to bear on the task by group members, the task strategies used by group members in carrying out the task and the knowledge and skills of group members that are effectively brought to bear on the task.

Critical features of the task are its difficulty, the amount of effort demanded, the ease with which it can be done and the multiplicity of solutions, the co-operation requirements and the degree to which the group would have familiarity with the type of task presented. Particularly important are group size and composition – the size should be kept to the minimum needed to contain all the skills required for the task in terms both of the technical requirements and the representation of interests appropriate in the decision-making process. Also impacting on group development and performance is the impact of the social structure from which the team has been drawn and operates, the status differences within the group and the authority relationships that exist within the social system in which the group is functioning.

So whilst we have identified many of the factors which impact on group performance, it is clear from the research evidence available to date that it is not possible to be prescriptive in terms of a formula for success. Also previous success is not a guarantee of continued high performance even where many of the conditions are held constant.

However we have now established many of the attributes to be considered when designing a team.

DEVELOPING TEAMS

No single theory

Turning our attention now to the processes of team development, here also research has not resulted in a commonly held view about how teams develop to be successful or not. B. W. Tuckman's[5] theory of group development which he propounded as early as 1965 has been influential in subsequent thinking about how teams develop and has also stimulated alternative views. B. W. Tuckman suggested four phases in the development of a group over time – *forming, storming, norming* and *performing*. He suggested that every group moves through these phases without necessarily recognizing it. The emergence of group norms (those informal rules governing behaviour based on similarities in attitudes and values) is a notable element in this process. Norms develop through expressive statements by fellow members, critical events in the group's history, primacy or carry over behaviour from past situations. They can have a major impact on the extent to which the group will conform to the aims of management. They can be just as dysfunctional as they can be productive. The more that the members conform to the group norms the more cohesive the group. Cohesiveness in turn is influenced by the amount of time members spend together, the more difficult it is made for new members to join, the size of the group, the greater the collective threat posed by the group and the group's record of previous successes. High cohesiveness can be both the cause and the outcome of high group productivity. A highly cohesive group committed to the organization's goals can be very effective.

B. W. Tuckman's model of group development can be criticized for its assumption that the group develops along a linear path, but nevertheless the model does identify stages that are recognizable in retrospect to many team members. However, later researchers have emphasized the cyclical nature of group development; the group is dynamic, responding to changes in its external environment as well as its internal membership. One particularly influential study is that carried out by Connie Gersick[6], into the workings of eight naturally occurring teams. She identified three phases in their development:

1 *Phase 1* which takes place during the early stage of the group coming together. How the group reacts will depend upon how members define the task, how they perceive outside requirements and how they organize themselves within the group. She found that the ways of working established by the group at an early stage lasted until about halfway through the group's task.
2 *Transition* – an abrupt change can be observed in the attitudes and behaviour of group members. The realization that a deadline is approaching leads to self-reflection and analysis by the group and then to a radically changed way of working.
3 *Phase 2* in which the group carries out the task along the lines agreed in the transition.

An interpretation of these findings is that group performance is related to the nature of the task and the time constraints under which the group is performing. Connie Gersick's model is one of *punctuated equilibrium* in that periods of relative stability are concluded with a major upheaval which leads to a new pattern of working. This transition phase for a task of defined time scale was about halfway through the time period. A *steady state alignment model* could not therefore explain group dynamics. We argue in Chapter 8 the need to incorporate conflict into models of the organization in contrast to the popular steady state alignment models which are often used.

Teams tackling projects

Joseph McGrath has developed earlier research further by categorizing group activities based on the dimensions *time, interaction* and *performance*. In developing this model Joseph McGrath based his work on the assumption that groups are continuously and simultaneously engaged in three major functions, i.e. production (meeting the task requirements), member support (mutual assistance) and group well-being (aimed at the maintenance of the social entity). He then suggests that groups carry out these functions in one or another of four modes:

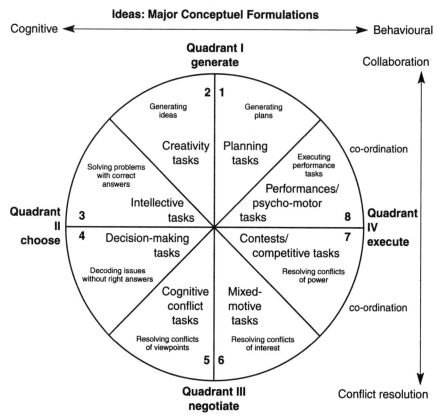

Figure 6.1 A model of group processes

Mode 1: inception of a project

Mode 2: choice of the means for solving technical issues (problem-solving approach)

Mode 3: resolution of conflict (political rather than technical)

Mode 4: execution of the performance requirements of the group task.

These modes are not a fixed sequence but rather four potential forms of activity by which groups pursue each of the three functions. Groups carry out their projects by means of time/activity paths consisting of mode/function sequences. Modes 1 and 4 are required for the completion of every group task, whereas Modes 2 and 3 are not essential. Joseph McGrath then presents a classification of tasks performed by a group. He divides the tasks into four main types:

1 To generate – ideas or plans.

2 To choose – a correct answer or a preferred solution.

3 To negotiate – conflicting views or interests.
4 To execute – in competition with an opponent or against external performance standards.

He sees these task types as varying in the extent to which effective performance depends upon the transmission only of information amongst group members. They vary in the extent to which effective performance also requires the transmission of values, interests, personal commitments and other similar features described as *media richness*.

The four task types are represented in Figure 6.1 as four segments of the circle. These task types are further subdivided in the diagram. Items to the right of the circle are more behavioural in nature while those to the left are more cognitive. Items to the top of the diagram are more based on collaboration and those to the bottom on conflict resolution. By breaking down tasks in this way it is possible, as we will see later, to assist teams in understanding the processes better and also to start matching tasks to the technologies available to support group activity.

TECHNOLOGY SUPPORTING TEAMS

Matching technology to task

Over the last few years, rapid developments have taken place in software to support teamworking. Probably the most important pre- requisite for teamworking is the ability to communicate effectively within the team. A second prerequisite is accurate and timely information to support the team in its task. A third requirement is to be able to communicate with the external world. Fourthly, as we saw in the last section, team performance is determined by the quality of the group interaction process – an area where improvement is usually possible and technology can offer some support.

Where groups are working in a face-to-face mode, methods of communication are well understood. However, a multiplicity of techniques to assist groups problem-solve have been developed and put to practical use including approaches such as brainstorming. While these techniques have considerable potential they are often not applied practically and the results are then disappointing. Also there is considerable understanding among human resource specialists of the role of *process consultation* in facilitating group

> **Over the last few years, rapid developments have taken place in software to support teamworking.**

interaction processes and in helping groups overcome blockages to progress. However, experience is mostly in the face-to-face situation. Where groups are working in a dispersed/distributed mode different methods are needed.

In Table 6.1 we have illustrated some of the technologies which might be used to support a dispersed team in the four main areas of its activity. In any situation team members will of course use a combination of communications media and supplement whatever is supplied by any means they have access to and feel are appropriate.

Table 6.1 Technology to support communications in the distributed team

Purpose of system	Type of system
Communications – Internal amongst group members.	Teleconferencing; video conferencing; fax; e-mail; bulletin boards; computer conferencing; voice-mail; groupware.
Retrieval of information.	Access to databases (internal to the organization and external) and search facilities; expert systems to filter and enhance usefulness of information.
Communications – External with both individuals and groups.	Same as internal communications, but including the telephone.
Structuring group task performance.	Group performance support systems·

Freeing meetings from time constraints

However, many distributed teams are not normally working together in real time. Synchronous communication is time-dependent as well as expensive if interaction is over a prolonged time period. So asynchronous systems are of particular use where the team is working in different time-zones and over large distances. Voice-mail, e-mail, and computer conferencing are well-established but electronic groupware systems are becoming especially useful in this context. The latter is the new generation of software tools designed to assist groups function in such conditions and which are capable of tailoring to suit particular needs. The extent to which these facilities enable simultaneous dialogue between group members with the certainty that all have received the same information varies between systems. Also the channelling of information can be managed through conduits such that each member only receives that felt to be appropriate by the person responsible for managing the information flows (this is done by setting up arrangements such as *closed user groups* for communication within a wider network).

External sources of information used by groups include each member's personal store of information and sources as well as accessible corporate information of both a quantitative and qualitative kind. Other external sources include both public and private information databases. The former include many which are accessible through Internet, the worldwide communications network, but which are difficult for the inexperienced to use effectively. These systems can be accessed directly in real-time or alternatively routines developed to enable automated searching at times when communications costs can be minimized. Whatever means are used to access information there is the distinct possibility that too much information will be presented to the team and at the wrong times. Tools to assist groups bring together information from several data sources and present it in intelligible forms are already available including those that use hypertext presentation for ease of movement in databases. But more interesting developments are taking place in the automated examination and sifting of information based on expert systems. Any system of this type can be used by distributed teams so long as they have the means for transmitting the data to other team members. In designing such systems the goal should not be lost sight of, it being to improve the effectiveness of the decision-making process by delivery of appropriate information in a way in which it is useful to, and usable by, the group.

Groupware systems can be programmed to interface with project management tools, software development tools and other software to plan and structure group work. However when looking at enhancing the performance of teams an increasing number of tools are becoming available which offer group performance support. These are available to channel or modify the group's task performance processes and task products. The tools structure the form in which the tasks are presented to the team and the form of the team's responses. They usually have components which assist in structuring ideas, evaluating them and developing agendas for action. These systems can be used alongside other communications tools, such as the groupware systems referred to earlier, to provide a powerful suite of programs to aid distributed teams in their work.

The limitations of technology

The advantages and disadvantages of means for group communication were identified in Chapters 4 and 5. They each reduce to varying degrees the set of *modalities* available to members to communicate with each other, e.g. auditory, visual, non-verbal, para-verbal. The loss of any one modality limits the way in which the group can function. Since each medium results in a different form of loss to a differing extent it is obviously good practice to define the purpose and specification before choosing the system or combination of systems. So, for example, where there is a high level of individual work with low task interdependence, the sharing of information may be primarily to report progress against a schedule and to seek help in solving technical problems. The system chosen in such circumstances may be a project management tool along with e-mail. In sharp contrast, where the task requires a high level of negotiation on sensitive issues it may prove impractical regardless of the kind of technology used and the team may have to meet face-to-face.

Table 6.2 gives an indication of the principal advantages and disadvantages of technologies that might be used to support communications between members of a collaborative team. However, a combination of technologies can overcome some of the drawbacks. As an example satellite transmission of video might be point-to-multi-point and be one-way; a back-channel might take the form of fax, e-mail or phone-in to allow spontaneous questioning. Some sophisticated systems already on the market combine video and computer-based information by using split screens and the capability of ISDN to transmit the data. Some of the problems inherent in early systems will be overcome by technological improvements in the hardware and software and the communications links.

Earlier we introduced the ideas developed by J. E. McGrath, who identified the four types of activity engaged in by groups as *to generate, to choose, to negotiate* and *to execute*. He further subdivided this categorization as shown in the second and third columns of Table 6.3. He also identified two other dimensions to describe the nature of the activities engaged in – those activities which are more behavioural in nature compared to those which are more cognitive, and those which are more based on collaboration vs. those based on conflict resolution. By breaking down the overall activities engaged in by teams in this way it is possible to form a view of the media richness required for effective teamwork. This we have done tentatively in the fourth column. This gives us a view of the extent to which the activity is

Table 6.2 Systems to support communications for distributed teams

Synchronous*	Asynchronous	Advantages	Disadvantages
Face-to-face.		Full modality. Process consultancy can be effective.	Team members have to all be in one place at one time.
Interactive video systems.		Team members can be dispersed. Allows no interactive text or data unless the system includes 'white-boards'.	Reduction of non-verbal interaction. All members must be present and connected. Limits to the extent of inter-connectedness.
	Non-interactive video.	Team members can be dispersed.	Loss of spontaneity and ability to question conveniently.
Telephone conferences.		Preserve the para-verbal aspects of speech. Relatively cheap and easy to set up. Issues can be addressed immediately. No text or data.	Loss of visual image. Difficulties in chairing and managing meetings, particularly as numbers grow.
	Voice-messaging.	Cheap and easy.	More difficult for recipient to gain understanding of anything other than simple issues. Time delays in receipt of replies and limited distribution.
Interactive computer conferences.		Instantaneous. Allows transmission of interactive text, graphics and data.	Generally inefficient because of the limitations of typing speeds and problems of co-ordination. Loss of all non-verbal and para-verbal cues.
	Asynchronous computer conferences.	Not time dependent. Time to consider personal contributions. Allows transmission of interactive text, graphics and data.	Loss of modality except for written communications. Contributions difficult to structure logically. Possibility of information overload. No certainty about the receipt of messages.

* The terms *synchronous* and *asynchronous* refer to the team members being simultaneously in contact and not the electronic method of transmission.

going to benefit from full face-to-face contact and the extent to which various media, by reducing the modalities, may inhibit teamwork to the point where progress is unlikely on the task. For example, we have already suggested that the more sensitive the issues and the greater the level of negotiation necessary the more appropriate that a full face-to-face meeting be convened.

Based on the type of analysis shown in Table 6.3, we can review the needs of the distributed team by examining in detail the nature of the activities required for them to perform successfully and matching the capabilities of technologies to their needs. Columns 1 and 6 allow space to complete the analysis for any particular activities to be carried out by a distributed team or even to assess its overall task.

Table 6.3 A framework for matching technology to task need

Task purpose	Type of task	Main activity	Nature of the activity	Importance of media richness	Most applicable technology
	1 Planning.	Generating plans.	Behavioural/ collaborative.	Relatively low.	
	2 Creativity.	Generating ideas.	Cognitive/ collaborative.	Relatively low.	
	3 Intellective.	Solving problems with correct answers.	Cognitive/ collaborative.	Moderate.	
	4 Decision-making.	Deciding issues without correct answers.	Cognitive/ conflict resolution.	Moderately high.	
	5 Cognitive conflict.	Receiving conflicts of viewpoints.	Cognitive/ conflict resolution.	Moderately high.	
	6 Mixed motive.	Receiving conflicts of interest.	Behavioural/ conflict resolution.	Very high.	
	7 Contests/ competitive.	Receiving conflicts of power.	Behavioural/ conflict resolution.	Very high.	
	8 Performance/ psychomotor.	Executing performance.	Behavioural/ collaborative.	Moderate.	

CREATING AND MAINTAINING THE HIGH-PERFORMANCE DISTRIBUTED TEAM

Design principles

We have already seen something of the characteristics of an effective team earlier in this chapter. In designing a distributed team there are four major areas to consider:

1 The purpose of the team and success criteria.
2 The make-up of the team.
3 The design of the technical infrastructure to support the team.
4 The process of team development.

We are assuming that appropriately empowered teams are more likely to be high performing than those subjected to closer supervision as in the more traditional organization. The following characteristics form the basis for the design of empowered teams:

1 Members have a range of overlapping skills and competencies.
2 The leader is a coach and facilitator rather than a supervisor in the traditional sense.
3 Problems are seen as bi-directional and not just to be resolved by management.
4 The team works out its own solutions wherever practical.
5 The team is party to establishing its own targets.
6 The customer is the prime focus of attention.
7 Team members have direct customer contact where practical.
8 The need for constant personal upgrading is recognized and encouraged by all members.
9 Rewards are diverse and situational.

The aim is to create teams with a rather different working atmosphere to that found in many traditional groups. The specific behaviours sought from the team and its members are likely to include features such as:

1 A recognition that members and the team will benefit most from mutual support.
2 A commitment to team goals.
3 Free discussion of ideas.
4 A working atmosphere of openness and trust.
5 Free sharing of members' views and encouragement to ask questions.
6 Encouragement of members by the team to seek training and development which will enhance their skills for the present and the future.

7 conflict is seen as a healthy way to resolve issues.
8 participation in decision-making is seen by members to be part of their role and responsibility.

Supporting moves to team-based work

Setting up teamwork in an organization where teamworking is not part of the normal way of working is a lengthy process. As we will explain in Chapter 8, this significant structural change requires a change in the culture and other organizational factors. This might involve bringing about new attitudes at all levels in the organization, from top management down through the rest of the workforce. There will be implications for changing work practices which will undoubtedly affect all interfacing functions and departments, not just those where teams have been set up. Implementing teamworking is often undertaken in conjunction with other change initiatives and in the case of the distribution of the team members is likely to include new technical support systems. It clearly requires careful planning, consultation with those involved and monitoring of progress. Teams need to be nurtured. They need the right amount of guidance, which will vary as they mature and can take on more responsibility.

Changing the culture of an organization takes considerable time and concerted effort. Attitudes cannot be changed overnight. People have to be persuaded that the proposed way forward is appropriate for the organization and themselves. They need time to think about and discuss how the new methods of working will affect them. Unless those in senior management who come into contact with those directly involved demonstrate their commitment and intent to make it succeed problems of implementation will be magnified.

> **Setting up teamwork in an organization where teamworking is not part of the normal way of working is a lengthy process.**

Most organizations view the development of teamworking as a long-term process. Organizations need to develop a frame of mind where they can cope with undertaking and seeing through such long-term change.

Learning from prototypes

In attempting to set up high-performance teams it is possible to create a prototype. Lessons learned from a prototype can lead to modification of the process adopted for later projects and if only a few people are involved it is possible more easily to make corrections as the project develops. As a result of some prototyping it may be found that dispersed teamworking is more appropriate for some types of activity than others and for some parts of the organization than for others. The areas more receptive to the approach may be the nucleus of later high-performance teams and establish the patterns of working for following teams to adopt.

However introduced, managers and employees are likely to be worried, or even suspicious, about changes in working practices which disturb the status quo with which they are familiar. They may feel threatened by the uncertainty of the unknown. Organizations have to work at overcoming resistance to change at all levels.

The nature and role of management is likely to be dramatically changed where teams are distributed. As dispersed teams develop skills and take on more responsibility in making decisions and become semi-autonomous or self-managing, the role of the manager and the supervisor will change. Managers and supervisors will undoubtedly feel threatened by the new ways of working, especially if it undermines their authority and they feel that it takes away some of their responsibility. As pointed out earlier, in the traditional style of working managers saw their role as controlling and directing their workforce. In a team culture, managers become coaches and facilitators. They are there to provide overall direction, and to guide and advise the team. As teams mature and grow, they will become skilled and confident to take more and more of the decisions which managers used to take. Managers are likely to need training and counselling in understanding and coming to terms with their new role both in relation to the empowerment of the team and its dispersal.

Training and high performance

Teams will not develop into high-performance units if simply left to their own devices. They need training. This may be in the form of informal guidance or more formal courses. Team members need training not only in how to work as a team, but also how to build the team, so that it is able to take on increasing levels of responsibility. Team members may also need training in new job-related skills, especially where the success of the team depends on its members becoming conversant with systems for remote working.

The creation of a new physical workplace environment can have a symbolic impact. It can signify change and a new beginning, and a clear break from the past. Consideration needs to be given to the design of the physical facilities for team members to ensure that they have convenient access to all the technology needed to support the new ways of working which are being encouraged and fostered.

It has to be recognized that the changes expected of people are likely to induce higher stress in the short term for team members and their managers. Changing towards new ways of working carries a high risk of stress. We are all habit-forming creatures, and it is natural to avoid change. We feel comfortable sticking with the ways we know. As individuals we need our personal territory – that is, we all need an area we can call our own, and we need some time to work on our own and to be alone with our thoughts. Nevertheless, working in a team where members are distributed may remove some of the former comfort derived from working in close proximity with colleagues. Companies need to be aware of the potential stress brought about by team-based working. They need to consider how well employees are equipped to cope with it, and whether the demands made of them are reasonable. Taking on additional task responsibilities as well as becoming involved in new ways of organizing the work can double the pressure on employees.

> **We are all habit-forming creatures, and it is natural to avoid change. We feel comfortable sticking with the ways we know.**

Supporting continuous improvement

Different teams will develop at different paces. Organizations need ways of monitoring this progress, in order to measure their performance against goals, and also to provide feedback and appropriate support to team members and their managers.

Team rewards must encourage teamworking but it is essential that members do feel that they receive personal recognition for their own efforts. Rewards need careful alignment with the organizational objectives.

Where members are distributed it may prove extremely difficult to manage the underperformer. This is an issue to be considered before the teams are created. Appropriate training and mentoring provision should be considered.

The technical infrastructure is being put in place to enable effective electronic communications between team members so it may seem unnecessary to consider how effective communications, both within the team and between the team and the rest of the organization, will be developed. However, whilst teamworking may improve and encourage informal communications between team members, it may be necessary to set up new formal methods of communication, such as team briefings to ensure that the team is kept in touch with the wider organization. Undoubtedly, if the introduction of teamworking is part of a wider process of culture change in the organization, communication systems may be needed to ensure that team members feel involved in the major changes affecting the organization, and are consulted about the changes which will affect them.

Where teams are distributed they are most likely to be successful if methodologies are employed which ensure that tasks are well-structured. This is particularly important in the early phases of the team working together. As experience is developed there is the possibility of introducing tasks where the interfaces between team members are less well-structured and explicit.

In establishing teams consideration should be given to the amount of time members will spend together, if any. We identified earlier the type of tasks which don't lend themselves to distributed technology-based work and are best carried out face-to-face. At the 'forming' stage of the group, clear advantages can be gained by members coming together to develop working relationships prior to moving onto distributed work.

As few projects in practice require a team of constant composition throughout the project lifecycle, consideration should be given to the means for managing the introduction of new members. Also consideration should be given to how to replace those who find the method of working unacceptable or fail to cope.

Finally the development of distributed teamworking will lose credibility if the technology does not work at least satisfactorily. So a considerable amount of effort may be necessary to ensure that generally facilities work as specified. Failure of the technology will very much interfere with the development of high performance and in the worst case result in demoralization and ultimate collapse.

MOVING FORWARD

Some key points for reflection are presented below.

Management summary

- Distributed teams are playing an increasingly important role in organizational life.
- Many organizations are failing to realize the potential of teamworking, particularly the distributed team.

- Team design needs matching to organizational expectations and performance requirements.
- Effective teams will not result unless there is a conducive and supportive infrastructure.
- Teams need coaching and support particularly during their early development.
- Technology can be a support to the high performance distributed teams but there is also the possibility – if not well-designed and supported – of it being a hindrance.
- Ever increasing targets for continuous improvement need to be agreed to ensure on-going team development.

References

1 KATZENBACH J. R., SMITH D. K. 'The Wisdom of Teams – Creating the High Performance Organization', Boston, Massachusetts, Harvard Business School Press, 1993.
2 PHILLIPS N. '*Managing International Teams*', London, Pitman Publishing, 1992.
3 MCGRATH J. E., HOLLINGSHEAD A. B. 'Groups Interacting with Technology', Thousand Oaks, California, Sage, 1994.
4 HACKMAN J. R., MORRIS C. G. *Group tasks, group interaction process and group performance effectiveness: a review and proposed integration.* In Berkowitz L. (Ed) 'Advances in Experimental Psychology', New York, Academic Press, 1975, pp. 45–99.
5 TUCKMAN B. W. '*Developmental Sequence in Small Groups*' *Psychological Bulletin*, 1965, 63, 6, pp 384–99.
6 GERSICK C. J. G. '*Time and Transition in Work Teams: Towards a New Model of Group Development*', *Academy of Management Journal*, 1988, 31,1, pp 9–41.

'Learning is not simply having a new insight or a new idea. Learning occurs when we take effective action, when we detect **and** correct error. How do you know when you know something? When you can produce what it is you claim to know.'

CHRIS ARGYRIS

Knowledge for Action – A Guide to Overcoming Barriers to Organizational Change, San Francisco, Jossey-Bass, 1993.

7

LEARNING IN ORGANIZATIONS

New approaches for Future Work organizations

INTRODUCTION

T he time and space independence facilitated by the use of technology is not only having a major impact on the way we work but also on the way we offer learning and personal development opportunities in organizations and within society more generally. New style organizations demand more capability from their workforce but at the same time employees expect their employers to provide them with better opportunities to upgrade skills and qualifications. The costs of traditional provision are increasing rapidly as are the numbers expecting access to opportunities. The effective use of technology to meet this ever increasing demand is essential if organizations are to maintain their competitive position.

Of possibly greater importance is the need organizations have to learn at the organizational level as well as individual and team levels. It is here that organizations will develop the capacity to compete more effectively. This is the area now seen as possibly the only one where businesses can gain advantage – learning quicker than competition. An organization that is in a perpetual state of learning benefits by having an adaptive relationship with its environment. The mechanisms of acuity and action that it needs in order to function in this way almost certainly prohibits it from lapsing into the *tactile* state referred to in Chapter 2.

In this chapter we look at the use of technology to support learning at three levels – the individual, the team and the organization. We examine the nature of competence and its development and then examine how technology can support this learning process. We outline some tools and approaches which can assist in decisions in this important area.

THE NEED FOR ORGANIZATIONAL LEARNING

Knowledge – the life-blood of future organization

We have seen in earlier chapters how the 1980s saw a number of forces combine to radically change the business environment. Information technology, global communication and the changed values and expectations of both customers and employees being among these forces. Business executives can no longer assume that they will be in control of stable production processes or systematized office routines where little change takes place during their lifetime. Organizations are being forced to adapt and change ever more frequently in order to survive. The rate at which change is needed is increasing to the point of change being a constant. Staff generally have to be capable of quickly changing to new working practices and managers at all levels are being required to manage change effectively. Most organizations, but some more so than others, are having to become highly flexible as they develop the capability to respond to customer demands and the challenge of increasing levels of competition.

> There is the need for a new breed of staff and management capable of working in these new style organizations where knowledge-based workers have replaced the low-skilled mass-production operative.

In responding to these challenges we have seen that organizations have delayered and adopted new structures more capable of a speedy response. These new structures are based more around temporary project teams than traditional hierarchies and often span the traditional organizational boundaries to involve more external parties. Much more work within organizations is being undertaken in such teams, often distributed and supported by electronic communications and where status differences must not interfere with the achievement of the task. There is the need for a new breed of staff and management capable of working in these new style organizations where knowledge-based workers have replaced the low-skilled mass-production operative.

Unlocking and leveraging potential

The focus on competition based on the value-added component of the organization's product or service has led many organizations to recognize the need to leverage corporate resources to maintain competitive position and the key part played by staff in this process in terms of their intellectual contribution rather than exclusively from physical effort. The proportion of contribution based on knowledge made by all of the workforce is increasing and for many organizations their productive effort is entirely knowledge-based. Unfortunately relevant knowledge today is likely to be irrelevant tomorrow as factors such as technology, market conditions and organizational structures change. So in response to the recognition of the importance of creativity in developing new business and the major contribution from training, personal development and education, many organizations are looking beyond individualized training and development to ideas about organizational learning and at the concept of the *learning organization*. They are setting out to develop and implement policies and practices aimed at achieving an appropriately qualified workforce to enable the implementation of a strategy based on change as a constant.

THE RELEVANCE OF THE 'LEARNING ORGANIZATION'

The 'learning organization' defined

We cannot overemphasize the need to link human resource development to the strategic direction of the business if the full leverage benefits are to be achieved. However, this is not a straightforward process, particularly as much of the workforce may no longer be direct employees. Organizations are recognizing weaknesses in traditional approaches to strategic planning as a strategic response to increasingly turbulent environments. A. Pettigrew and W. Whipp[1] showed that strategic planning should be viewed as a continuous process rather than resulting in a steady state affair. Given the impermanence of a firm's strategic position and the fragility of bases of competition, they highlighted the need for continuous review and change. This is made more difficult where major activities have and are being continuously outsourced. In response to these factors, organizations must develop learning processes at all levels on the assumption that the ability of the firm to learn faster than its competitors may be its only form of sustainable competitive advantage. Many are seeking to become 'learning organizations' described by D. Garvin[2] as '*an organization skilled at creating, acquiring and transferring knowledge, and at modifying its behaviour to reflect new knowledge and insights*'. This in itself, however, is insufficient unless it is explicitly understood that the purpose of such entities is still that of maintaining or improving competitive position. A rather different definition which emphasizes the competitive element but also indicates the features present in the organization which will lead to the desired outcome was proposed by A. Jashapara[3] – '*a continuously adaptive enterprise that promotes focused individual, team and organizational learning through satisfying changing customer needs and understanding the dynamics of competitive forces*'.

The concept of the learning organization is based on the notion that new ideas and experiences are essential for learning to take place. But ideas in themselves do not lead to organizational improvement, only people can translate ideas into action. Improvement only comes about through the introduction of new and more effective ways of working. The translation of ideas into action cannot be left to chance, the processes have to be managed even if the experiences are outside the organization's boundaries, i.e. upstream or downstream.

D. Garvin further insists that the concept of the learning organization will only be useful if there is a well-grounded definition which is actionable and easy to apply; he emphasizes that for it to be of use it must be possible to translate the definition into clear management actions and also be possible to measure the extent to which a learning organization has been achieved.

In an attempt to clarify further what is involved in being a learning organization A. Jashapara, based on B. Garratt's[4] three-level hierarchy of policy, strategy and operations, proposed the three levels of learning shown in Figure 7.1.

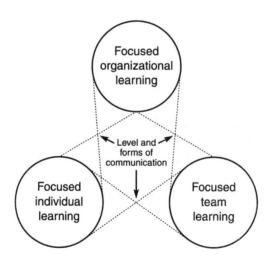

Figure 7.1 The relationship between learning at three organizational levels

At the individual level the D. Kolb[5] learning cycle is adopted (*see* Figure 7.2). This revolves around:

1 Concrete experience.
2 Observation and reflection leading to
3 The formation of concepts and generalizations resulting in
4 The development of hypotheses which are to be tested in future action, leading in turn to new experiences.

In this model, in addition to *knowledge and understanding*, the subject also undergoes changes in *attitude* and develops the vital skills of *learning how to learn*.

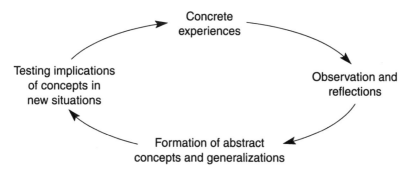

Figure 7.2 The Kolb learning cycle

Mental models and learning

P. Senge[6], in his widely acclaimed book about the learning organization, refers to both *personal mastery* and *mental models*. In his concept of personal mastery individuals develop their learning through a creative tension between their future vision and current reality. Mental models are often the basis of those defensive routines which form barriers to learning. For effective learning to take place at the individual level it is essential to foster an environment where individuals are encouraged to take risks and experiment, where mistakes are tolerated, but where means exist for those involved to learn from their experiences. So the design of a learning programme (course design, delivery and learner support) in itself is insufficient, without follow-up action and reflection on the learning coming out of the change the knowledge acquisition will be in a vacuum. Those concerned with, and directly involved in, training and development

> **For effective learning to take place at the individual level it is essential to foster an environment where individuals are encouraged to take risks and experiment, where mistakes are tolerated, but where means exist for those involved to learn from their experiences.**

must be engaged in activities going well beyond course design, they support the organization's move towards the creation and maintenance of a *learning culture* which encourages and supports personal development as well as rewarding personal achievement.

Individual, team or organization focus?

Much traditional training and development has been concentrated on individual learning although this may have been achieved through interaction with other learners in team-based exercises. However an important dimension of learning when examining the overall development of the organization is the learning that takes place at the level of the team. This is particularly important in the project environment, which is becoming so prevalent in organizations, where people are often required to quickly function as an effective team but then only work together for the short period of time needed to achieve project objectives. Clearly team working as pointed out in Chapter 6 is more than just being a member of a group. The ability to function at peak performance and achieve more than the sum of the individual parts is every leader's aim for his/her team. Nevertheless we know much less about 'team learning' than we do about individual learning. The learning cycle proposed by D. Kolb does still seem to be apposite but to the collective rather than the individual. In practice it implies that there will be observation and reflection by the team collectively rather than just on an individual basis. It also implies that there is a shared goal or mission and that members are willing to openly discuss individual and collective contributions to achieving the goal and modify their individual behaviours in response to feedback. Also, rather than recriminations and blame for substandard performance, the team has to be supportive in helping members develop capability and contribution. Further it implies that members will learn each other's strengths and weaknesses and devise ways of working that accommodate individual differences but at the same time give people the opportunity to develop personally.

Above the level of the group as the unit of analysis, organizational learning may be seen as the ability of the organization to develop strategies and tactics to respond to the changing environment and for members to learn collectively from a range of impulses, translating the many cues into appropriate action. It is the ultimate responsibility of those in senior positions to constantly examine the underlying assumptions and governing values of the organization and to aid the organization in this learning process and the management of change. But to be effective the searching activity must incorporate cues from throughout the organization and its environment. B. J. Jaworski and A. K. Kohli[7] suggest the basis of a market orientation, so important in modern organizations, as *intelligence generation, intelligence dissemination* and *responsiveness*. Generating intelligence is of little value unless it is disseminated to all areas of the business where that intelligence is needed, referred to by B. J. Jaworski and A. K. Kohli as requiring *response design*. Networking technologies can support rapid information dissemination but there is the obvious danger of overload and rather than intelligence being shared a lot of uninterpreted information, consuming the time of executives and others, hinders the ability of the organization to respond. Having distributed this intelligence the organization then has to be capable and motivated to respond effectively to the resulting plan – a process described by B. J. Jaworski and A. K. Kohli as *response implementation*. This process seems to us to be at the heart of the competitive learning organization representing as it does the mental models and organization memory underpinning actions. Mastering the processes involved is vital to the long-term success of the business and learning how to learn is central in this endeavour. Technology has a role to play in this process.

Learning design then is part of a learning strategy which to be really effective must not only tackle the individual and team level but also learning as an organizational process. This will not be achieved unless top executives are engaged in the whole process, by owning the need and the solutions adopted and by actively promoting a learning culture.

DEVELOPING PERSONAL COMPETENCE

Defining competence

A well educated workforce, whilst a laudable goal in itself, is not sufficient to enable organizations to respond in the ways being demanded at present and into the future. The need for alignment of tasks and competencies at any point in time is essential. However people need to be developed not just in order to perform competently in current roles but also to be able to create and adjust to the new workplace demands. Before proceeding to look at the specific means for developing personal competence, we need to first look at what we mean by the term.

Personal competence is those qualities that the individual brings to the job in order to perform its various aspects at the required standard of performance. These standards may be those established for a profession or they might relate to the particular occupation. Without some form of recognized standard measurement it is not possible to assess the extent to which the organization has the necessary personal competencies to achieve its strategy, and then one of the prerequisites as identified by D. Garvin for the learning organization to be a reality is not present. An organizational competence framework seems vital for decisions about the priority needs and for the deployment of resources for training and development.

The models of individual competence which have been devised can be divided into three broad types:

1 Input models

These are the characteristics that are expected of the job-holder before appointment to the job. This cluster of competencies will include knowledge and understanding, skills and abilities, motivation, values and style. Input models draw from a list of general characteristics to produce the particular set for any one job. The list will describe competent employees by the kind of person they are, the level of education they have attained and the skills they possess. They may describe the minimum level of competence required for the job, i.e. the 'threshold competence' or they may be the result of an analysis of excellent job-holders. They may also be described as 'entry-level competencies'.

> **Personal competence is those qualities that the individual brings to the job in order to perform its various aspects at the required standard of performance.**

Input models of competence are useful in staff selection and for the design of assessment centres for appraisal. However they are essentially conservative, describing expectation rather than competence, difficult to use and, particularly importantly, they can reinforce stereotypes.

2 Process models

Process models of competence describe individual behaviours, tasks and procedures and contributions to group behaviour and action. They are often divided into 'basic competencies' and 'high performance' or 'meta-competencies'.

Basic competencies are essentially task-related effectiveness skills which are needed to perform the more specialized technical and/or functional areas that make up the role. They include such competencies as planning, organizing, controlling, developing and interacting. Based in part on the earlier work of R. R. Boyatzis[8] who studied over 2,000 managers in 12 US organizations the American, Harry Schroder[9] identified 11 high-performing competencies as follows:

a **The cognitive competencies**
   Information search
   Concept formation
   Conceptual flexibility

b **The motivating competencies**
   Interpersonal search
   Managing interaction
   Development orientation

c **The directing competencies**
   Self-confidence
   Presentation
   Impact

d **The achieving competencies**
   Proactive orientation
   Achievement orientation

Competencies as defined here contribute to the ability in particular of managers to transform an organization and are believed to be of particular relevance in turbulent environments.

3 Output models

Much work has been done in the United Kingdom on the development of measures of output competencies, normally referred to as 'standards'. They are statements of what an employee has achieved as a result of his/her actions. The standards are threshold competencies derived by a process of functional analysis which is the top-down disaggregation of the occupational role. In the case of management, in the analysis carried out for the UK's Management Charter Initiative, at the first level four key roles are identified, i.e. managing operations, managing finance, managing people and managing information. Units of competence are related to the four roles. In turn these units of competence are further broken down into elements of competence against which standards of performance are established. Assessment of competence includes observation of workplace behaviour as well as a review of outputs from the workplace such as reports of investigations, minutes of meetings, budget reviews.

Whilst this approach does have some merit including an attempt to standardize the measures, it has been criticized particularly for higher level work such as that carried out by managers for a fragmented approach to assessing performance when the job does not really lend itself to fragmentation. Also they tend to ignore the underpinning knowledge required to enable transfer of skills to other work environments.

Applying competence models

These competence frameworks can be adapted to the specific situation in any organization and become the framework against which the organization may judge the extent to which it has an adequately qualified workforce in order to achieve its prime aims.

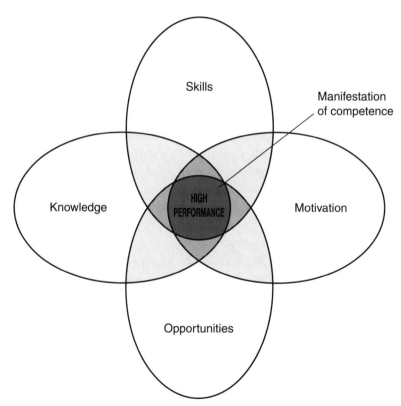

Figure 7.3 A model of job performance

However employing staff with competence in the job in itself is insufficient to guarantee high-organizational performance. As we have identified
in the earlier section dealing with the learning organization, individual competence is but one factor in achieving the state of a suitably adaptive
organization. Even at the level of the individual competence is only one
component in performance. In Figure 7.3 we present in diagrammatic form
a model describing the four components which lead to effective workplace
behaviour. These are:

1 Knowledge

All employees have a knowledge set, however complete or otherwise, which
underpins their workplace performance. The extent to which this includes a
basic understanding of the technologies being employed at the workplace,
both to provide the technical solution and the means for delivery, will vary
depending upon the specifics of the role. As an illustration the demands for
specific detailed technical knowledge will be very limited at senior management levels in most situations but obviously imperative for those
responsible for installing and maintaining equipment. Also the extent to
which there is the need for an understanding of the principles of business
management will vary but to some degree be essential at all levels in the
organization, as will the extent of sophistication of underpinning conceptual frameworks or mental models required.

2 Skills

In addition to knowledge and understanding, performance at work
demands a range of personal and job-related skills. All tasks have an element of personal management and most require interpersonal skills to
ensure that the interfaces between roles are satisfactorily managed. Many
jobs require direct contact with external customers or suppliers and interpersonal skills are important in this area.

3 Motivation

No matter how skilled and knowledgeable the staff, without a high level of
personal motivation the individual's skills and knowledge will remain
underemployed and performance fall short of what could be achieved.

4 Opportunities

Even where staff are skilled, knowledgeable and motivated they still need
opportunities in which to test and further develop their skills. Just as in the

case of sports stars without the challenge of competition, reactions lose their sharpness, confidence saps and development slows down. Without opportunities motivation and interest will begin to degenerate.

To maximize the return on investment in training and development the employer needs to ensure that all four components are addressed at the workplace.

Many traditional courses principally focus on the acquisition of knowledge and the development of skills. However, when designing training and development systems organizations should really address all four components.

Developing team competence

In the last chapter we examined the principles for the design of high-performance teams and indicated that there are four major areas for consideration:

1 The purpose of the team and success criteria.
2 The make up of the team.
3 The design of the technical infrastructure to support the team.
4 The process of team development.

If the first three conditions for effective working have been met the key to effective performance will be the way in which the team develops. In Chapter 6 we examined many aspects of team development and the reader is referred back to this material.

One key point coming out of the work of C. J. G. Gersick in relation to team competence is the concept of *punctuated equilibrium* – which may be interpreted as the notion that groups keep plateauing in their development. This has parallels in personal learning. Stages of rapid personal development seem to be followed by periods of relative stability and lack of development during which there may well be consolidation. A similar phenomenon seems to apply to team development.

The need for external coaching may well be strong. This may take the form of process consultation aimed at assisting the group develop to its full potential. This will at times include assisting the group in reducing barriers to progress.

The organization's prime aim is likely to be high team performance but specific behaviours which might be looked for so as to bring about this high performance were identified in the last chapter as including empowerment and features such as:

1 Members having a range of overlapping skills and competencies.
2 The leader as coach and facilitator rather than supervisor in the traditional sense.
3 Problems seen as bi-directional and not just to be resolved by management.
4 The team works out its own solutions wherever practical.
5 The team is party to establishing its own targets.
6 The customer is the prime focus of attention.
7 Team members have direct customer contact where practical.
8 The need for constant personal upgrading is recognized and encouraged by all members.
9 Rewards are diverse and situational.

This set or one similar could be the basis for measuring progress towards the competencies needed to perform at high levels alongside the success criteria referred to earlier.

DEVELOPING ORGANIZATIONAL COMPETENCE

Defining core competence

At the heart of the notion of developing organizational competence is the concept of *core competence* – those competencies which facilitate the bringing together in a unique blend the many technologies employed by the organization together with a deep level of customer knowledge and understanding into products and services which give the organization a distinctive edge. C. K. Prahalad[10] suggests that a core competence can be identified by applying the following tests:

1 *Is it a significant source of competitive differentiation?*
2 *Does it transcend a single business covering a range of businesses both current and new?*
3 *Is it hard for competitors to imitate?*

He goes on to suggest that it is not something that is easily observable but it does permeate the whole organization and represent its tacit learning.

Competence in C. K. Prahalad's view comes about when the organization has the appropriate technology, appropriate management processes and can generate collective learning. For many organizations there are considerable in-built barriers to the development of collective learning – including lack of recognition of the need, functional and geographic divisions, risk averse cultures, promotion systems perceived to be based on factors other than past achievement, lack of example and encouragement from those in leadership positions.

Core competence then is, in part, the accumulated wisdom of those within the organization, its memory, and those to whom the organization has access. But it also includes the technologies to which the organization has access as well as the ability of the organization to share knowledge and understanding across organization boundaries. Most importantly, it is the distinctive competence which the organization marshals to enable it to out-perform competition.

Many different areas might form the basis of the organization's key competencies, for example, a business might have one or more of:

- Efficient manufacturing of specific types of high quality products.
- Unsurpassed service support to customers.
- Project initiation and management skills.
- Skills in developing and utilizing networks.
- Expertise in managing partnerships.
- Effective means for maintenance of customer loyalty.
- Expertise in new product development.

The competencies which give the business its competitive edge are those which it can effectively structure to meet the customer need but at the same time which are most difficult for others to emulate. They are probably unique to a particular market, however defined, and most commonly developed and accumulated within the organization through its own internal activities. To offer sustainable advantage these assets must not be easily acquired by potential competitors, the greater the barriers to entry the better. P. Verdin and P. Williamson[11] identified a number of impediments to the cheap and rapid accumulation of assets:

1. *Time compression diseconomies* – the extra costs of doing things under time pressure in order to catch up with the market leader.
2. *Asset mass efficiencies* – many assets are more costly to accumulate if the business has few of them to start with.
3. *Asset interconnectedness* – a business will find it easier to accumulate assets when it already has assets in complementary areas.
4. *Causal ambiguities* – the difficulty in identifying those specific assets required to produce success in any particular area.

Leveraging core competence

So effectiveness in the use of those parts of the asset base which produce value-added may well be the principal determinant of the long-term prosperity of the organization. However this in itself is only one contributory factor. C. K. Prahalad helps here by identifying two aspects of future value creation. First there is the *performance gap*. Business needs to be constantly improving its efficiency in areas such as costs, quality, lead times. But probably more difficult to deal with is the *opportunity gap*. This is those areas where resources could be profitably deployed to create new opportunities whether new markets, products or businesses. The competencies required to reduce a performance gap lend themselves to investigation and analysis. Identifying the competencies required for reducing a particular performance gap is relatively straightforward compared to the challenge of identifying core competence, matching it to future market opportunities and then identifying means for reducing the competence gap in order to make the strategic vision a reality. He does go on to suggest that opportunity gap management comprises four interlinked parts:

1 *Establishing an opportunity gap which gains employee commitment and which requires innovative approaches.*
2 *The development of a strategic architecture* – an informed view of how the market and the industry will evolve over the long term.
3 *The ability to leverage resources to achieve the vision* – this should focus on functionalities rather than specific products or services.
4 *Energizing the whole organization to concentrate efforts* – this involves developing a shared mind-set and shared goals and developing strategies for acquiring and deploying competency.

This is clearly not a sequential once and for all process but rather interactive and on-going.

He goes on to describe core competence as the following:

Competence = Technology × Governance Process × Collective Learning

He defines the governance process inside the organization as the quality of relationships across functions and across business units and sees collective learning also spanning boundaries.

This equation may be a key to helping managers design the new organizational forms to ensure that the key elements that comprise competence are either within the organization itself or otherwise manageable. For organizational learning to take place there must be more than just information passing, there needs to be sharing of individual and team learning (illustrated in Figure 7.1). In many organizations the achievement of this sharing across boundaries seems a long way from the current practice and intent. But this sharing does seems to be a major corner stone of the concept of the **learning organization** and the development of **core competencies**.

Tom Peters[12] in his book '*Crazy Times Call for Crazy Organizations*' warns of the danger of putting too much energy exclusively into core competencies:

> 'It's a good idea for many unfocused companies, which the majority of big corporations are, but to say that the strategic competence concept can be followed too closely is an understatement. The times are changing, and strategic competence must change right along with them.'

So a balance needs to be struck between investing in core competencies perceived today to be needed for planned future action and ensuring that the organization has access to enough people who are ideas generators and innovators, so as to create new business opportunities and keep questioning the status quo.

In the next section we will see how information technology can aid and hinder the development of learning, first at the individual level but then also at the team level and at the pinnacle; the organization itself.

INFORMATION TECHNOLOGY AND INDIVIDUAL LEARNING

The JIT provision of training and development

One area where information technology is really starting to fulfil the promise made during the early days in the development of computing is in the area of learning. Rapid strides have been made in the technologies for delivery – satellites, CD-Rom, CDi, telecomputers, groupware, to name a few generic products. Costs are also coming down to the point where these systems are offering viable alternatives to more traditional classroom based approaches to training and development. However, whilst technology is developing very rapidly skills in its deployment are lagging well behind. As in other areas where technology is being deployed there is considerable time lag between the emergence of technology and the widespread development of skills enabling its effective application.

Rather than starting with a description of the technologies for delivery it seems more appropriate to start from the needs of organizations and then look at means for matching technologies with needs.

From the previous sections we have identified the need for learning to be taking place at the individual, team and organizational levels. We have indicated that learning goes beyond specific skills to enable the individual to perform competently on any specific task to something which is much broader and enables the individual to make an effective contribution to the organization overall and its development. At the organizational level we have seen that a focus solely on incremental performance improvement is equally inadequate. The organization has to have the capability to leap forward so as to take advantage of the opportunities available to leverage core competencies in exploiting new opportunities.

The starting point for intervention to develop core competencies may well be the needs of the workforce for training and development. If the competence of individual job-holders is inadequate there will be a shortfall in performance and a tendency to become preoccupied with reducing the performance gap rather than the wider issues relating to the development of core competency. If the workforce has major competence shortfalls in key business areas it is even questionable whether these should be considered as core competencies.

Designing JIT provision

The development process for training programmes is illustrated in Figure 7.4. The development needs of each member of the workforce will vary. The first step for the training executive is to establish precisely what needs exist in relation to the organization's strategy by carrying out a needs analysis. This involves either each person being assessed and training needs identified for each individual or where there is a clear change of direction for the organization with obvious training implications a sampling procedure may be adopted. This review process should be included as part of the annual appraisal system. Assessment is ideally carried out against competence criteria established earlier and presented in a matrix for all roles within the organization. However, for key roles, e.g. the development of high flyers, specially developed assessment centres may be used with the review of a group of personnel being carried out by a small team of senior managers. The assessment centre attempts to simulate the kind of decisions the job-holders have to make in their normal routine and a group of the same or prospective job-holders under assessment work together on the tasks being observed by the assessors. The assessors are then required to form a view of the development needs of each individual in relation to the competence set identified in the matrix. This approach may be seen as more objective than the review by immediate superiors. However, the assessment centre needs careful design by expert practitioners. It also takes a lot of executive time and effort and without a high level of commitment on the part of the executives will not be successful.

Here we have assumed the desirability of a comprehensive competence framework covering the whole organization. This framework may be based on a national scheme such as the UK's National Vocational Qualifications with adaptation to any particular situation. Because the situation every organization finds itself in differs, ideally a competence matrix is created for the particular situation. However, there is perhaps a more important reason for going through the process of creating a situation-specific matrix and that is to involve key decision-makers in defining the competencies needed within the organization to meet the strategic plan. By their involvement in the process commitment can be gained to the programme of human resource development which it precedes.

Gaining commitment

Why is the process adopted by the organization for defining the competence matrix so important? The defining of which skills are needed in the organization for it to be successful in achieving its strategic goals is a vital stage in the implementation of the strategy. It is vital that the key decision-makers commit themselves to the total process needed to implement the strategy. The proper development of employees is a vital part of this and is one which requires the commitment of expenditure just as other parts of the strategic plan require investment. It is the area of expenditure given the least consideration in many plans. All too often people assume that the employees will be able to adapt to new roles without any training or that staff can be recruited with the necessary skills. Expenditure on training and development in many organizations lags well behind that needed to achieve the goals being set. By involving senior executives in defining the needs they can become aware of the costs involved and they will then want to see the training budget well-targeted and expenditure monitored against outcomes and achievements. They can also form a more realistic view of the feasibility of achieving their long-term aims from the current capability of the organization and if necessary be encouraged to work on alternative approaches.

How then can we set up a process to achieve this competence matrix which is built up by the key decision-makers? Some large businesses are

1 **The identification of training and development needs**

- organizational requirements for training and development
- the learning needs of individuals and groups

↓

2 **The design of training and development strategies**

- Training and development strategies and plans
- organizational strategies to assist individuals and groups to achieve their objectives

↓

3 **Provide learning opportunities, resources and support**

- secure and allocate resources to deliver organizational training and development plans
- provide opportunities and support for individuals and groups to learn

↓

4 **Evaluation of the effectiveness of training and development**

- evaluate the overall effectiveness of the strategy
- evaluate individual and group achievement against learning objectives

↓

5 **Put the experiences into the wider framework of developments in training and development**

Figure 7.4 The process for developing training programmes

now taking this area so seriously that they have established working parties to carry out the task chaired by the Chief Executive or a director colleague. The Chief Executive's group will determine the overall aims, the structure to carry out the task and then monitor progress and review the final matrix and action plans. It is recognized by many training executives that without at least the involvement of line management in the process there is unlikely to be the commitment necessary for implementation

Expenditure on training and development in many organizations lags well behind that needed to achieve the goals being set.

of a comprehensive training programme. Also without the clear and explicit support of a senior executive it is unlikely that line management will devote the necessary time to the activity. However, particularly where it is made clear to all managers that their annual review will include an evaluation of their contribution to the development of their subordinates and that poor performance in this area will carry equal weight to underperformance in achieving other targets, the culture of the organization can be changed so as to accept the need for commitment to people development against specific targets defined through a competence matrix.

It is important that the validity of the competence matrix is recognized. If an in-house approach is adopted for the development of a framework, the resulting matrix will be based on practising managers' perceptions of the competencies required for effective performance rather than carefully controlled research. In consequence the model needs to be constantly reviewed and refined in the light of experience and the changing needs of the organization.

The needs analysis exercise will probably result in some needs which are common to a number of staff and others which are individual. It may also result in a view that some of the job-holders, even with training, are unsuited for their current role even though they have a range of competencies needed in the organization. Following on from this latter outcome it may be necessary to counsel some staff out of their current role and relocate them into more suitable work. Before introducing widespread competence assessment it is vital that executive management are aware of the possible outcomes and have agreed the way in which the process will be managed.

Technology can play an important part in speeding up the assessment processes and standardizing feedback. Computer-based systems can process the data derived from psychometric and other tests and give instant output of results. Expert systems have been developed which interpret results without the intervention of professionals, leaving the latter to help the individual interpret the results and relate them to their own personal situation. Competence assessment can be linked to databases containing information about how the knowledge and understanding or personal skills might be developed so that the interrogator can make decisions about how best to achieve those areas they need and want to develop.

Matching technology to need

The outcome of this assessment process will be a collection of needs and now the training executive has to work out cost-effective means for providing the development. So what choices exist?

The training executive has probably a much wider range of options than have existed at any time in the past. The rapid development of sophisticated distance learning approaches to management development, the availability of face-to-face off-the-job training in both lecture room and in the outdoors, coaching at the workplace and many other approaches exist to make the choices difficult.

In developing cost-effective training programmes as well as opportunities for individuals to 'better' themselves, technology can play a part. The technologies available for training and development processes can be classified into synchronous and asynchronous methods. Synchronous methods are those that deliver training in real-time. Asynchronous methods are those that allow the learner to decide the time and place of study – they include storage systems which make it practical to deliver just-in-time training anywhere and at any time. Systems can also be classified by the extent to which they permit interaction between the learner and either the system or the tutor. Some systems have built-in feedback for the learner. Others depend upon the learner taking a personal view on whether he/she has achieved the necessary competence. These contrast with systems that permit interaction between learner and tutor. In Table 7.1 we present a broad classification of technologies and their uses/limitations in the learning environment (based on J. Bang[13]).

One major point to note about these various technologies is that used separately or in combination they can offer considerable opportunities for

Table 7.1 Categorization of technology for learning

	Synchronous	**Asynchronous**
Person to person dialogue.	Tele- and video-conferencing; telephone.	Fax; computer mediated communications; voice-mail; e-mail.
Person to system dialogue.		CAL delivered on CD-Rom, disc, interactive video; CDi.
No interaction.	Broadcast radio and TV	Print, audio and video cassettes

providing the workforce with training. A wide range of delivery styles can be adopted aiming to meet the personal learning preferences of individuals. Technology can be applied throughout the process of individual learning, i.e. competence review, review of development opportunities, provision of learning materials, tutor and mentor support and assessment of learning. Expert systems are particularly useful in providing feedback as part of assessment processes. Multimedia applications are providing rich experiences for learners. Computer mediated communications and groupware systems are providing opportunities for interaction between tutors, mentors and peers. The possibilities of just-in-time training provision using technology are already being realized by some organizations.

Limitations of technology-based solutions

While technology can greatly assist in provision it falls short of being able to provide for all the needs of the learner. It has to be remembered that for development to take place the individual has to be receptive to change. The process may be conscious or otherwise. However, in the terms used many years ago by Kurt Lewin[14], for change to take place there has to be a process of *unfreezing, moving* and *refreezing*. People have to be prepared to expose themselves to what may be a painful process which starts with an analysis of themselves and their strengths and weaknesses. They have to recognize that their current behaviour is not as effective as perhaps they at first thought or is inappropriate for the new situations they or their organizations find themselves in or wanting to move to. They have to go through this stage of unfreezing in which they start to open themselves up to self-reflection and this will result in a degree of self-doubt. This will be a stressful process for some and even a traumatic experience. Having recognized the need to change and having become receptive they can then start to move to a preferred state. Once the old ways of working have been modified to a new, more acceptable, behaviour pattern this is then internalized and a refreezing take place. Support during difficult periods of change is not achieved through technology alone. A mix of different provisions should be in place to support learners. The need for face-to-face counselling will still probably remain. As we saw earlier remote working using technology results in a degradation of media richness and not all processes lend themselves to remote working.

While Kurt Lewin's model has merit it does seem to assume that a new and more acceptable state can be achieved which should be a lasting condition. However, on-going change is now such a feature of business life that there is unlikely to be anything other than a transitionary state as the outcome. For many managers the next set of changes will already be required before the last has been frozen. In the technical development of the organization we argue that understanding and driving the *change vector* is more important than understanding with precision the starting point or final destination of the change. The ability to cope with this lies not in fluid environment nor in the organization's adaptive structure but within the core competencies of its people. These new behaviours enable them to cope more effectively with on-going change. The model illustrates well the need for a change in the person for development to take place and highlights that it may be an uneasy process for the individual concerned.

We have made no attempt to distinguish training from development. We see learning as more concerned with an increase in knowledge or enhancement of an existing skill where new knowledge is translated into different behaviour that is replicable. Development, however, is seen as a move towards a different state of being or functioning. C. Argyris[15] talks about 'single loop learning' as that needed to develop skills in using current processes to meet current job requirements. 'Double loop learning' is then the process of challenging the existing status quo with its underlying assumptions about how organizations best function, then developing an understanding of how they can be redefined and transformed to another state. These distinctions are useful in that they help us recognize that we can be attempting to achieve different objectives through a development process. At one level we are attempting to improve the individual's performance in his/her immediate job. This is very important for many at an early stage following appointment to their job. However, as people become familiar with their immediate task needs they are unlikely to be satisfied with the limited perspectives and approaches adopted for the first-level training and many will start to seek a more self-directed development approach. Also, the organization is likely to be encouraging the individual to take responsibility for his/her own learning and development and be actively encouraging this state of independent learning.

In encouraging individuals to take this responsibility for their own development the organization has to develop means by which it can provide the training needed to meet the demands being created. Here technology has to be integrated in appropriate ways into the delivery processes at all stages of the training cycle. But probably the more difficult task is to create a climate where learning is encouraged, experimentation is supported and the learning from failure is shared.

Designing the workplace to support the learner

In order to encourage the workforce to develop the use of technology in support of their work and related personal development the organization must provide them with convenient access to those facilities which will enable them to achieve the established goals. Open learning centres are already accessible in many large organizations and they serve a useful purpose. They can act like a traditional library in that they permit browsing and the exploration of materials which are not strictly focused on individual needs at the point in time. However there are barriers to their use. They are centrally located and so physically separated from the workplace. They require physical attendance and these barriers to be broken down. They may well not have the specific training and development materials available and just like a traditional library there may be a delay whilst they are obtained.

So technology needs to be better used to deliver the just-in-time training that has been advocated here and it can be used effectively to do so but only if facilities are designed to meet organizational and personal requirements. Ideally the learner should be given direct access from the workplace to the technology-based training needed to improve work performance. This is shown diagrammatically in Figure 7.5. (from P. Dalsgaard)[16]. Here we show the integration of PC-based systems at the workplace so that there is access to both task-related software and learning opportunities provided through the PC. But rather than having different systems that have to be accessed it is suggested that all should be integrated so that the user has few problems in accessing and using the learning materials and opportunities once familiar with the systems used for task achievement. This leads to the concept of the virtual training centre with multimedia training materials 'on tap' as well as access to the virtual library to supplement these learning materials.

The distribution of learning opportunities in this way is essential to support the distributed organization, particularly when the workforce is also in part home-based.

TECHNOLOGY TO SUPPORT TEAM LEARNING

What is team learning?

We earlier distinguished differences between single-loop and double-loop learning. In the latter, our mental models are challenged and reformulated. These models are deeply held internal images of how the world works and

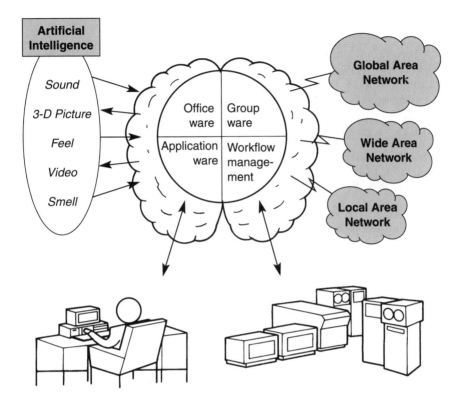

Figure 7.5 Office architecture

they influence how we view that which is happening around us and thus our behaviour. As well as assisting us interpret what we see happening around us, these models inhibit the very way in which we see the world, acting like filters in interpretation, storage and retrieval from memory. Individually-based learning is particularly suited to acquiring specific operational skills and the mastery of routines. However for this second order of double-loop learning to occur the individual needs to have beliefs and internalized models challenged – a process which is easier to achieve when sharing ideas and concepts with other people. Team-based learning provides a powerful means for developing this conceptual level of understanding.

However in the context of the organization we are particularly concerned here to understand more fully how teams develop their own capability to function at higher levels of performance. Many organizations run team-building and leadership development programmes. Some use well-tried techniques and processes, many using experiential learning as the principal methodology. On the face of it, it is difficult to see how technology might assist in what is essentially a very personal experience when as we saw earlier technology tends to reduce media richness – the basis of much of the sensitive feedback processes required for such personal development to be achieved.

How can technology support team learning?

However, we see technology assisting in six ways in particular:

1 Dispersed teams have to work effectively together despite not being able to spend time in face-to-face dialogue some of which would bring about team development and probably performance improvement. Communications technology can substitute for face-to-face contact and such media as video conferencing and e-mail can offer opportunities for sharing and have the potential to be more effective than more widely used means such as fax and letter. The team, if given access to a range of communications facilities, can decide how best to use them for their own particular purposes.

2 The models of team development which shape our expectations are based primarily on face-to-face experiences. When given access to communications technology as the alternative people will pay attention to different things, have contact with different people and in different ways and begin to depend upon each other differently. In consequence, we can assume that where teams are motivated to do so they will develop enhanced performance by rather different methods than they would in conventional settings and that low cost, speedy communications will facilitate these new approaches.

3 Communications technology can complement other team-building activities. For example, where a key team is being put together comprising people unknown to each other who have to work remotely, the process may be initiated by a face-to-face encounter with team-building exercises built in. The working methods established at this stage can then be adopted using communications technology to maintain relationships and progress the group task. As pointed out earlier, negotiation both when people first meet and then on particularly sensitive issues is often also best carried out in face-to-face discussion.

4 Teams, whether working remotely or face-to-face, might find one of a number of structured approaches to work-flow management or problem solving helpful. Group Decision Support Systems (GDSS), standardized methodologies for project management, workflow systems and systems

design methodologies can be utilized to assist by structuring problem-solving processes or work routines and standardizing the language used between team members. Their use can assist team performance by enabling the team members to focus on issues relating specifically to the task in hand rather than having attention deflected because of concern about team processes. Team learning then can be related to the nature of the task and focused on technical aspects of the work.

5 Communications technology can provide the team with access to a wealth of information from both inside and outside the organization to assist with the task. Such information can be quickly shared and analyzed by team members. This can create feelings of being very much in touch with the problem and the task of jointly finding a solution. By using technology in this way team members can con-

> **There is little doubt that communications technology and group systems can aid in the process of team learning.**

siderably enhance their learning as they work on tasks together. To some degree this will lead to questioning of mental models and their reformulation, particularly in technical fields .

6 Communications technology will change interaction patterns, social groupings and organization in ways which are difficult to predict. This will make it possible for people to work in quite different ways to those that we envisage at present. These new networking opportunities will give individuals the opportunity to form their own teams to support them in their activities. Individual learning will result which in turn will transfer into increased capability to work together in distributed teams. People will start to think in new ways and work differently both individually and in teams as well as start to do completely new things.

7 Teams can have much better access to a shared memory. The collective learning of team members can be stored and accessed to assist in later problem-solving or task activities. This memory capacity will change the dependence upon individual memory or file storage. With much enhanced team memory, team learning can focus on those areas of non-routine activity which are of greatest intellectual challenge and where the highest value-added is achieved for the organization.

There is little doubt that communications technology and group systems can aid in the process of team learning. Organizations seeking to achieve high performance in distributed teams will not do so if they fail to manage this process.

In the next section we will see some of the conditions that have to be created within the organization to foster double-loop learning at all levels. One point to make here, however, is that the processes may need some intervention from managers with responsibility for training and development in order to facilitate the processes of learning. This is particularly likely during early stages in the development of the communications infrastructure to support the distributed organization. Also of particular importance is the design of the infrastructure systems to ensure that they promote rather than hinder team learning.

TECHNOLOGY TO SUPPORT THE LEARNING ORGANIZATION

Integrating individual learning into the wider organization

Organizations ultimately learn via their individual members. However individuals within organizations often get into a mind-set and stop challenging the assumptions underpinning organization functioning. This may be the result of commonly shared views about 'how we do things round here', it might be fear of crossing a strong manager, it might be an unwillingness to be seen as a deviant by stepping outside the accepted ways of doing things, the organization might have well articulated standard operating procedures.

Organization learning comes about when there is a transfer of knowledge between individuals and an exchange of individual and shared mental models. This requires individuals to make explicit their mental models. Learning is seen to have taken place where there is an increase in the organization's capacity to take effective action in response to changing stimuli. The new mental models will make it possible for the organization to introduce discontinuous steps of improvement with radically different approaches to tackling issues and solutions to problems. The extent to which this sharing can take place will be influenced by both organizational structure and management style.

The aim of the organization with regard to learning is to share the learning that takes place from each and every interaction with a customer/client, vendor, supplier, employee and competitor. The challenge for management is to create a climate which encourages this open sharing and particularly the practice of learning from mistakes. This process has to be encouraged across hierarchical levels and organizational boundaries. It also has to transcend time and geographic boundaries as well as the external boundaries of the organization. A learning culture encourages responsible risk-taking on the part of individuals and groups, it fosters reflection, open discussion and debate about experience and it is willing to acknowledge mistakes but at the same time individuals are prepared to take away the lessons from them. Managers at all levels have to be seen to be practising the principles and themselves facilitating open dialogue and discussion. Information flows are a major support in developing the learning organization. Timely, accurate, available and relevant information which is presented in a form which is usable by those who need it is a prerequisite for the learning organization. Reward systems must recognize and reinforce desired behaviours as must other human resource practices.

Creating the drive, generating the outputs

The organization needs to generate a large number of learning opportunities, generalize the learning beyond one or a few individuals, do this more swiftly than competitors and build in the desire and opportunity to learn from others. Learning from failure is not possible if the actions which resulted in the failure were not well-planned, thought through and based on an explicit model of the organization's functioning. Careful review and planned response can complete the learning cycle described earlier for those individuals involved and dialogue and sharing can lead to the modification of mental maps. However the learning is of limited value unless it then has impact on the ways of working such that it adds value to the stakeholders of the business over the longer term.

Bench marking can enable comparisons in performance and produce the setting of targets for future improvement. It can give clear focus for organizational objectives and measured improvement offers an indirect means for assessing the extent to which the organization is achieving this learning state. Examination of best practice both within and outside the organization can assist in the process of developing mental models. Centres of excellence within the organization can be useful in assisting people develop insights and build their personal models. Laboratories and simulated exercises make it possible for individuals and groups to experiment and time-compress experiences thus resulting in concentrated learning. A major issue however in this whole area is how one gets transfer of learning from one-off experiences into the wider community such that it has the desired type of impact on the wider actions within the organization. The use of ad hoc teams, job rotation, training programmes, the acceptance of people from outside on short assignments and other similar measures can all aid in this process of learning transfer.

Technology supporting the learning organization

The principal area where technology can have a major impact on the implementation of the learning organization is in the design of the information systems such that they support both the learning process and the transfer of learning. As an example, we saw in Chapter 4 that groupware had been implemented by one major consultancy to enable the sharing across the worldwide network of consultants of tools and techniques and information about the outcomes of assignments. But very quickly the consultants or anyone else on such a system, rather than learning from such information, could be overwhelmed by information overload so there has to be built into the system means for filtering and retrieving information such that it is timely and usable.

However it is clear that the development of the learning organization, since it depends upon the development of shared mental models and attempts to change basic understanding, is going to require much face-to-face effort in small meetings which bring people close together. The loss of media richness associated with the use of technology for communication will result in sharing being superficial and many misunderstandings which result in limited constructive impact on personal mental models. So electronic communications systems offer a useful complement to other concerted actions aimed at developing this learning organization.

Another area where technology can be deployed effectively to assist and develop understanding of mental models is in the use of computer-based simulations. It is feasible to operate these across an electronic network with learners physically dispersed throughout the network. They can provide the opportunity for participants to gain an holistic view of the functioning of a system but of course they are only as good as the model forming the basis of the design of the system.

The role of management in the learning organization

However well-designed the information systems and communications infrastructure, the learning organization is unlikely to develop on its own. There is the need for concerted management action to create the conditions to encourage its development as well as maintain it as an on-going process. It is not something that can be turned on and off like a water tap. Once the organization has committed to such a development it will have difficulty turning back and if it does so the impact on the later initiatives to encourage learning within the organization will be highly detrimental.

Moving forward in developing learning and capability

The links between individual, team and organizational learning are shown in Figure 7.1 where the importance of communication links are highlighted. Below we list some key points for reflection.

Management summary

- Organizational learning will increasingly be the basis of an organization's competitive strength.
- Organizational effectiveness will result where training and development is targeted towards achieving strategic goals.
- Real learning requires a reformulation of personal mental models.
- Competence frameworks give a yardstick against which to measure individual development.
- Team learning needs collective effort against agreed goals for team improvement.
- Individual, team and hence organizational memory can be supported by the use of the storage capacity of IT and the ability of systems to speedily retrieve information.
- Organizational learning needs to be focused on developing core competencies against a performance gap. Targets and a monitoring process are essential.
- More cost-effective delivery of training and development in some areas is possible using technology but it does not offer a complete panacea.
- In designing systems for delivery using technology the needs of the organization should be the starting point and means should be sought to match technologies to needs.
- The learning processes need active management if strategic goals are to be achieved.

References

1 PETTIGREW A., WHIPP R. '*Managing Change for Competitive Success*', Blackwell, 1991
2 GARVIN D. 'Building a Learning organization', *Harvard Business Review*, Volume 71, Issue 4, July/August 1993, pp78–91.
3 JASHAPARA A. 'Competitive Learning Organization: A Quest for the Holy Grail, Henley-on-Thames, England, Henley Management College Working Paper, 1993.
4 GARRATT B. '*The Learning Organization*', Gower Publishing, 1987.

5 KOLB D. '*Experiential Learning*', New Jersey, Prentice-Hall, 1983.

6 SENGE P. '*The Fifth Discipline: the Art and Practice of the Learning Organization*', New York, Doubleday, 1990.

7 JAWORSKI B. J., KOHLI A. K. 'Market Orientation: Antecedents and Consequences', Journal of Marketing, Volume 57, Issue 3, July 1993, pp 53–70.

8 BOYATZIS, R. R. '*The competent manager: A model for effective performance*', Wiley. New York, 1982.

9 SCHRODER H. '*Managerial Competence: the Key to Success*', Kendall Hunt, 1989.

10 PRAHALAD C. K. 'The Role of Core Competencies in the Corporation', *Research-Technology Management*, Nov-Dec 1993, pp 40–48.

11 VERDIN P., WILLIAMSON P. 'Successful Strategy: Stargazing or Self-examination?', *European Management Journal*, 12,1, March, 1994, pp 10–19.

12 PETERS T. '*Crazy Times Call for Crazy Organization*', New York, Vintage Books, a Division of Random House Inc., 1994.

13 BANG J. 'Curriculum, Pedagogy and Educational Technologies: Some Considerations on the Choice of Technology for Open and Distance Learning', EDEN conference, June 1994.

14 LEWIN K, '*Field Theory in Social Science*', (Ed, Cartwright D.) New York, Harper, 1951.

15 ARGYRIS C. 'Teaching Smart People How to Learn', *Harvard Business Review*, Volume 69, Issue 3, May/June 1991, pp. 99–109.

16 DALSGAARD, P. *Case Working Towards Year 2000*, Group Vision, Drammensveien 134, Po Box 228, Skøier n.0212, Oslo, Norway.

'The mark of a first-rate intelligence is the ability to hold two opposed ideas in the mind at the same time and still retain the ability to function.'

F. Scott Fitzgerald

The Crack-up, 1936.

8

APPROACHING FUTURE WORK

INTRODUCTION

In this chapter we prepare managers to start creating tomorrow's organization. Such a challenge of significant change makes demands on managers that go far beyond those required in maintaining and developing the traditional organization. Many of the comments we make will apply to *any* major change programme; others are specific to the special nature of the transformation to *Future Work*. Whilst the entrepreneur may create something new out of nothing, the manager in an established setting has the harder task of creating tomorrow's organization from existing structures which may be resistant to change. Moreover, the on-going established business must be maintained while the very systems that it relies upon will themselves become the subject of transition.

Our main interest is to bring about dramatic, radical and beneficial change by creating something that is differentiated and new. We look to managers who will take their organizations into new markets; to change the very basis of competition in their existing markets; or at least to find traditional performance improvements of one or two orders of magnitude. This briefing is intended primarily for the serious and committed practitioner. These creative and determined managers comprise the architects and sponsors who will put into action the building programme that will create tomorrow's organization out of the components that are available today.

Our preparation first involves commitment to a *strategic approach*. Such an approach is vital to secure and to sustain the impetus of *Future Work* practices, and to ensure that effort is always expended to the benefit of the business, and not dissipated elsewhere. *Interdisciplinary skills* for managers represent the second vital element for our opportunities to clearly emerge in the traditional organization and are a prerequisite to any transformation actually taking place. Lastly, the confident design of an organization presupposes a strong and reliable understanding about the nature of organizations and how they operate in practice. This is covered with a topical discussion on *organizational models*. The scope of this chapter and its relationship to Chapter 9 is shown in Figure 8.1.

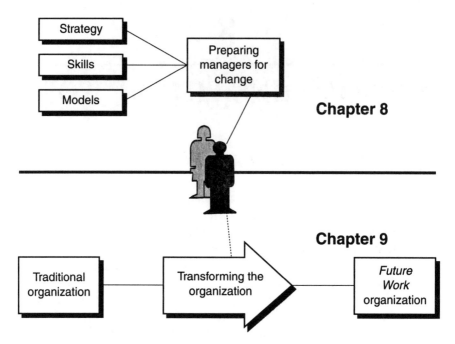

Figure 8.1 Preparing managers for the transformation towards the *Future Work* **organization**

THE EXPANDING STRATEGIC HORIZON OF POSSIBILITY

From the moment that we entered the *era of the negative gap*, that point in time when the potential of IT started to exceed its current level of business demand, the *'horizon of possibility'* for organizations expanded. Quite simply, strategists can now dare to truly dream.

In any strategic vision, the cornerstone of any strategic plan, the strategist (a person or group) describes some 'better future' whilst assuming or recognizing beliefs about certain current constraints. Once such constraints have been established, we then find it very difficult to challenge the beliefs that have always supported them. They become embedded in our thinking; they become written in concrete. Today, *Future Work* can offer the strategist an 'even better future'. *Future Work* implies that we may need to dent, if not shatter, the concrete that confines some of our currently accepted beliefs.

But as our horizon of possibility expands, and as we start to dream, we must ensure that the actions we are about to take in transforming our organization really do make genuine progress along the direction of the organization's mission. That is to say we must resolve to remain strategic in our outlook. Only when we are able to describe this better future, and can provide a viable context that encourages it to come about, will we be able to start work on reshaping or removing the concrete constraints.

Pioneering top level commitment

'He who rides on a horse is a king . . .

He who has shoes is rich . . .

But as for the one who has no shoes: he who is inactive is better off than him.'

The Babylonian Talmud[1]

With a few notable exceptions, *Future Work* techniques have been used in large organizations to avoid difficult situations and to dodge immediate obstacles. Typical instances include the provision of teleworking facilities to staff whose life partners have started a job in a new uncommutable locale, or those on maternity leave. These people then work from home. Thus the human side of the organization has been making demands and has been prodding the technical side with some success. *Future Work* in these organizations rests relatively comfortably with middle managers, but where top level commitment is lacking, its full potential has not yet emerged. *Future Work* is on the move. It is going *somewhere* – but detached from the mainstream of work practice. In search of a proper home somewhere within the organization, *Future Work* still wanders and floats, confused and diffused. How may it become properly established?

> *Future Work* is on the move. It is going *somewhere* – but detached from the mainstream of work practice.

Anyone who has tried to walk barefoot on a pebbled beach will know this problem well. Many of the stones will be sharp and threaten to cut the feet; such stones the traveller will avoid. Some areas of beach will appear to be safer than others to traverse; such areas will be preferred. As we observe from a distance, we come to realize that the route is in fact prescribed not by the wishes of the traveller, but by the patterns and dispositions of the stones.

> **Given sufficient drive, enthusiasm, determination and shared commitment, the major *Future Work* project has a chance of success.**

At best, tactics are standing in for strategy. At worst, tactics are driving some unknown strategy. In a similar fashion, *Future Work* has until recently been rambling barefoot across the rugged landscape of the organization. Top-level commitment towards some goal – or at least in some attractive direction (*which we describe as a 'vector of change'*) – has to be established even before the first step is taken.

With the exception of the very lucky, organizations merely dabbling in *Future Work* without committing adequate resources, are not likely to gain benefits that are worth their efforts. Without ever having sufficient commitment, they probably would have been better off not even starting out. Their resources spent on the project together with the opportunity costs will have been completely wasted. They will be less motivated to try again, even if sufficient resources were to become available. Of course, piloting *Future Work* concepts may be an excellent idea for some, but only if this is done within a proper design framework and when a clear understanding of the criteria for success is established at the start.

Given sufficient drive, enthusiasm, determination and shared commitment, the major *Future Work* project has a chance of success.

A vital ingredient: the business imperative

Serious commitment and determination to change will tend to flow from some recognized and unassailable business imperative. It is only within such a strategic context that *any* major change implementation should be considered. The imperative to change may stem from:

- Opportunities that emerge when considering *Future Work* ideas themselves, or
- Within another major change programme, such as JIT, TQM or BPR
- Results from review systems such as staff appraisal or strategic monitoring.

The transformation of the organization from today to tomorrow (*see* Figure 8.2) must produce a benefit so large as to justify the very significant amount of management energy demanded in designing and implementing the change programme, as well as managing the risk of failure.

Experience in change management has shown that the ability to recite the business imperative throughout the design and implementation of the

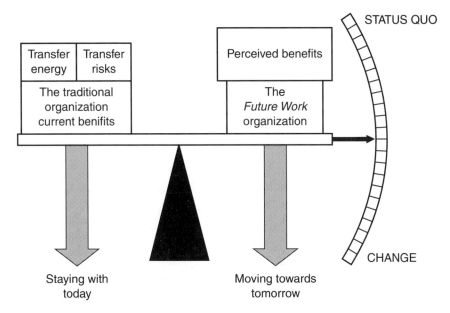

Figure 8.2 Tipping the balance towards tomorrow's organization

change is a factor that is critical to success. A visionary script can be very inspiring at the start of a change programme. But scripts that are phrased more in a language of *noxiant avoidance* – that is the prevention of the undesirable consequences of today's collision course that will inevitably result in a projected business failure – without a doubt have a better track record during the later stages of implementation as a means of persuasion to motivate behavioural change.

Thus, once analysis has been completed, the first job of the pioneer is to compose a mantra of change that crystalises the business imperative. Whilst its tempo will be vibrant and uplifting, some variations on its theme will be capable of introducing more sombre harmonies if necessary.

Managing metamorphosis

Future Work pioneers will recognize that the transformation programme being embarked on must first be seeded and then launched from within a *traditional organization*. It is within the *traditional organization* that the work on planning has to be justified, budgeted and then performed. It is within the *traditional organization* that the case has to be aired, argued and agreed. It is the *traditional organization* that has to design, to truly commit itself to, and then to implement a plan that will change its very fabric.

The traditional organization will provide the setting, if not the battle-ground, wherein the struggle towards its own radically different future will take place. In order for such a metamorphosis to be successful, we are implicitly expecting the traditional organization to be capable, both in technique and in motivation, to reinvent and to rebuild itself whilst maintaining its current operational levels. This need to perform on two or three fronts simultaneously, puts the emerging organization under extreme pressure (*see Exhibit 8.1*).

Exhibit 8.1 Pressures on the emerging organization

1 Maintaining current levels of business.
2 Designing and planning the change.
3 Implementing and learning from the change.

Organizational climate

Today, as the enormous potential of *Future Work* emerges within the context of the business organization, it throws down a new challenge. The extent to which the business will benefit may turn out to be directly proportional to the willingness of board members to destroy, or at least to rearrange, their own traditional functional boundaries.

Within the company, the close inspection of the present state of individual functions, which is necessary in the planning of any major change, has been described by those involved as a 'white-knuckle ride'. Difficult and sensitive issues are bound to surface. It is therefore vital to establish a safe and supporting climate in which change issues may be openly raised and worked on.

A possible *Future Work* script

What in reality is *Future Work*? What should it mean to managers and their businesses? We offer here a script (*see* Exhibit 8.2) as a starting point to help managers introduce a discussion and stimulate ideas.

Those who champion *Future Work* will, of course, want to produce a script for their own company. We present some preliminary considerations that should be taken into account in Exhibit 8.3.

Exhibit 8.2 A possible *Future Work* script

Our management style will emphasise units of productive service and measurable beneficial output, rather than a commitment to complete or exceed a certain number of hours sitting behind a desk in one of our offices. Many of our people may not even work in an office. Some may work from home. Many others will utilize the various new kinds of workplace that are neither within the confines of the traditional office nor inconveniently force-fitted into the residential home.

Our capital requirements, especially our property exposure, will be significantly reduced. We will always have the optimum number of people working for us, as and when needed. Some of these people will be employed, others will work on more flexible arrangements; there will be minimal costs in switching work between people and locations.

More local work will be performed abroad. With all the benefits from cost-effective computer networks and time-zone-shifting, we will strive to complete work for customers in what seems to them to be no time at all. This will give us tremendous service advantage over our competitors. We will be less exposed to local demographic fluctuations.

We will look for new customer segments that are unavailable to us today. We will exploit quite different markets. We will take the opportunity to define completely new products and markets for ourselves.

Many of today's fixed costs will become variable. Costs that are unavoidable today will become avoidable. Tangible assets (and the very significant costs of servicing them), will become less-costly virtual assets.

We know that our business world and the opportunities from new technology are changing at a frenetic rate. We will actively inform ourselves about these changes and constantly upgrade our skills and organizational capabilities. We value a culture of innovation and a climate of openness in which new ideas are tried, evaluated and experiences are speedily shared.

With new products; new markets; better customer service; lower overheads; less space requirement; more productive, motivated and innovative people, we will be truly unbeatable in our chosen markets.

Exhibit 8.3 Some considerations around the *Future Work* transformation

Some Considerations

1 Actively seek out *Future Work* business benefits.
2 Determine whether there is a business imperative for investigating, piloting or implementing a *Future Work* programme.
3 If it is not possible to identify a genuine imperative to change radically, then don't change radically.
4 Doing nothing can sometimes be better than failing. But not in the long term. Work on the assumption that someone – you or your competitor – will get to the high ground first.
5 If there is uncertainty as to whether the *Future Work* imperative is strong enough, balance your risk of implementing against the risk of not implementing, and investigate whether a pilot programme will help to inform your decision.
6 As with all major change initiatives, top-management support, determination, learning and adaptability will be needed throughout.
7 If another major change initiative is under way, then seek to inform it of *Future Work* opportunities, or even extend its scope.
8 Major change means upheaval.
9 *Future Work* may involve scrutiny of existing functions. This will require an appropriate open climate in which sharing can take place.

ETIQUETTE FOR CHAMPIONS

Here we turn our attention squarely on the *Future Work* champions. These are the directors, executives and managers who, having passed the preliminary stage of inquiry, are starting to interpret these opportunities in their own business, and who wish to initiate a wider evaluation of the principles *within their own organization*. Hopefully, they will want to introduce a debate at boardroom level to identify company-wide business benefits, and to develop an action plan.

Future Work champions will have certain key qualities. Of course, they will be inquisitive and creative in grasping the richer business vision. They will also need to be able to cope with some discomfort and ambiguity that the change programme is bound to introduce. But they also need to be highly-skilled managers who are able to communicate and persuade *within the framework of the traditional organization* as it migrates into the future. They therefore must be excellent managers of change.

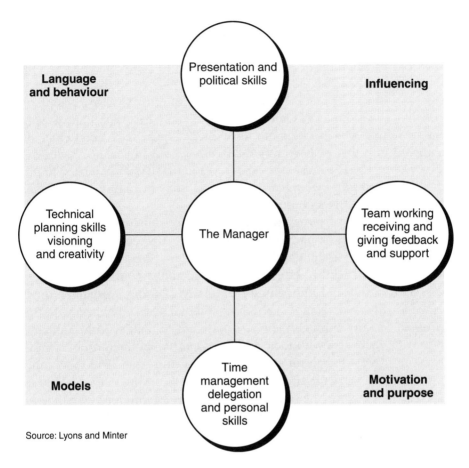

Source: Lyons and Minter

Figure 8.3 A basic skills framework for change-managers

A skills framework introduced by Laurence Lyons and Anne Minter[2] that has been used in the development of senior and middle management teams is given in Figure 8.3 and provides the basis of a useful management skills inventory.

Yet, however outstanding any individual *Future Work* champion may be, a time is bound to come when the initiative will have to be shared and performed by a team.

The inter-disciplinary conundrum of three circles

In defining our subject of *Future Work* at the beginning of this book we drew three circles and declared their central overlapping area to stake out its perimeter. After studying the *content* of the subject matter in this central region, our champions will of course *themselves* become familiar with the opportunities that are on offer. But when introducing the subject *to others within their own traditional organization* they will recognise that they will be talking about issues that are radical as well as sensitive, so that their introduction will therefore require careful handling. In order to have a chance of succeeding just as far as this initial stage, it becomes necessary to turn away from the simple *content* within our three interlocking circles, and to look at the implications that we have introduced *through the very act of drawing the circles themselves.* The most striking observation is that when related to the structure of a *traditional organization*, each circle in Figure 1.1 is today represented by a different business function.

This leads us to the view that any strategic transformation towards *Future Work* has to be underpinned with, and overseen by, an effective and cohesive multidisciplinary team. In Chapter 7 we identified the four components that lead to effective workplace behaviour as knowledge, skills, motivation and opportunity. In many of today's organizations, *knowledge* of the emerging *Future Work* potential when combined with the *motivation* to work through the issues pertinent to their specific company will provide managers with their first *opportunity* – in the form of a business imperative – to migrate to the new learning style. The remaining component necessary for effective progress lies in the area of *skills*. These skills may be based on the framework in Figure 8.3 and must combine to produce a strong emphasis on interdisciplinary working. The 'training and development' thrust must be towards producing organizational competence through the development of team performance.

In September 1992, The Strategic Planning Society News[3] reported a case study at McKechnie Vehicle Component Division (McKechnie is a *Times 500* company) in which a group of four senior line managers, each from a different business function in the UK company, were coached in a 'safe support and challenge' environment within a specially formed 'strategic cell'. The aim of this exercise was to satisfy a business imperative that demanded the rapid production of high-quality and practical interdisciplinary and strategic plans to be presented to the board. In addition

> **The 'training and development' thrust must be towards producing organizational competence through the development of team performance.**

to the reported 'measurable business benefits' and 'reduced business risk', this three-month exercise created a strong and effective management team that fostered a learning climate throughout the division. One key to the *strategic cell development* approach is that the coaching combines multidisciplinary consultancy, personal and interpersonal skills, specially-designed workshops, personal mentoring and role modelling. This case study indicates that the skills required for effective interdisciplinary management team working may be learned and are transferable.

The new horizon of *Future Work* is multidisciplinary in its very nature. In order to find a place in which to live and grow, it requires that a cross-functional home exists for it somewhere in its organizational host. Where within the traditional organization will this challenge be picked up?

Who is responsible?

The question of responsibility, in fact, becomes the root of much confusion within boards and companies involved in any major change that crosses traditional boundaries. As *Future Work* resides within three functional spheres, who should be responsible within the organization for championing *Future Work*? The HR Director? The IT Director? Or should it be the CEO, managing director or chairman? Or, even non-executive directors? Or perhaps no one has been given this responsibility. As the subject in many traditional organizations is spread across two or three functional areas, it may surface in each only weakly.

Interdisciplinary teams

In order to establish a business imperative, or indeed to research whether such an imperative could exist, it is necessary to translate the techniques of IT-enabled work practices into a strategic statement for a particular company. To do this requires a relationship to be established between *Future Work* concepts and strategic benefits. Such benefits may include improvements in the value chain inside the business; or in the value system around the business; in potential for market differentiation, and so forth. When we drew *Future Work* at the centre of three circles, we effectively implied that people can come together across functions to achieve the synergy needed to help the business reorganise itself. This is not a trivial task and has to be the first order of business for the interdisciplinary team that is championing the *Future Work* programme. The new business imperative is only likely to materialize through team collaboration in which strategy, marketing, IT, HR and real estate colleagues can contribute, and this exercise initially may require careful facilitation.

The new rules and roles

But the challenge is not just to work across functions: it also requires the extension of the boundaries of existing disciplines. To appreciate the real challenge, it is necessary to recognize that there is now a new set of rules in play that have been in force since we entered the *era of the negative gap*. These rules establish newly-expanded horizons for many familiar business functions.

Future Work concepts have opened up opportunities within the marketing function through refurbished business processes. This is not new; it is merely an extension of the approach pioneered by Michael Porter[4] that has encouraged businesses to look not only to markets, but to their own industry, as well as finding efficient internal processes as sources of competitive advantage.

The new rules also recast the real estate function from the mundane to the strategic. The greatest expansion in role perhaps falls within the IT and HR functions. In the past, the role of planning within these functions broadly ensured that resources were available to carry out some given strategy. Today these functions must work on the input and ideas side of change, as well as on their traditional resourcing and implementation of it. Figure 8.4 demonstrates where they have a new role to play in *formulating* vision and strategy as well as in delivering it.

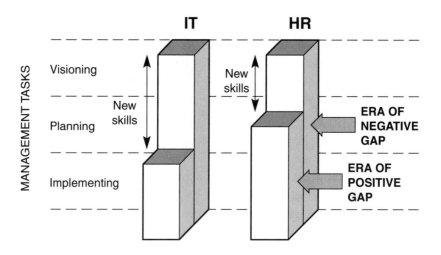

Figure 8.4 Mapping the new roles for IT and HR executives

MODELLING THE ORGANIZATION

'Grau, teurer freund, is alle Theorie,
Und grün des Lebens goldner Baum.'

Dear friend, theory is all grey,
But the golden tree of actual life is ever green.

JOHANN WOLFGANG VON GOETHE
Faust part I, Prologue in Heaven, Apprentice Scene

One limiting factor in our capability when designing the organization lies in our ability, or lack of it, to state and to agree what an organization actually *is*. Even if we are able to reach agreement on this – or are simply able to map out the alternative available perspectives – there remains the question of design. Is it possible to design an organization in the same way, let us say, as a car can be designed? By 'design', we mean the ability to construct or tailormake an organization to our specific requirements. Such a 'designed organization' would be consciously inspired and purposefully built. Indeed, many owners and directors would claim that this is exactly how their own businesses have evolved – through deliberate design. Many consultants seem to be willing to prescribe specific ways of tuning the design of organizations. Somewhere in today's collective management psyche there lurks a tacit belief that it is indeed possible to design a bespoke organization, and that almost anything imaginable is specifiable and achievable.

But what are the limits on our ability to design, and how good are we at it? To what extent can an organization really be designed, as opposed to learned or negotiated?

The need to learn and negotiate will stem from the recognition that not everything that needs to be known maybe available at the outset. Some of the assumptions that surface at the design stage will need to be tested, verified, accepted or replaced during implementation. Such assumptions may relate to an understanding about the organization's present state, the true nature of its environment, or how the specific organization's change dynamics may operate *in practice* during the planned change.

What does it take to design the organization 'correctly'? What factors must be considered? Most importantly, what are the rules of good design? Before discussing *tomorrow's organization* and how we might purposefully create it, let us pause for a while to examine the current state of management understanding from which that organization will have to emerge.

The nature of the organization

Until now, a major, if not the central, difficulty in designing organizations is that – in spite of many articles and books having been written on the subject – we are still at an early stage of understanding or agreeing its true nature. One definition that was originally put forward in a tentative manner, yet seems to have stood the test of time, is that an organization is:

> **'The rational co-ordination of the activities of a number of people towards a common purpose or goal through a division of labour and function, and an hierarchy of authority and responsibility.'**
>
> ED SCHEIN[5]
> Organizational Psychology

In a world in which management structures are becoming flatter, the word *hierarchy* may seem to be a little dated and in need of review. We shall argue later that the term *context* is perhaps more appropriate today, as it removes the connotation of the traditional 'management hierarchy' which seems to cut across the modern ideas of peer-to-peer distributed and self-managed teams as well as self-organised professional individuals. But *hierarchy* and *context* concepts are still absolutely vital to management theory, however flat the physical structure may appear. A move towards flatter organizations should not encourage us to jettison these essential concepts. In the same way that we argue against 'boundary-less' organizations in favour of new boundaries that are being drawn by emerging taxonomies, we support a view of *context* as a fundamental consequence of those very taxonomies. Examples of these taxonomies were introduced in Chapter 3. Later, we will argue that the building and collapse of *context* provides a sequential model for a successful change management programme capable of creating tomorrow's organization.

In reviewing popular approaches we will consider:

- Alignment Models, and
- Micro and Macro Models.

and discuss their appropriateness to *Future Work* and organizational transformation in general.

Alignment models

The manager as designer, has tended to concentrate on one or perhaps two favourite perspectives derived from one of the many 'alignment' models that are available. These models declare that certain elements such as strategy, structure, people, purpose, technology and so forth must somehow interrelate and mesh.

One popular model prevalent in the 1980s is the McKinsey 7-S Model. This model (together with an excellent exposition of *mission* that is also useful in linking to ideas of *culture* that we introduce later) is described by Campbell *et al.*[6] in their Book *A Sense of Mission*. The 7-S Model is based on the alignment of the following organizational factors:

- Strategy
- Shared values
- Skills
- Staff
- Systems
- Style
- Structure

A more recent model, that specifically sets out to introduce information technology as a factor in organizational behaviour and design has been used to underpin the *Management in the Nineties* Research Programme launched in 1984. This model, which is presented in Michael S. Scott Morton's[7] book *The Corporation of the 1990s* recognizes the following interrelated factors:

- Strategy
- Structure
- Technology
- Individuals and roles
- Management processes

All these factors reside within an 'organization boundary' and the whole is set within external socio-economic and technological contexts. The elements of *structure, management processes*, and *individuals and roles* appear within a context of *culture*. The model also recognizes changes in *strategy, structure, people* and *IT* as a consequence of the agency of managers in the change process.

There is no doubt that alignment models have been useful, with each model having its own merits. However, there are certain limitations and problems with alignment models that are worth noting:

Language

One of the difficulties in using alignment models has to do with our use of words and language. Problems with language can often stimulate heated debate about what the basic labels on the factors actually mean. Given an alignment model, it seems to be possible to derive any other alignment model with appropriate explanation. The strength of any model seems to rely on the *richness* of understanding of the words that are used to identify its components. Many of the terms used in these models have both a simple, narrow and highly-restricted meaning, as well as a more complex *rich meaning*. When using such terms it is vital for the designer to declare clearly the extent of what is meant.

Theoretical rigour

Another concern with the alignment models has to do with their degree of rigour. These models are often abstracted from the undeniably valuable insights that their proponents have gained through years of practical experience and in a variety of applications. But upon close scrutiny, some models are often nothing more than anecdotal summaries.

One popular approach that is often used in social science and borrowed by management theorists, is to triangulate situations from the three standpoints of:

- Structure
- Content, and
- Process.

This approach has been shown to be extremely useful in describing what must now be thousands of situations, and has surfaced important insights about inner relationships and alignment. We could ask: Why does the model use three and only these three axes for description? Are these three axes totally exhaustive; can everything important be contained and explained within them? From where are these axes derived? What theoretical underpinning do they comfort us with? A critical question might be: would we feel safe using this model not simply to *describe* a situation, but to determine *policy*?*

In the world of management we have to ask ourselves whether our confidence in the organizational models that we use is indeed sufficient to justify our construction of real-world businesses from them, with all the responsibilities that this implies. Are we yet at the stage where we can put our hand on our collective management heart and say, yes?

---

* This model may be derived quite simply from Figure 8.7 shown later.

Conflict

One test that may be put forward in addressing the question of validity of a model, is whether important characteristics that practising managers will recognize in their own organizations are actually to be found within the model. We have confidence that a real-world organization can be tested against a definition such as Schein's, and it would pass. But are there other important characteristics of organizations – especially those undergoing change – that we might miss? We believe that there are.

In their role as persuaders, decision-makers, champions and negotiators, managers will be unable to avoid one pervasive if not universal organizational element that is very difficult to determine within an alignment model: conflict.

It is easy to see from the *stakeholder model* we introduced earlier in Fig. 3.3 that the various demands of value, interest and expectations that are around the organization offer an abundant source of conflict. This conflict does not simply disappear within the organization's boundary, but it may seem to diminish, and become more manageable, the more we consider the organization as if it were purely an operational machine.

Alignment implies elimination of conflict. Management is the recognition and balance of conflict. Conflict is necessary to propel change. Indeed, we have already implied that conflict between an established business imperative and the ability of today's organization to satisfy it, is *the key motivator for successful change*. We have also suggested that where no business imperative exists then strategic change should not be contemplated. Alignment models, by their very nature, find it difficult to accommodate conflict and therefore change – yet it is this very characteristic that is of paramount interest to managers when transforming their organizations.

The traditional organization poised to introduce *Future Work* may well at the same time be in a state of:

- Operational alignment, and
- Strategic misalignment.

In this fairly common state of affairs we seem to be prepared to tolerate greater levels of conflict, and over longer time periods, as the degree of 'context' expands. The key difference between operational and strategic conflict is one of degree. The latter

> **Alignment implies elimination of conflict. Management is the recognition and balance of conflict.**

may only be properly addressed through a *significant* alteration in the way the business operates, typically suggesting a change in its structure. The *strategic* gap can never be bridged by simply tinkering with present operations, or trying to run them faster. This is shown here in Fig 8.5

Recent emphasis on quality typified by the total quality management school has nudged the dominant approach in many organizations from the *operational* into the *adaptive* region. In contrast to the prevailing ad hoc approach that we find today, the strategic introduction of *Future Work*, if it is to achieve its full potential, indicates a shift in approach to a high-context and potentially high-conflict area. There are clear implications in this for the personal attributes of those in any team working on *Future Work* opportunities.

The implication for the organizational models is in their need to permit a degree of conflict in order to motivate change, and not to pretend to eradicate all conflict by choosing to define it out of the model's scope.

The tactile organization will typically adopt a low-context, low-conflict perspective. *Future Work* challenges it to go beyond quality improvement and to apply a strategic perspective just for the time needed for it to chart

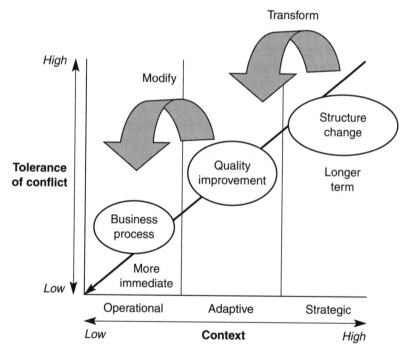

Figure 8.5 Tolerance of conflict in different organizational contexts

its transformation. Once the change process is under way, an adaptive approach may become more appropriate as we have outlined in Chapter 7: Learning in Organizations.

Micro and macro models

In addition to alignment models that emphasize key internal organizational variables, other approaches may be grouped broadly into two popular categories residing at either extreme of a spectrum. At one extremity there is the microeconomic model which describes the organization in terms of men, money, machines and materials. The other extreme, typified in Figure 3.3 regards the organization as one of several players in a wider macroeconomic setting.

> *Future Work* **organizational transforms demand an extremely sophisticated single model to meaningfully integrate all of the micro, alignment and macro descriptions.**

The micro and macro models force us to choose between individual building blocks or complete houses. As organizational architects we need to also map the space between the raw materials and the finished product – in design and construction – and this is where the alignment models complement the picture.

Future Work organizational transforms demand an extremely sophisticated single model to meaningfully integrate all of the micro, alignment and macro descriptions. From our discussion in Chapter 3 it is clear that the model should be able to show the connections between, for example:

- The introduction of IT-enabled work practices and the impact on employees' families.
- The impact and demands of *Future Work* on the current legislative environment.
- The structural impediments to change that could be experienced from professional lobby groups.
- The introduction of *Future Work* in an organization and environmental benefits to society.

Until now, the lack of such an integrated model has been shown up on many occasions by unanticipated disastrous consequences. Anecdotes are rife among managers about projects that intended to improve a core-business process, but actually alienated the staff causing them to fail*. The designers of such disasters may point to the murky area between the polarized micro and macro models, and the complex multiplicity of possible relationships within the alignment models, and say that these dire consequences were unpredictable.

Some will invoke the Chaos Theory. They will tell a story about the butterfly's wings to explain that small perturbations within a complex system may become amplified and then surface dramatically and suddenly without warning in an unexpected place. They may say that the interrelationships are almost indefinable. Others close to the BPR School may describe the organization as if it were a machine. If machines can be designed and tuned to peak performance – why cannot an organization? Is a machine really a good metaphor for an organization? Of course, many practising managers will point to the *soft* aspects of the organization and answer, 'no'.

Towards a new model

Thus at the dawn of a new era of organizational structure, we find that we need a new backcloth, which itself is a type of model. It must be capable of describing *all* types of organization; traditional organizations, *Future Work* organizations, and especially the organization that is in transition between the two. We have to aim for a model that does not require any modification to accommodate the vast variety of organizational species we encounter, even during their development. While the organization is free to evolve and change, the robust framework on which it rests must remain unchanged. We need this solid platform on which we can design, redesign and transform our organization out of today and into tomorrow. It is simply not acceptable to say that new organizational forms require a radically different form of model to describe them. If we cannot describe both the old and the new *on a single canvas*, we risk the danger of jumping across a discontinuity of understanding that no seasoned change-manager would ever wish to attempt.

Our ability to provide such an organizational canvas is central to addressing the design conundrum. We need this canvas to provide the permanent spatial backdrop on which the designer can test a variety of comprehensive representations of the organization. When working on the canvas it must be possible to sketch out draft outlines and road maps that will move the organization effortlessly and cohesively from one stage of development to another.

Figure 8.6 depicts the focus of several themes, dominant in current management thinking. It highlights the need for a new fusion at the triple point of the following intersections:

* We will provide some relevant comments from the change management field in Chapter 9.

1 **Micro-Alignment-Macro axis**. There is a need for a framework which identifies meaningful elements of organizational design, incorporating and uniting the familiar micro and macro descriptions as well as approaches based on the alignment of organizational variables. The framework has not only to identify these key elements, but have the ability to record their characteristic interrelationships and inclusion properties with respect to the accompanying elements. We will show that these essentials are needed to underpin good design practice when transforming the organization.

2 **Stable-Conflict axis.** Sound organizational design requires that organizational models must be able to describe alignment between design elements, but also to recognize and record tension and conflict. Indeed, this tension is the very force that will propel the organization away from today and towards tomorrow. Good change management has a lot to do with orchestrating and managing the misalignment (and thus the conflict) during transition, so that a better aligned future may be reached.

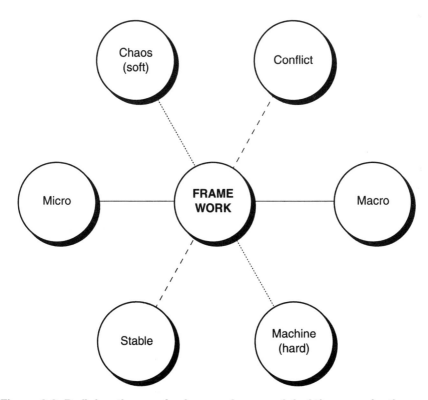

Figure 8.6 Defining the required scope for a model of the organization

3 **Chaotic-Machine axis.** Each of these views has some validity in its own right, yet a unifying framework on which to integrate and contrast them has been missing. At one extreme is the complex/chaotic view. This declares that the multiplicity of interest around the organization, together with the frenetic rate of change brought about by ever-new demands on processes, makes a comprehensive and orderly design inappropriate if not impossible. At the other extreme, there is the view of the organization as a machine, typified by the 'Re-engineering' School who may leave the impression that a mechanistic design approach, similar to that used in designing aircraft or televisions, will always lead to success when applied to designing organizations. Our requirement, then, is for a framework that can accommodate both of these extreme 'soft' and 'hard' factors as well as the full spectrum that lies between them.

The model we will present integrates the perspectives we have set out, so as to offer a comprehensive insight into Organizational Development. Most importantly, for *Future Work* managers, it is useful for plotting appropriate routes for *informing strategy*, a development activity that is specific to our subject. It is also helpful in charting the transformation of organizations in general. We will develop rules to inspire managers with confidence to design and transform a traditional organization from a sound theoretical footing.

A BRIEF INTRODUCTION TO ORGANIZATIONAL METALANGUAGE*

'Anything that happens, happens.

Anything that, in happening, causes something else to happen, causes something else to happen.

Anything that, in happening, causes itself to happen again, happens again.

It doesn't necessarily do it in chronological order, through.'

DOUGLAS ADAMS
Mostly Harmless
Heinemann, London 1992

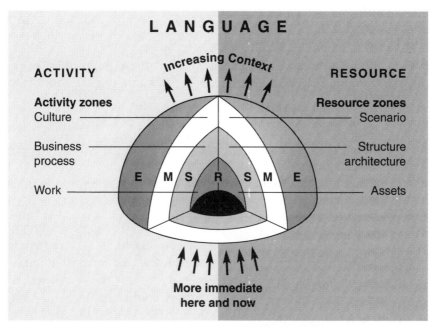

Key   R = Immediate S = Scientific M = Motivational E = Environmental

Figure 8.7 The basic MetaLanguage Model – a canvas on which to place the organization.

* The full theory of Organizational MetaLanguage is outside the scope of this book, but sufficient basic concepts are introduced here to enable managers to gain deeper insights into *Future Work* transformations so as to assist them in practical design and implementation programmes.

Organizational MetaLanguage is not a theory – it is a meta-theory. At its core lies a framework upon which many organizational theories can be placed and positioned, and, most importantly, on which sound organizational transformations may be designed. This framework allows us to make connections between elements. Design rules are themselves theories about the framework, or meta-theories.

Scope

It is important to make it clear that the approach to be described is intended primarily for use in the design and implementation of *significant* organizational transformations. By *significant* we mean that there is sufficient conflict between the current state of the organization and the business imperative for change. Our *Future Work* champion is most likely to be introducing a change programme that is major and will demand fundamental structuring and radically new behaviours. Some typical questions that we expect to emerge will include:

- What repercussions can be expected, and where might they emerge, when a major change is introduced in the whole organization or in a part of it?
- In what order should the change programme tackle the key issues it sets out to address?
- How should the timescales, rate of change, and intermediate stepping-stones be determined?
- What otherwise unanticipated consequences could emerge from the change programme?

In a wider sense, Organizational MetaLanguage is also a comprehensive advanced system of management thinking, enabling multiple perspectives of the organization to be mapped, contrasted and analyzed.

We believe this approach to represent an essential and desperately needed new step forward in unravelling many of the problems and current confusions in management theory. Its essential thrust is to help managers as architects think through all kinds of organizational transformation, specifically the move towards *Future Work*. In a wider sense, Organizational MetaLanguage is also a comprehensive advanced system of management thinking, enabling multiple perspectives of the organization to be mapped, contrasted and analyzed. As it is based on language, it is the preferred framework for providing a truly rich, yet comprehensible, description of the organization, and for this reason it has been shown to be extremely powerful in articulating and promoting change through multidisciplinary teams.

The organizational canvas

The fundamental concept in Organizational MetaLanguage is the framework known as the *organizational canvas*. A canvas is a prepared cloth for painting on, and this is exactly what the organizational canvas provides. It is the exhaustive conceptual space onto which we can map all our perspectives of the organization. The canvas is the board on which the organization's games are played. It is filled with a number of *zones* which are in constant interplay.

Three strategic questions

Managers will be familiar with the three questions of strategy which are given in Exhibit 8.4:

Exhibit 8.4 The three questions of strategy

> **Q1** *Where are we today?*
> **Q2** *Where do we want to be tomorrow?*
> **Q3** *How do we get there?*

Each of these questions is important when designing organizational transforms, yet each is of a different nature.

Mission

The first question is a **positive** question; it is concerned with the condition that the organization is actually in.

The second question is **normative**; it asks not how things *are*, but how we would like them to be.

In the Organizational MetaLanguage approach, these two questions are strongly associated with the organization's mission and are represented by the zone labelled 'scenario' in Figure 8.7. The organization's mission lies in its ability to create and distribute value to its stakeholders. A diagrammatic representation of the *scenario* zone is given in Figure 8.8. The *stakeholders* in Figure 8.8 will be different for different companies but will in general contain many of those to be found in Figure 3.3. Their identification and the distribution of value by the organization towards them will depend on displacements taking place in other zones in the canvas. *Value*, of course, has to be measured not by the company, but by the stakeholder who receives it.

One strength of the Organizational MetaLanguage approach lies in its ability to relate the scenario zone to other zones. It is thus able to make appropriate connections between, for example, the introduction of new processes or technologies, and the consequent redistribution of value or effect on new stakeholders.

System duality

Business transformations are organizational transformations. As such they are extremely difficult to manage. For this reason it is important that the tools that we use are strong in addressing those challenges that occur during change. We will briefly mention how the Organisational MetaLanguage approach incorporates vital ideas from systems theory to help managers design and operate better change management programmes.

A powerful perspective that systems theory brings to management is its ability to describe an organization as an *open system*. In the broadest sense, an open system is a 'living' or social system, whereas a *closed system* is usually not. Systems that are open will have *soft* elements; a closed one will have only *hard* components. Systems theory is interested in the differences in behaviour between systems that are open and those that are closed*.

One reason that organizational transforms are difficult to manage is that organizations comprise both soft and hard components within them. Culture is a soft element, building premises are hard. Both are to be found within the organization's perimeter. Each may require a different management approach.

Organizations also have within them managers who will often perceive the organization from a single perspective – either soft or hard. On the Organisational MetaLanguage canvas the division (or boundary) between hard and soft lies somewhere between the *scientific* and *motivational* shells**.

---

* See Bertalanffy[8] for a detailed discussion.
** For example, we have elsewhere mentioned the formal (hard) and informal (soft) variants of structure in the traditional organization.

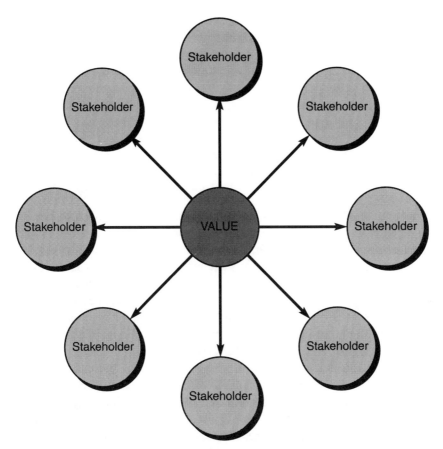

Figure 8.8 Mission as scenario – the organization as a distributor of value

The judgement of managers that is applied in mentally 'drawing' this bound-ary will directly affect the quality of their planning and presentation, the language they use, the degree of influence that they may exert and the suc-cess that they may achieve (*see* Figure 8.3).

Transformation as a vector of change

In declaring the organization to be an *open system* and when discussing some important difficulties in implementing an organizational transform, Katz and Kahn have to say:

> **'The major misconception is the failure to recognize fully that the organization is continually dependent upon inputs from the environ-**

> ment and that the inflow of materials and human energy is not constant. The fact that organizations have built-in protective devices to maintain stability and they are notoriously difficult to change in the direction of some reformer's desires should not obscure the realities of the dynamic inter-relationship of any social structure with its social and natural environment. The very efforts of the organization to maintain a constant external environment produce changes in organizational structure. The reaction to changed inputs to mute their possible revolutionary implications also results in changes.'

KATZ AND KAHN[9]
The Social Psychology of Organizations

We return to the latter questions of dynamics in Chapter 9. For the moment, let us consider simply the third question of strategy which asks the question *how do we get there*? This is the 'active' question of strategy that directs the implementation of the change programme. It is concerned with the *actions* that are to be taken in the redeployment of its *resources* and the changes to be made in its activities or practices in order to approach the future scenario. In mathematics, a *vector* is any entity that possesses both magnitude and direction. In Organisational MetaLanguage, the business transform is a *vector of change*.

In any business transformation, the magnitude of the change will be determined by available management effort and the rate at which the organization can absorb change. The main determinants of this 'magnitude' are given in Exhibit 8.1. The direction of change is, of course, along a path that will eventually tend to satisfy the business imperative. *Equifinality* – a systems theory concept – will insist that for *open systems*, such as business organizations, there will be several ways to reach tomorrow's scenario. As soon as we accept that equifinality applies to the organization as it is an open social system, we concomitantly have to reject the description of a business as purely a machine which is a closed physical system. Very often change-managers will forget this vital point to the detriment of their programme. As Katz and Kahn go on to remind us:

> **In any business transformation, the magnitude of the change will be determined by available management effort and the rate at which the organization can absorb change.**

* See the discussion of 'damping' in Chapter 2.

'One error which stems from this kind of misconception is the failure to recognize the equifinality of the open system, namely that there are more ways than one of producing a given outcome. In a closed physical system the same initial conditions must lead to the same final result. In open systems this is not true even at the biological level. It is much less true at the social level. Yet in practice we insist that there is one best way of assembling a gun for all recruits, one best way for a baseball player to hurl the ball in from the outfield, and that we standardize and teach these methods. . . . The general principle, which characterises all open systems, is that there does not have to be a single method for achieving the objective.'

KATZ AND KAHN

The hallmark of a good change programme is therefore to be found not only in its initial plan that it draws up at the outset, but also in the choices that are made along its journey of change. It is these choices, reflecting the quality of the change programme, that will determine the actual direction taken, and hence the well-being of the company under change. The determination and review of the *vector of change* in a particular transformation involves the continual exercise of sound management judgement and the making of quality decisions about the magnitude and direction of change. Indeed, we see these qualities in the journey as more important than trying to gain total clarity about the conditions of the starting point or even the details of the destination.

'Chi Wen Tzu always thought three times before taking action. Twice would have been quite enough.'

CONFUCIUS
Analects 5th Century BC

Many strategists will spend a disproportionately long time in researching Question 1. Is this the most important of the three? Why analyse to the ultimate degree a situation that we already know needs to be changed? Question 2 provides a stronger impetus for development *towards* the future, and should be the primary focus of initial work in planning change. Even so, it is very likely that a number of assumptions will be needed, and some of these may only be tested during later implementation. It is clear from this that a *learning organization* must be the preferred type for implementing strategic change. Organizations that are not already in a learning mode may need to prioritize this as the initial step towards change.

The question that will motivate real action is Question 3. The true value in asking Question 1 stems from the ability of its answer to inform Question 3; *the precision aimed for in Question 1, therefore, should not go beyond the scope of providing this information.* Any organization in transform would find it extremely difficult to specify exactly where it may be today, or indeed precisely where it would like to be tomorrow. This is not a great problem, as beyond some degree of precision, the additional information could not be used. What we do know is that the developing organization is on some journey. The focus of strategic effort has to ensure, so far as possible, that the general direction is charted and is one of improvement. The strategic thrust is a *vector of change* for the organization.

In declaring that the canvas forms an open system, and by insisting that the vector of change possesses equifinality, Organisational MetaLanguage embeds with it the full power of systems theory and helps to prevent the misconceptions that Katz and Kahn identify from entering into the design of the transformation.

Constructing the canvas

The canvas may be constructed by crossing it in two different ways. These are described as: (a) language sweep, and (b) context sweep.

A language of activities and resources

When designing change programmes within organizations, it is essential to distinguish between what organization do *(i.e. their activities)* and what they have *(i.e. their resources)*. These are elements in the strategy question Q1: *Where are we today?* When applied to the second strategy question: *Where do we want to be tomorrow?* they represent *what the organization would like to do,* and *what it would like to become.* Of course, the specific deployment of all the activities and resources of the organization now or in the future will prescribe its identity, and so define it. The consideration of activities and resources often gets them muddled, and where confusion exists, there is usually little scope for sound change.

To take an example: *Strategic Gap Theory* – a concept from MetaLanguage Theory – explains that, at certain times such as at its inception, the activities of the organization and its deployment of resources try to mirror its perceived role and bring about its feasible aspirations. But over time the activities may persist although the environment may have changed in a way to make the old role inappropriate or the aspirations unachievable, or even undesirable. In this state, many of those who are in the organization tend to justify its role in terms of the maintenance of the activities that have become established. Motivating such an organization, and the people within it, towards change underscores the need to sever the association between the established activities and the emerging new role, which now may be expressed in terms of changes to the structure within the organization. The 'language sweep', which is of a far more fundamental nature than described here, provides just this distinction on the canvas shown as the *activity* and *resource* quadrants in Figure 8.7*.

A sweep of context

Context is the other dimension that sweeps across the descriptive canvas of the organization. As it does so it sketches out a number of concentric *shells*. These are shown in Figure 8.7. to reveal six *zones* that have been labelled and will shortly be described. A straightforward way to explain the meaning of these zones is to conduct a *walk on the canvas*. Starting at the innermost shell, we meander through both quadrants before emerging into the next shell. Along the way we simply describe what we find in each zone.

A walk on the canvas

The context sweep reveals the full range that is possible for the depth of description we may choose to use. Within the 'immediate' central shell in Figure 8.7 *(technically known as the R-shell)*, we are able to talk about the obvious and the here-and-now. In this low context, child-like world, everything is perceived very much at face value. Everything is simple. In the resource quadrant, assets such as raw materials disappear into the organization whilst finished goods emerge. Elsewhere, people work. At this low level of context there is little else that can be said of the organization as it remains barred from using any deeper form of explanation.

In order to gain a more scientific understanding of the organization it is necessary to delve into a richer contextual depth. The *scientific S-shell* enables us to appreciate that the obvious outward appearance of the organization is possible only through the operation of certain business processes and within structures that lie behind the organizational veneer. The business processes orchestrate work and synchronize assets to arrive and interact with each other at certain places and times. Structures declare and enforce how the work and assets are divided up and shared. The threading of work into meaningful business processes, and the grouping of

---

* The term *language* comes from the technical MetaLanguage descriptions of these quadrants as *Verbs* and *Nouns* which also relate the framework on the Canvas to Systems Theory and Hierarchy Theory.

assets into strategic or synergistic resource sets becomes recognizable and describable within the S-shell.

It is particularly worth mentioning that so far as the processes are concerned, these are not only first-order. A first-order process will simply synchronize operational work activities. A second-order process may be needed to modify an existing process. This is perhaps best understood by considering a change process such as TQM. Once a TQM team has been set up, or structured in some way, it will operate a process whose purpose will be the improvement of some existing processes. All change processes are at least second-order – they are a process for a process – and require quite different handling to the simpler first-order ones.

> **But change-champions cannot afford the apparent luxury of ignorance. Major structural change demands wider thinking.**

This *S-shell* may appear to be the architectural fabric upon which the organization rests. For design purposes it may seem that in order to change the organization it is necessary only to redefine the structure *(e.g. the organization chart)* or to modify or repair any delinquent processes. For small-scale 'change' programmes that involve only cosmetic improvements and that do not challenge any of the current organization's assumptions, this lower-context approach may prove to be adequate. But in the major change programmes that are of concern to us, it would be far too simplistic to regard the organization as just a collection of changeable structures and modifiable processes. To succeed in our quest, a higher and richer degree of context is required.

In recognizing the fact that organizations are populated with people, organizations can be said to have collective norms of behaviour. Within the identity and motivational *M-shell*, these norms become embedded in the subculture of the organization to declare what general behaviours are expected, acceptable and tolerated; and which are not. Culture is *how we do things around here*, the 'here' being within the organization's boundaries, however perceived. This zone is the repository of shared values and style. Although it may be described as a very 'soft' zone of the organization, its ability to construct real and extremely 'hard' barriers to change has been demonstrated time and again. Ignorance of the factors and dynamics in this zone has caused many change programmes to fail.

The *scenario* zone declares the organization's unique role and aspirations in the world. The internal structures that determine the divisions within the

organization are an extension of the division that separates the organization as a whole from the world outside. In attesting and asserting its wider
identity, the organization will state how it intends to distribute the value it
creates. Such a distribution may be spelled out in a mission statement,
where this exists. A mission statement can thus provide a powerful and
more modern alternative to the financial determination of stakeholders
that we discussed in Chapter 3 (*see* Figures 3.1 and 3.3). This zone provides
an extremely useful basis for identifying otherwise hidden stakeholders and
relating the value they are to receive from the organization to specific policies, work practices, process and technologies etc. that are within the
organization's design plans.

For organizations that do not have an articulated mission statement, it is
incorrect to assume that no mission exists for them. To the extent that they
continue to create and distribute value, they have a positive yet unstated
mission. Because of this, the scenario zone can never be void: at least, the
organization continues without self-determination, it becomes a follower of
events that are in its environment. The first step that is needed to convert a
tactile organization (*see* Chapter 2) into a leader, is to reconstruct this zone.

In defining the scope of Organizational MetaLanguage, we said earlier
that the design is suited to a *significant organizational transformation*. We
are now able to locate this as the *business change imperative*, (or simply
business imperative) emanating from within this zone. This zone is often
physically difficult to access (it may not exist), hence the need to construct
it and populate it – with a forum of the top team – must be the first priority
of the change programme. History has shown that however well they may
be conceived technically, change programmes without a business imperative, endorsed and promoted at the most senior level within the
organization, have no chance of success*.

However sharply we may try to cut the organization off from the rest of
the world *(E-shell)*, we can never isolate or insulate it completely. The
organization's very existence as a separate entity playing and acting out its
unique role makes its total isolation impossible. For most of the familiar
organizational activities – such as introducing a new product variant; raising prices; introducing a quality circle; or recruiting an individual – this
wider role of the organization is so far removed from perceived reality that
it is of no concern. Indeed, managers would not be able to cope if the

* A *skunk works* project — in which people work 'unofficially' is unlikely in itself to produce major
and sustained change, but it may succeed in providing a stepping-stone towards getting sufficient
attention and resource mobilized to populate this zone.

widest repercussions of each and every action had to be considered prior to any action. But change-champions cannot afford the apparent luxury of ignorance. Major structural change demands wider thinking. We are forced to recognize that the organization exists within what is known in systems theory as *semi-permeable* boundaries. We have to accept that the future organization will have to reside and justify itself within the environment that, in part, it is determining through its present action towards change.

It is also important to note that organizations may incorporate a business environment monitoring programme as a prerequisite to qualifying a change programme. Such a programme will monitor the outside world for key indicators so that a change programme can be triggered and launched at an appropriate time.

Canvas variants

There are three main variants of the MetaLanguage canvas. When drawn on paper, all variants look identical due to the exhaustive property of the canvas (that is in its ability to contain all possible descriptions of the organization). Indeed, were the variants to appear visibly different, then it could easily be shown that the canvas would fail its quest as a meta-theory framework. The variants are:

- **Positive (*Type P*).** A state that actually exists in the organization at a specific time. In this variant, the zones in the framework may or may not be 'aligned'.
- **Normative (*Type N*).** A state that describes how we would like the organization to be. A normative state of the organization may contain alignment between some or all of the zones. Normative space may be used to describe a stable organizational state.
- **Transitional (*Delta-space*).** A transitional space to describe the organization in change. This description will identify conflict between zones or shells.

These three variants loosely correspond to the three strategic questions of Exhibit 8.4. The notation **P, N,** δ (delta), is used to identify the variant being used on any occasion. A change programme design will include a number of variants, typically with one for today (P), another for tomorrow (N), and a number of stepping-stones (δ) along the way. The stepping-stones will ensure that a thread of *intelligent continuity* runs throughout the change programme. As we have mentioned before, the transitional space is the most important and demands the most work. We are not overly concerned with strictly mapping *today*, or – perhaps surprisingly – *tomorrow*. A learning organization may not be able to specify its ultimate destination with complete clarity. What is of the most importance is that the organization is progressing in an appropriate direction, and learning whilst it does so. The delta-space provides us with a canvas upon which the *vectors of change* can be mapped.

> **A change programme design will include a number of variants, typically with one for today (P), another for tomorrow (N), and a number of stepping-stones (δ) along the way.**

Management summary

- A business imperative together with top level commitment are prerequisites for any change programme.
- Identifying a *Future Work* champion may be difficult because of the multidisciplinary nature of the opportunities.
- Multidisciplinary teams are essential for real *Future Work* opportunities to emerge.
- Models used in the design and implementation of organizational change must be able to accept conflict necessary to motivate change.
- Organizational MetaLanguage provides a useful framework for managers involved in designing and implementing significant change in their organization

References

1   Talmud The. Tractate Shabbat p.152a. For a translation see Freedman, H. *The Talmud*, Soncino, 1938, p.775.
2   LYONS, LAURENCE S. AND MINTER, ANNE. *Strategic Cell Development: A method for accelerating strategic behaviour in individuals and organizations within the work environment*, SCD Monograph Series, Metacorp, Reading, England 2 RG31 6JZ, 1992.
3   NEWS of the Strategic Planning Society. 'Innovative method outlined for bridging strategy and management development', *NEWS*, September 1992, p.1.
4   PORTER, MICHAEL E. Competitive Advantage: Creating and Sustaining Superior Performance, The Free Press, 1985.
5   SCHEIN, E. *Organizational Psychology*, Prentice-Hall, 2e, 1970.
6   CAMPBELL A, DEVINE M AND YOUNG D. *A Sense of Mission*, Pitman Publishing, 1993.
7   SCOTT MORTON, MICHAEL S. (ed.) *The Corporation of the 1990s: Information Technology and Organizational Transform*, Oxford University Press, 1991.
8   BERTALANFFY, L. VON. 'The theory of open systems in physics and biology', *Science*, vol.111 (1950), pp.23–29 *in* Emery (1969).
9   KATZ, D. AND KAHN, R. L. *The Social Psychology of Organizations*, Chapter 2, Wiley, 1966, pp.14–29, *in* Emery (1969).

Further Reading

ANSOFF, H. Igor. *Strategic Management*, Macmillan Press, 1979.

BERGER, PETER L. & LUCKMAN, THOMAS. *The Social Construction of Reality: A Treatise in the Sociology of Knowledge*, Penguin University Books, 1971.

EMERY, F. E. (ed.) *Systems Thinking*, Penguin, 1969.

MERTON, R. K. 'The unanticipated consequences of purposive social action', *American Sociological Review*, vol.1, no.6, 1936.

PASCALE, RICHARD TANNER AND ATHOS, ANTHONY G. *The Art of Japanese Management: Applications for American Executives*, Simon and Schuster pub., New York, 1981.

'There is nothing so practical as a good theory.'

KURT LEWIN

Field Theory in Social Science, Tavistock, p.169, 1952.

9

MANAGING THE TRANSFORMATION TO FUTURE WORK

INTRODUCTION

In the previous chapter, we prepared managers to champion the *Future Work* initiative from within their own traditional organization. Here we cover issues in the *management* of the transformation towards *Future Work* using Organizational MetaLanguage as a basis for description.

Taking the initiative

Change-managers are unlikely to feel comfortable passively watching new boundaries emerge around themselves and their businesses. Managers prefer to change things rather than look on as things are being changed. They will be keen to play their own part, not simply in observing the pressure that results from shifts outside the business, but in actively managing their responses by drawing some boundaries of their own. As we have argued, in order to understand and hence exert any influence on the movement and establishment of boundaries, it is necessary to look at the context in which those boundaries are coming under pressure to change. This is the province of a taxonomy in which alternative interests and drives compete to determine where the resultant boundaries will eventually come to be drawn. It is in this area of conflict that the manager is able to introduce judgement and exercise choice.

> **Change-managers are unlikely to feel comfortable passively watching new boundaries emerge around themselves and their businesses.**

Addressing the strategic gap

For a company that has recently woken up to realize that it has become strategically misaligned, the initial work of managers must be devoted to articulating or profiling the scenario to which it now aspires. This is its response to the second question of strategy: *Where do we want to be tomorrow?* The answer to this will, of course, be at variance with the present destination and today's present course of action. Where the company is going, and where it should be going are likely to be located at different places. We have already described a motivation to change the direction of the business as the *business imperative*. To introduce the business imperative into the company is to introduce conflict between today's actions and today's aspirations. Conflict radiating from the business imperative provides the energy needed by the organization in its struggle towards establishing its new identity.

As the organization stretches out to exercise its self-determination new boundaries are able to emerge. One such boundary may introduce *Future Work* into the organization. But the conflict propelling this has to be harnessed by change-managers. At one extreme, too much conflict can be destructive. At the other, no beneficial directional change is likely to result if conflict is not introduced at all.

The power to change

From this it becomes clear that a key role of the change-manager is to appropriately introduce and manage the conflict that will guide the company towards its better future. The notion of introducing conflict as a deliberate management activity may strike a note of alarm for many. But it is this very characteristic that sets the change manager apart from the 'operational manager' who will be working within a more limited set of assumptions about adjustments that need to be made to the business. The operational manager aims to align the present activities of the business with its present design, whereas the change-manager has to accept that there is some *misalignment* between the present design (in its deployment of activities and resources), and what the business needs to become in order to develop and to survive into the future.

As a major organizational transformation, the adventure into *Future Work* will require change-managers to introduce and manage the conflict that unavoidably flows from the new business imperative. In so doing, they cannot avoid replacing old boundaries with new when this becomes neces-

sary. Provided that they are guided by a solidly supported business imperative, that they are careful with the degree of conflict being introduced and
dissipated (through their actions and the consequences of their actions),
and that they are receptive as they test their assumptions by learning as
they progress, then they will be poised for success.

Style and scope

Business executives sometimes expect management science to provide pat
answers packaged into a one-shot methodology that is guaranteed to
succeed. Those who cling to this expectation of a sure-fire painting-
by-numbers approach to change-management will find that they are
in for an uncomfortable ride. Managers who have experienced major
organizational change, will often correctly claim that the end result is
highly dependent on the qualities of the change-management practitioner,
and that no amount of theory – by itself – will ensure a safe arrival into
the better future.

Change-management – just like the organization that it manages – is socio-
technical in nature. It requires a combination of a solid theoretical approach
and sensitive change-managers. Rather than feel overwhelmed, creative
change-managers will welcome the rich variety of options that *Future Work*
opens up for them, in the hope that they may discover a highly-valuable and
unassailable source of differentiation for their own companies.

Although we do not recommend attempting to transform your organization
strictly 'by numbers', nor do we seek to replace the sensitive skills of a seasoned change-manager, we do offer some modern design rules derived from a
consolidated framework and much
field experience. That framework is
Organizational MetaLanguage and
has been used as the basis for designing and implementing many change
programmes and has been central in
establishing a common business focus
and language across change-management teams whose members have
come from different functions within
their companies.

> **Business executives
> sometimes expect
> management science to
> provide pat answers
> packaged into a one-shot
> methodology that is
> guaranteed to succeed.**

A RE-ENGINEERING BACKDROP

'This is what they all come to who exclusively harp on experience. They do not stop to consider that experience is only one half of the experience.'

JOHANN WOLFGANG VON GOETHE
Maxims and Reflections

From beneath a mountain of hype, misnomer and confusion, a real and new management approach has been struggling to emerge. Under the general banner of 'Re-engineering', it reflects the practical experiences of managers, and provides a source of practical feedback to management science (*see* Figure 9.1.)

It currently represents a response to:

- The failure of business processes to meet customers' needs and deliver customer satisfaction.
- The challenge of organisational politics.
- The yawning gap between strategic intent in the boardroom and the day-to-day practice of the business.
- Disappointments following the application of IT to businesses during the 1980s.

With regard to the last point, managers were only just coming to realize that in addition to its appearance as a 'good' that is supplied and 'consumed' by organizations, IT also has the ability to mutate structure. The following quotation, in summarising a number of surveys, expresses the need for a business-pull – as opposed to technology-push – approach, with the dominant drive emanating from the needs of the business:

'There is growing evidence that the majority of companies have failed to reap the hoped-for returns from their investment in IT. A number of key surveys have shown that the prime reason for this is the failure of senior management to align their IT strategy with corporate objectives.'

HARVEY & LEESON[1]
The Management Barrier, Pergamon Infotech Ltd., 1987

The essential characteristic of Business Process Re-engineering is in its emphasis on *processes* as a powerful change mechanism that aligns and locks the operations of the business into some defined purpose. One such

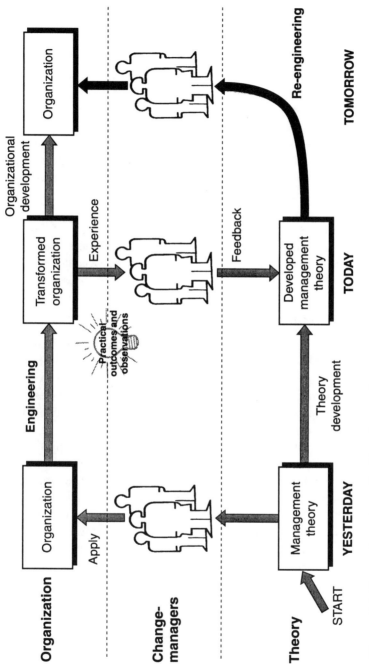

Figure 9.1 Re-engineering – the learning cycle

'purpose' may be to ensure that the way in which the business presents itself to the outside world appears to be sensible as perceived from the customer's point of view as well as beneficial to the business.

It is certainly true that the consideration of process before structure can have the effect of challenging the established structural boundaries in a dramatic way. These boundaries may either expand the scope of the business further into the supplier's or customer's arena*, or may jar against currently established professional demarcations. In their pioneering book *Reengineering the Corporation*, Michael Hammer & James Champy give an excellent example of the latter in their IBM Credit Corporation case study in which multitalented generalists replace professional specialists. They define Re-engineering as:

> **'the fundamental re-thinking and radical redesign of business processes to achieve dramatic improvements in critical contemporary measures of performance, such as cost, quality, service, and speed.'**
>
> HAMMER AND CHAMPY[2]

The Re-engineering of *Future Work*

The BPR definition given by Michael Hammer and James Champy offers to make the vital connection between the BPR approach and *Future Work*. Surely, *Future Work* has something important to contribute to the fundamental rethinking and radical redesign of business processes? All that seems to be required of *Future Work* is to inform a BPR exercise about candidate processes for change.

By *informing* we mean 'to identify and communicate opportunities to revise any resource or activity in and around the organization'. Such resources and activities are to be found within any of the Organisational MetaLanguage zones (*see* Figure 8.7). When contemplating the transformation of an organization, the concept of *informing strategy* can propose, for example, culture change, asset acquisition, restructuring the organization, and, of course, process modification. In this way, the Organizational MetaLanguage meaning of *informing strategy* recognizes BPR as a 'scientific activity' on its canvas. This establishes the important positioning of BPR within Organizational MetaLanguage as one of many significant perspectives.

---

* See, for example, the SUCCESS programme Supplier Customer Co-operation to Efficiently Support mutual Success *in* Matthyssens and Van den Bulte[3].

But whereas BPR will stress the process improvement as its vector of change, the Organizational MetaLanguage approach will appeal instead to a higher level of context and motivation – the business imperative. The difference is one of perspective. We suggest that in *Future Work* the motivation has to be the business imperative. However, a review of existing processes may pave the way. Consideration of the results of a *process improvement* exercise may suggest the need for more fundamental terms of reference. Ultimately, the most robust transformations will be those that attract the most commitment, which in turn implies an appeal to nothing less than a genuine business imperative. For example:

Exhibit 9.1 Informing processes can lead to informing strategy

'In the course of reorganizing our business functions, we are discovering that the traditional paper-based functions of purchasing, receiving, invoicing, and payment, are being completely transformed through information technology.

We are discovering that simply automating previously paper-based functions is a mistake, and that we need to completely rethink these functions so that we can take full advantage of technology . . .

We originally started out to plan for a computer system. It has now become apparent that the important issue is how we decide to do business.

Jim Holman[4]
Oregon Health Sciences University

In theory, we have shown that the Organizational MetaLanguage canvas is capable of helping us make the intellectual link between a scientific process approach to organizational transformation (BPR) and a business imperative. But is the linkage being made in practice?

There are two emerging problems with the notion that *Future Work* is capable of informing a successful BPR transformation. The first is that the connection is not being made in practice. The second problem has to do with the high degree of failure of projects that lay claim to being of the BPR type. This raises the question as to whether BPR is a sufficiently robust vehicle on which to launch *Future Work*.

Experiences with BPR

In reporting that 'Business Process Re-engineering is having a negligible impact on work patterns despite its reputation for radical change and revolution', Management Consultancy quotes Professor Colin Coulson-Thomas, leader of the European Commission's Constraints and Opportunities in Business Restructuring Project (COBRA), who bases his comments on the results of over 100 pan-European BPR exercises focusing on teleworking. He says:

> 'Virtually all the new models of more flexible organization and new ways of working and learning which are emerging have been created quite independently of BPR . . . In appropriate circumstances, where inspired by a vision of the future and when properly used, BPR can represent a useful element of a corporate transform programme...'
>
> COLIN COULSON-THOMAS[5]
> Management Consultancy, October 1994

These findings echo similar experiences reported by Professor Dan Jones from the Cardiff Business School who has said:

> 'A lot of companies have already told us that they have done quite a lot of process re-engineering and it doesn't work. This includes both manufacturing and service organizations . . . BPR has to be part of a much more fundamental culture change that is bottom-up as well as top-down.'
>
> PROFESSOR DAN JONES[6]
> Cardiff Business School

Exhibit 9.2 provides a detailed and comprehensive account that comes with much insight from a seasoned change practitioner and represents high-quality feedback of the type we referred to in Figure 9.1.

Our response to such feedback is to suggest that change-practitioners are demanding a more advanced management theory that is beyond the current state of 'Re-engineering'. David Greenstein is reminding us that an organization is more than a set of processes, and that to transform the organization successfully requires us to recognize and incorporate a wider range of factors into our thinking and actions. To achieve this will require us to delve deeply behind the cosmetic gloss of the organization and uncover the important interactions and dynamics that are at work within its very fabric.

Exhibit 9.2 A feedback report for the learning cycle

I caught myself wondering why most of the people working on BPR are not addressing all issues and aspects of the change it brings into the organization.

It would be very amaturistic to assume that BPR addresses only the process. I studied the effect of 'change' on organizational behavior for a quite long time. It is very important to understand, that any change – in the structure, in the personnel, in the technology, procedure, philosophy of operation, culture, etc. – has a significant effect on every area of the business. It means, that if someone is trying to 'slightly' change or modify the operational procedure for the sake of improving the performance, for instance, it will effect other areas, such as cost, quality, speed, management reaction, enthusiasm, etc. In a complex system, such as a modern organization, a small change in the initial condition will bring very significant change in the end. This is chaos theory.

Modern systems, such as organisations, tend to get more and more complex and more dynamic. The speed of change is increasing. Network based interconnection of modern organization and societies is increasing even more the dynamic complexity of systems. This process just started; the fun just began.

We have to start to investigate the effect BPR brings to all aspects of an organization. I observed that the best intention to improve a process in a factory not only didn't improve the performance, but had an opposite effect, even though the process *was* improved. There were other factors that suffered from that change that brought the anticipated performance improvement to the negative territory.

The 85% failure rate of BPR is largely due to a simple view of the effect BPR brings into an organization. We have to investigate the 'complex reaction' of a system in response to a change. A collective response of a complex system to a change, is extremely difficult to predict, never mind to measure.

The problem lies in our lack of ability to predict the reaction of all the individual components of a system to that (initial) change, and then the collective behavior of the system to that (consequential) change. In some cases, even the speed of reaction of individual components of a system could cause significant problems.

I believe, we have to start to include in the equation *all* important aspects of the organization. Some aspects are very subjective, but important. One example is perception. If management of the organization is not totally supporting the transformation, and just providing lip service, the project is doomed from its inception.

In my work, I am trying to anticipate the effect the change will have on the physical, moral, organizational, psychological, structural, etc. aspects of the system. We are trying not to impose the change, but co-evolve the organization with the evolution of individual components through the change process.

We are taking into consideration the 'integral' reaction of the system to the change that is caused from the changing behavior of all its components.

Eventually, I believe, we will learn to understand the dynamic reaction of complex systems. Very important is the transition period, and the 'multicultural' effect of the system.

Without taking the multicultural aspects into consideration, most transformation projects such as BPR will fail.

David Greenstein[7]
Project Manager, General Motors Corporation, November 1994

The apparently high (around 70 to 85 per cent) anecdotal BPR failure rate seems to confirm an expected estimate of 70 per cent suggested by Michael Hammer and Steven Stanton[8]. They argue for BPR – as we do for *Future Work* – that for any such major change programme to stand a chance of success two ingredients are vital. These are 'intellect', together with committed executive leadership. In order to bring the failure rate down dramatically, progress has to be made along the twin paths of intellect and leadership. We have already made the case for committed leadership in promoting *Future Work*. As for the intellectual challenge, we now summarise the above observations which set the new challenges for Re-engineering (*see* Exhibit 9.3), and we discuss how Organizational MetaLanguage is able to assist managers in meeting it.

Exhibit 9.3 Feedback from the BPR field

- Businesses are complex; *Process* is but one of many organizational factors.

- Small adjustments in one factor (e.g. in a process), may provoke large consequences in other factors.

- Without adequate recognition and supervision, such unanticipated consequences can be major, highly disruptive, and even overwhelming.

- A frenetic rate of change will tend to magnify conflict.

- Learning is critical in order to monitor and respond to any unanticipated consequences.

- A two-way dialogue (bottom-up and top-down) is essential for learning.

- An *holistic* understanding of the business would at the very least identify the areas in which these consequences might occur.

- Inspiration from a (normative) vision of the future helps the change to succeed; a business imperative is a source of stability.

- Culture change is strongly connected to process change and *vice versa*.

RE-ENGINEERING WITH ORGANIZATIONAL METALANGUAGE

In this section we use the Organizational MetaLanguage model to provide an intellectual backdrop that will assist change-managers in conducting a successful significant organizational transformation towards *Future Work*. The intellectual dimension is crucially important as it is only in the depth of our perception and understanding about the dynamics of the organization that we will find the knowledge and confidence to manage its change safely. Theory as the gloss on intellect, should therefore inspire the confidence that is needed in order to underpin committed leadership.

Populating the company

Our description of the organizational canvas comes to life when it is populated. As a socio-technical system the organization contains both people and designs. Each brings beliefs. People bring ideas and ideologies; technical designs bring functional conventions and assumptions. Thus a finance director may hold a belief that the company should enter a new market, and may back this up with arguments relying on accounting conventions. Furthermore, the Organizational MetaLanguage canvas recognizes machines as legitimate members of its population, so it does not insist that all 'activities' have to be performed by people alone. Any organizational assumptions embedded in such automation will be incorporated to become part of the organization's technical fabric.

Within the organization *conflict always exists*. As a socio-technical system the organization contains two types of conflict. One type of conflict will stem from technical misalignment, the most obvious example being an ineffective process where an organization is fighting against its own purpose. But even if all technical processes were to become 'perfect', the second type of underlying organizational conflict would remain – that which is generated between differing beliefs and assumptions. Indeed, an organization that was not forever experiencing some degree of dynamic conflict would become tactile, unresponsive to its environment, and could not survive into the long term.

> **People bring ideas and ideologies; technical designs bring functional conventions and assumptions.**

Levers of change

A taxonomy reflects a technical set of rules. When applied to the world (or to an organization) a taxonomy will provide a series of discrete boxes. These divider-boxes will include or reject parts of the world. They produce, for example, market-segmentation schemes and organization charts. The boxes, or zones, are normative: they assert where things should be, or where they will be assumed to be. As such, taxonomies are predicated on some set of beliefs. These beliefs are not absolute in themselves – they are held by people. As conflict always exists within organizations, beliefs may be challenged and the current taxonomies may be disputed.

In order to express the current amount of conflict in an organization it becomes necessary to discuss the degree of agreement between the individuals within and around it. The term 'culture' is used to express the general sharing of ideas, customs, symbols and art across a society. Culture can only refer to a group of people, not to a single individual. We use the term *culture* broadly to denote the ability for the organization to gain within itself some general agreement about today's dominant business taxonomies. Given a business climate in which the organization struggles to transform itself into something new, a need will emerge to replace today's taxonomies with those of tomorrow. To introduce *Future Work* is therefore to instigate a new culture, whether consciously or otherwise. *Future Work* does not present a technological challenge, but an intellectual and social one. We argue that the preferred route for the change-manager is thus *scenario* and *culture* before *process* or *structure*.

The special role of change-managers

For many in the organization, conflict will seem to swell at times of major change. During change, the competition between the taxonomies of today and tomorrow will add to the background level of conflict and will present the unsuspecting manager with what at best may be described as a 'messy' situation, characterized by much deliberately-introduced conflict. Change-managers have a special role in communicating, inspiring and encouraging the move towards the better future by explicitly recognizing this currently unresolved conflict. They must clarify the situation and take a leadership role in managing the transition. We argue that in terms of the Organizational MetaLanguage model, the guiding principles for change managers should be:

1. The appropriate and scheduled introduction, monitoring and resolution of conflict, and
2. The control of context.

Developing the context of the organization is another idea that many will regard as an unusual management activity, especially when this spills outside the company and into the business environment. Activities in the environment are often overlooked, or regarded by managers as irrelevant, unworkable or impossible to undertake. A more modern and holistic management approach, however, will recognize the need for *lobbying*, i.e. managing the context of the organization. This activity is highly-relevant to the introduction of *Future Work*, as new work practices impinge on the traditional environmental mould in which today's organization rests. The organization has its unique role to play in the dialogue that is required to realign today's legislation with the emerging work practices. It is only able to participate in this through the dialogue that its managers enter into outside the organization's boundary.

The *environmental shell* of the Organizational MetaLanguage canvas easily accommodates context-conditioning as an activity that takes place beyond the organization's traditional boundary. It also recognizes that the organization operates within the context of a legislative environment. During organizational transformation, these environmental zones may be 'in dialogue' with the organization's scenario: the organization may be in a two-way negotiation with its environment. We believe it is important that any modern management model must explicitly incorporate these environmental zones into its description of the organization. Indeed, such inclusion is absolutely essential for any organization that is trying to impress its new identity into a world of full-ripple economics, whether this relates to *Future Work*, or otherwise.

Change-managers will also recognize the difference between what they know and what they do not know, and so act accordingly. *Where the organization is today* is a positive question in the sense that the answer is knowable, so that with sufficient resources the present organizational state can be established. *Where the organization will be tomorrow* is normative in the sense that managers

> **Gravity will dictate that a drop of rain falling on a window will travel downwards; local conditions such as surface tension will navigate its particular course.**

may have some vision of the better future, but, because of the very nature of the strategic challenge this future cannot yet be experienced. Equifinality suggests that there are potentially many paths to that future, and the strategic question *how we get there* must contain assumptions that as yet remain unproved. The vision may be realizable, yet the specific and particular path that the organization is to follow, although known in outline, may not be known in detail. We have already argued that the original state of the organization would require much work to establish in detail, even though it is knowable. In contrast, absolute knowledge about the transformation, containing as it does many complex interrelationships and as yet untested assumptions, is not possible to attain. Thus the business imperative may dictate a direction whereas managers who are implementing the change will determine their local courses of action. Gravity will dictate that a drop of rain falling on a window will travel downwards; local conditions such as surface tension will navigate its particular course.

Business vision will produce a top-down imperative. Learning is a mechanism that provides a bottom-up feedback. The reality that is experienced during a successful transform is a blend of these two elements. The change-manager must be capable of monitoring and adjusting to this blend.

Basic transformation concepts

Organizational MetaLanguage insists that 'all aspects of an organization' as suggested by Greenstein (*see* Exhibit 9.2) are capable of contributing to its strategic position. The 'aspects' that are of interest to us are zones on the canvas that we introduced in Chapter 8. We are now in a position to paint a fuller picture and establish the relationship between strategy and transformation. The *general strategic position* is a rich description of the organization and is shown in Figure 9.2.

General strategic position

The general strategic position is based on:

- The three questions of strategy (Exhibit 8.1).
- The Organizational MetaLanguage description of the organization (Exhibit 8.7)

When consolidated as in Figure 9.2, the model incorporates all the common connotations of the term *strategy*. Specifically these are:

- The relationship of the organization with its environment.
- A significant degree of change.

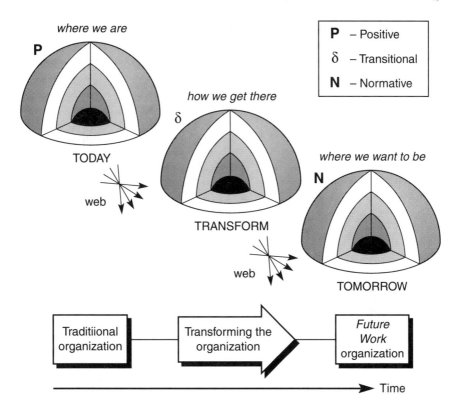

Figure 9.2 General strategic position

- A medium to long term planning horizon.
- The (re-)creation and (re-)distribution of value.

Complex and Dynamic Interrelationships

The dynamics of an organization are complex, not simple. If we are to shift our focus of perception away from a purely 'process' description such as BPR, we must ensure that we do not simply substitute it for some other simplistic single-factor description. Thus, for example, it would be as dangerous to define a business as simply the sum of its processes as it would be to describe it as just a set of structures. The modern change-manager is faced with a number of perspectives of the organization from which to choose a preferred model. An important subset of these is presented in Table 9.1

Table 9.1 Organizational perspectives compared

Perspective	Description	Component	Strengths and Weaknesses
Traditional Functional *professional*	The organization is comprised of a set of functional structures.	Business functions	**Strength:** Easy to determine responsibilities. **Weakness:** Organizational politics often wins over sensible process management and a sense of business purpose can get lost.
Process (BPR) *operational*	The organization is represented as a set of core processes.	Business processes	**Strength:** Process places purpose prior to politics. **Weakness:** The *introduction* of new core processes requires a supporting strategic and cultural context outside the scope of this perspective.
Organizational MetaLanguage *change management*	The organization is a complex interrelationship of resources and activities that reside within a strategic and cultural *motivational* setting.	The holistic canvas	**Strength:** Constant appeal to the *business imperative* encourages a sense of identity, enforces a business logic and helps prepare the commitment required to instigate genuine beneficial change. **Weakness:** Mainly applicable for *significant* transformations.

A simple version of Organizational MetaLanguage will declare that an organization is comprised of resources and activities; structures and processes; a mission and a culture; an environment and a legislative context. Yet managers who work in organizations from day to day will recognize that in practice the real world does not seem to distinguish sharply between any of these entities. Practical reality presents the organization to them as a blended mixture of elements, so that a more advanced management theory is needed to accommodate complex interrelationships. This is where the organization differs from the machine. For the machine in the world of physics, these so-called 'second-order' effects of interrelationship often cause a calculation to be modified in only the second or third decimal place. Within organizations, second-order effects may produce unintended consequences that are best described as order-of-magnitude surprises. The intellectual challenge lies in our ability to describe the organization with sufficient complexity. The management challenge is to contain the dynamic conflict that is generated between the factors during a change programme.

In the Organizational MetaLanguage description of transformation, a web of complexity runs forwards and criss-crosses each and every zone. Each point of contact suggests a potentially important relationship. This web accommodates into our thinking the linkages and interrelationships. These relationships may be current, historic, or may even incorporate beliefs about a possible expected future state of the company or its environment. We repeat that a model of such richness is normally only necessary if the transform that is being undertaken is significant. Conversely, if a significant transformation is being undertaken, the use of such a rich model is mandatory. Change-practitioners will want to know what counts as 'significant'.

We have suggested that one characteristic of a significant transformation is that it enables the organization to break free of the current way that business is done. Simply doing more of the same things, or doing things slightly different does not qualify as significant. By significant we mean that a new rationale and culture is being introduced as the 'world view' of the organization changes. The organization is undergoing a shift in paradigm; important boundaries are eroding and reforming. Drawing together some of the threads we established in earlier chapters, we are now able to present a rule-of-thumb:

Exhibit 9.4 Rule-of-thumb for significant change

Organizational MetaLanguage is most appropriately used in cases where the organization is undertaking a significant transformation. To qualify as significant we suggest that the current business imperative demands some new taxonomy that will redraw boundaries in and around the organization.

One-shot vs. on-going transformation

Another important observation from Figure 9.2 concerns the extent of the transformation into either the medium term or long term. It is absolutely vital for designers of organizational transforms to distinguish between the resources and skills that are needed only temporarily, simply in order for the transformation to take place, and those resources and skills that will be needed for running and operating tomorrow's organization.

For organizations expecting a constant and unrelenting change, these skills may be identical. Such organizations will be forever learning. These are continuously 'Learning Organizations'. But other organizations may be undertaking a step change in their structure and may expect to revert to a more familiar operational style once the transformation has been completed. These organizations will have very different design requirements to their more frenetic cousins.

Thus there are two kinds of 'learning' in organizations. One type of learning is needed essentially to implement a single change programme: this would be shown as a skill requirement in the transform δ-space. The other type of *on-going* learning will demand to be placed in tomorrow's normative culture-zone. Putting the 'learning' label in the wrong place can be damaging. The example given here profiles the difference between a 'hands-off' approach, suggesting the need for external consultants only for the duration of the transformation programme, or another that would encourage the participation of the company's own managers towards the development of an adaptive and learning organization*.

Exhibit 9.5 Two kinds of learning

Distinguish between the knowledge and skills that will be:

- Ongoing and critical in tomorrow's transformed organization, and
- Temporary yet necessary in order just to implement the change.

Strategic transformation

Figure 9.2 also indicates the relationship between strategy and transformation. It insists that *transformation* is a part of strategy, or *strategic intent*. As the means that will take today's organization into tomorrow, it is clear that informed transformation is the *vector of change* that we discussed earlier. Its more mundane tasks may include the translation of today's technical procedures into tomorrow's new processes. But it is also able to transform today's assets into strategic resources that are vital for meeting quite new challenges. For example, it will translate qualified customer lists into new markets; it can charter the transformation of an automotive manufacturer into a credit card company. The richness of the model is particularly relevant at a time when many managers are reporting serious

* An increasingly fashionable twist on this is the use of interim executives who are recruited during the period of change simply to run today's existing business, so that the top team can concentrate their energies on designing and implementing the change.

disappointment about the gap between the strategic intent of their business and the actual development of operations 'on the ground'.

Shells of inclusion

One major difference between Organizational MetaLanguage and many of the alignment models lies in the concept of *shells of inclusion*. The normative form of the canvas presented in Figure 8.7 is based on just four shells. It is, of course, possible to draw additional shells when needed, for example to specifically incorporate products and services into the model, or to incorporate lobbying and legislation (activities and resources) in the organization's environment. Products and services are resources and activities that could be fitted within the innermost shell to provide an additional T-shell (trading). Such a model has been used by one of the authors in charting the cultural impacts for a large IT manufacturer when moving in to providing consultancy services. In another application with a corporate communications directorate, an additional outermost shell was added to incorporate a specific legislative environment in the canvas description.

The idea of *context* insists that on the canvas, the smaller concentric shells are *contained* within the larger ones. In our normative model it is possible to directly read such statements as:

- (Operational) Work should be done within a context of some business process or procedure.
- Processes that involve people are carried out within some cultural setting.
- Assets should be organized to assist or deliver business processes.
- The entire deployment of assets and activities within the organization should be in support of creating value as determined by the mission statement.
- An organization exists within, and interacts with, its wider environment.

The nature of *Future Work*

We said at the outset that *Future Work* is to be found at the junction of three circles of information technology, people at work and business strategy. Each of these factors is of a fundamentally different nature to its two companions, and the manager needs an organizational model that is capable of accommodating and combining all three in a way that will help the business. This is no trivial intellectual task.

We argue that these components are most meaningfully related only when considered at a sufficiently rich level of context. The choice of a business imperative as our primary reference point effectively provides us with level ground upon which all three factors can comfortably coexist and interplay. Thus we insist that our dominant viewpoint must be located within the motivational shell and must incorporate some understanding of the cultural context before change is even contemplated.

Informing strategy in context

The introduction of *Future Work* concepts is a first step towards informing strategy. In today's organization, this information will impact the current scenario. The act of informing strategy in Figure 9.3 involves the precipitation of business opportunities far beyond simple scientific 'process improvement' opportunities.

Business imperative as conflict

From the moment that a new business imperative has been established, a tension will exist between the organization's aspirations and its current reality. A scientific perspective, such as that adopted by the BPR school, may view the resultant misalignment of business processes as the most important symptom. This is shown in Figure 9.4a.

Practitioners who have led change programmes that focus on modifying the business processes as *the* central lever of change, have observed wild,

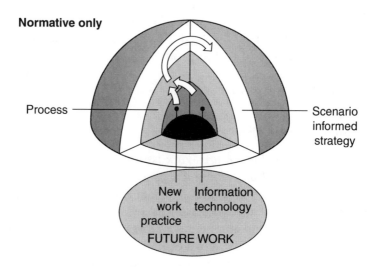

Figure 9.3 *Future Work* informing the business processes and scenario

unanticipated consequences. We illustrate this effect in Figure 9.4b. This dynamic falls within David Greenstein's 'negative territory' (*see* Exhibit 9.2) by which he means that the damage from unanticipated consequences far outweighs any benefits even though the original single-factor objective was achieved.

In this instance the complex interrelationships have overwhelmed the organization because the control of context has not been properly managed. Although it may appear that the introduction of a new business process has been *scientific*, it is in fact *unmanaged* if a strategic context has not first been established. *What is at issue here, is a fundamental difference in belief. Those who champion a pure process approach may suggest that culture will follow process. We believe that this is to misunderstand the nature of organizational change, and that a more reliable starting point is to be found by working first in the higher-context motivational shell in the relationship between strategy and culture and then move on to action on the ground.*

The kind of relationship to which we are referring is described in 'Long Range Planning' by Toyohiro Kono's[9] virtuous and vicious circles. After observing that 'the company's culture also affects its strategy', Toyohiro Kono goes on to make a key point that: 'there is a close relationship between the type of product a company makes and its culture.' We believe that culture is also a dominant contextual element in the implementation of change as well as in the development of strategy, and as such must be considered prior to the manipulation of business processes within which the immediate product or service of the company resides.

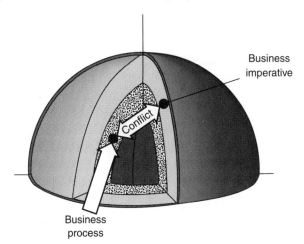

Figure 9.4a Conflict between business imperative and processes motivates change

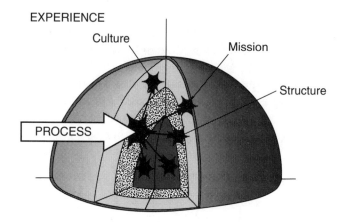

Figure 9.4b Unanticipated strategic consequences from an unmanaged process intervention

Avoiding the pitfalls in managing context

> **At its very best, decision-making orchestrates an informed search for a new identity that is intended to be followed by a scientific implementation plan.**

As we show in Figure 9.6 *decision-making* is the filter between 'informing strategy' and the actions of implementation. But it is more than just a filter. Decision-making makes the fundamental link between the intended purpose of the business and practical operations on the ground. It transforms motivation into design, and thoughts into actions. It is at the very foundation of the enterprise. It propels aspirations and ideas that stem from the motivational sphere into resource redeployment and new procedural designs at the practical and scientific level. It is the first link between intellectual reasoning and the real world, the essential thread that ties operations into strategy.

At its very best, decision-making orchestrates an informed search for a new identity that is intended to be followed by a scientific implementation plan.

Using the canvas to assist decision-making and avoid ingestion

When transforming the organization, it is essential to get the vital element of decision-making right. The quality of tomorrow's organization will fundamentally depend on the quality of the decision-making that brings it into being. By *quality decision-making* we do not mean paralysis by analysis. We mean that work has been done to establish an *informed vision and strategy* that is shared and promoted by enthusiastic and committed executives. Yet all too often, experience has shown that this crucial decision-making component is weak.

When this happens the organization has in effect lost its identity and self-determination; it has become driven not by the will of its executives, but by the vagaries of its environment. Where quality decision-making is absent, the organization is open to 'ingestion'. The most obvious, and highly pervasive form of ingestion relates to IT.

There is a wealth of experience from organizations that have acquired technology because its label seems to offer an attractive benefit, but failed to anticipate all of its organizational consequences and burdens until after they have ingested and then become dependent on it. One way to avoid such ingestion is to be able to identify the 'hidden' organizational variables in advance, and the Organizational MetaLanguage canvas can be helpful in achieving this as it can be used to provide a check-list of possible consequential zones. We have already outlined this technique in Figure 9.4b.

Appeal to context

Technology is not the only 'asset' that can be ingested to upset or impede the organization's strategic stability. One popular device in strategic planning is to profile tomorrow's organization from today's core competencies. This is to say that the organization is not prepared to review the relevance of today's competencies in the light of tomorrow's needs. Similarly, the SWOT model suggests that planning may be assisted by assessing strengths, weaknesses, opportunities and threats. If, indeed, the factors are addressed in the order suggested by the SWOT mnemonic, there is the danger of determining tomorrow's 'opportunities' simply on the basis of today's strengths. A stronger strategic approach, however, is to assess the opportunities and threats first, and only then go on to make an assessment of strengths and weaknesses. In saying this, we are arguing for a strategic position that is predicated on addressing anticipated environmental needs and internal aspirations rather than on simply projecting existing internal strengths. When stated simply, this is to declare a bias towards a proactive rather than reactive strategic stance.

When and how to think inside-out

During the decision-making stage, managers need an approach that will address the factors and issues *in the right order*. The differences in order that we are about to introduce may appear at first to be subtle, but the consequence of missing the subtlety may be a flawed business imperative. In the area of *Future Work*, the difference is yet more subtle, as the opportunity for change emanates not from the environment of the organization, but from within its own asset base.

When looking for opportunities to match an organization to its environment, Figure 8.8 (*see* page 217) may be combined with Figure 3.3 (*see* page 51) to produce a map of reciprocal needs, values and impacts shown here in Figure 9.5 as a skeleton 'stakeholder-value' chart. In practice, organizations will determine which stakeholders to include in such a chart and how to evaluate it. Only when this

> ### *Future Work* offers an opportunity to change structure.

has been done, the organizational design can proceed. This suggested approach starts with a high-context need and only then goes on to design a low-context solution; this decision-making takes place in a period of *decreasing context*.

Decreasing context is an unavoidable ground rule in the design-through-implementation stages of a change programme once the objectives of environmental matching have been determined. But it is not a *general* rule. A climate of *increasing context* is required if the organization is to be able to learn from its practical experiences. Increasing context is also required to get *Future Work* on the agenda of opportunities in the first place.

Future Work offers an opportunity to change structure. Its IT component is likely to imply an acquisition of assets. The source of the opportunity lies not in the environment of the organization, but from within. Decision-making in this type of situation requires managers to think first in a climate of *increasing context* so that low-context or scientific assets can be explained and than translated into motivational terms. Introducing *Future Work* requires operational managers to think in reverse. Whereas decision-making that typically may be applicable to a market opportunity will be progressed *outside-in*, opportunities to restructure must be approached *inside-out* in order to avoid the pitfalls of ingestion. The decision-making rule is first to inform strategy, then to implement strategy. Some questions that need to be asked in order to successfully surface and select strategic options are given in Exhibit 9.6.

Subsets of the Organizational MetaLanguage canvas conveniently provide managers with the strategic shorthand necessary to avoid technology ingestion and similar pitfalls. Figure 9.6 distinguishes between informing strategy and implementation. The elements on the left and right sides of

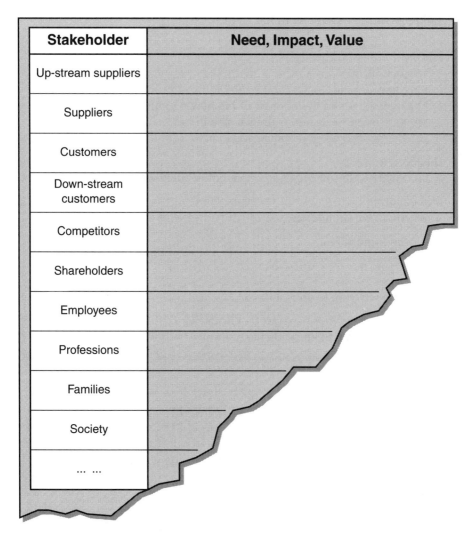

Stakeholder	Need, Impact, Value
Up-stream suppliers	
Suppliers	
Customers	
Down-stream customers	
Competitors	
Shareholders	
Employees	
Professions	
Families	
Society	
... ...	

Figure 9.5 A skeleton stakeholder-value chart

the figure are identical, except that the factors have been transposed. Thus in the first example (Figure 9.6a), strategy formulation takes place *within the context* of opportunities in information technology: information technology informs today's strategy. However the order of containment is reversed during implementation: information technology has been selected to satisfy the business imperative. The containment model conveniently and appropriately treats information technology in its very different roles of *input* to strategy, and as a strategic *outcome*.

Exhibit 9.6 Some questions to help inform strategy

Inform:
1 What implications are there in the Stakeholder-Value chart (*see* Figure 9.5), and across the *general strategic position* of the business (*see* Figure 9.2), within the context of the new hypothetical factor (*Future Work*, IT opportunity, etc.)? Are we able to redraw any boundaries? Are any boundaries being redrawn around us?

Business Impact:
2 In the light of this knowledge, where better could we be tomorrow?

Motivation:
3 Where do we want to be?

Business Imperative:
4 Where *must* we be?

Outcome:
5 What do we want to do and have?

Method:
6 How do we want to implement (e.g. pilot)?

Our second example in Figure 9.6b shows how a new process (possibly suggested as a result of a BPR exercise) may impose conflict upon current culture. The implementation model will accept the conflict but insist that the new process should be introduced only when it can be accommodated within a developed and receptive culture. In this way the Organizational MetaLanguage canvas can be used to establish sound design rules for the change manager. Some of these rules are summarized in Exhibit 9.7.

Similar containment models can be drawn for other factors. The thinking rules for informing and implementing strategy are:

1 Elevate the new factor around the organization's context. Create a vision of the organization in this alternative hypothetical setting.
2 Answer the questions in Exhibit 9.6 to analyze the business impact of the new context.
3 Return the factor to its place in Figure 9.2.
4 Communicate and commission any implementation plan in terms of the resulting *business imperative*, not in terms of the factor that stimulated it.

In all cases the 'implementation' must eventually follow the context arrangement shown in the normative canvas of Figure 8.7. This formula will ensure

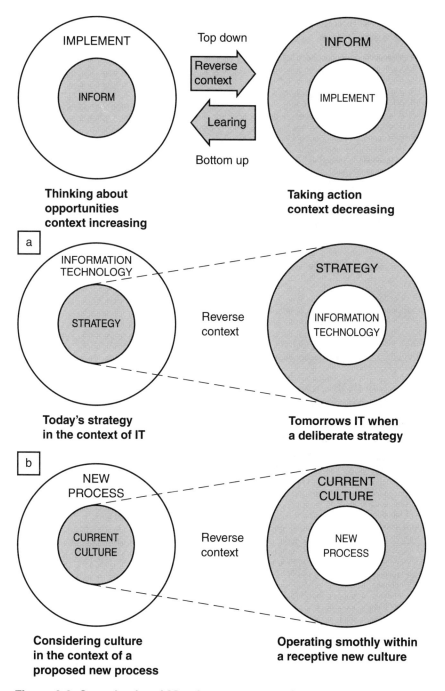

Figure 9.6 Organizational MetaLanguage containment

that the organization is not aimless, nor will it be product-led, technology-led or even market-led or customer-led. It will be business-led by taking into account its interaction with all stakeholders it chooses to recognize. It will lead itself.

Exhibit 9.7 Design rules for change-management

> ## Some Design Rules
>
> - Inform then implement.
>
> - Establish a learning culture for change.
>
> - Use *stepping-stones* where necessary in order to learn cross-impacts and to manage conflict.
>
> - The business imperative is the ultimate taxonomy.

Flowchart – introducing *Future Work*

The introduction of *Future Work* into the traditional organization will typically follow the four stages that are shown in Figure 9.7. These are:

1 **Introduction** of the topic at the senior level in the organization.
2 **Making the decision** whether to introduce a *Future Work* programme.
   Even if the outcome of stage two should be *not* to proceed with a programme, the opportunity should be taken to formalize the monitoring of the business environment by setting up a Monitoring Team. The valuable and company-unique information that has already been gained in the decision-making stage is potentially highly-useful and should become the basis of the briefing for the Monitoring Team. In the event that a programme is launched it will proceed to the next stage.
3 **Implementation.** Assumptions that were made at the time the programme was launched will now be tested in practice. Provided that the change programme has been carefully introduced (the context has been managed), the risk of conflict and unanticipated consequences will have been reduced. Change-managers will be sensitive to the degree of conflict, and look out for any unexpected side effects during implementation so as to navigate accordingly.
4 The organization will **learn** as it implements. It will modify and adapt its behaviour. In the extreme and unlikely event that the environment becomes so turbulent, or that basic assumptions turn out to be wildly wrong, the programme can be respecified or even terminated. Even organi-

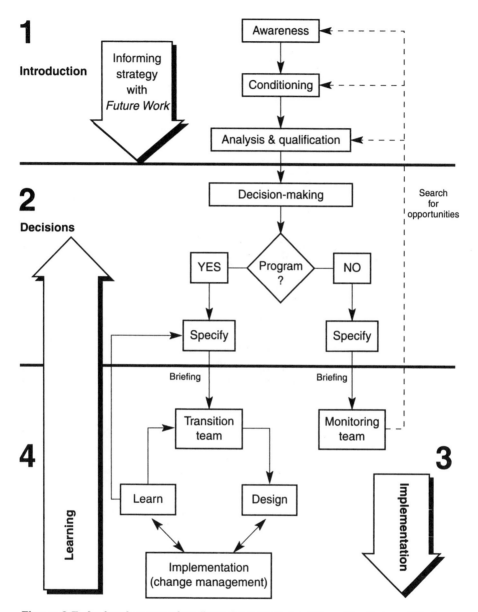

1

Introduction

Informing strategy with *Future Work*

Awareness

Conditioning

Analysis & qualification

2

Decisions

Decision-making

Search for opportunities

YES

Program ?

NO

Specify

Specify

Briefing

Briefing

Transition team

Monitoring team

4

Learning

Learn

Design

3

Implementation

Implementation (change management)

Figure 9.7 An implementation flowchart from traditional to *Future Work*

zations that come to experience such a tremendous degree of difficulty will stand the best chance of survival if they are already in a learning mode.

Detailed activities that may take place during the different stages are given in Table 9.2.

Table 9.2 Activities for introducing *Future Work*

Phase	Description	Notes
Awareness	Collect information on *Future Work*, read case studies, develop ideas. Typically this phase will end with the production of a short report to promote an activity such as the Analysis and Qualification Workshop in the next phase. A draft business case is useful at this stage to encourage people to start to think about opportunities from a business standpoint. It will be necessary to identify a champion (or to become that champion), as well as the people who will be the sponsors and supporters of the initiative.	Ideas from Chapter 2 can help to make a business case.
Conditioning	This is the preparatory stage in which an environment is created which will be able to evaluate the impact of *Future Work* within a traditional organization. In some cases it may be possible to integrate this with the stage that follows – the Analysis and Qualification Workshop. The components of the conditioning will be dependent on the degree of 'unfreezing' in the organizational climate. Where it is necessary to unfreeze, a team activity or programme may be conducted to include: • Strategic thinking. • Challenging assumptions. • A learning culture.	Many of the ideas and concepts in Chapters 6 and 7 can be applied to this activity.
Analysis and Qualification Workshop	A workshop, typically one-day duration, comprising the board and senior managers. The workshop may be promoted through memos, briefings or stand-up presentations relating *Future Work* to the business and illustrating some potential opportunities.	Information from selected parts of this book can be used to help promote the setting up of the workshop.
	Participants: These should include board members and senior managers to represent: • Information technology. • Human resources. • Real estate. • Marketing. • Production/operations. • Strategy. There must also be a facilitator and an 'expert' or champion who is able to relate *Future Work* to the particular business. Ideally, the champion will be a senior manager within the organization, supported as necessary by external consultancy.	**Selecting Participants:** Job titles are less important than the ability to contribute to the discussion. Equally, it is important to ensure that there will be commitment to the outcomes at the most senior level.

Table 9.2 continued

Phase	Description	Notes
	Agenda: This should cover: • Purpose of the meeting – to identify genuine business opportunities for further action, or, alternatively, an agreement to monitor the environment for key changes that would require another workshop. • A brief overview of *Future Work* and Organizational MetaLanguage principles of change-management. • A review of the current business definition and strategy, identifying current objectives, current trade-offs and wish list. • Workshop dialogue. • Identifying opportunities. • Scope. • Conclusions and actions.	**Purpose:** There are two desirable outcomes from this workshop: a) A monitoring activity to be performed by a nominated person or team. The task is to monitor the environment for conditions under which the workshop participants identify that a further review of *Future Work* will become necessary. b) A transition team. **Scope:** One important question that must be addressed in the workshop is that of scope. Does the transform apply to a geographic office, or a division of the company, parts of the supply chain, or the whole company? Will there be a pilot, and if so what profile should it satisfy? The qualification of scope is a key determinant for the actions that follow.
Decision-Making	Decide whether or not to pursue a *Future Work* initiative. If **yes** then specify the business imperative and set up a transition team to achieve it. If **no** then set up a team to monitor the business environment for opportunities and the activities of your competitors.	Refer to the rules of context in this chapter.
Transition Team	The role of the transition team is to drive the implementation. It must be able to maintain the priority of *Future Work* towards the top of the organization's agenda, and to maintain the purpose and direction of the implementation team.	It is vital to recognize that the 'implementation' phase refers to a change management plan as opposed to a routine tactical implementation. During this phase MetaLanguage should be used to determine cross-impacts from the structural changes being introduced.
Monitoring Team	Monitor the business environment for opportunities, examples of best practice, and also the activities of your competitors.	
Design	Design the change programme that will achieve the business imperative.	Refer to the design rules in this chapter. Ensure that all assumptions are made as explicit as possible and that mechanisms are in place to manage conflict.
Implementation	Monitor and contain conflict. Test out assumptions. Appeal always to the business imperative as the rationale for change.	
Learning	Adjust the scope and timing of the programme in response to experience.	

THE ULTIMATE TAXONOMY

One challenge that has appeared throughout this book has been how to position *Future Work* in and around the organization. We have described how developments in information technology and in new work styles have presented *Future Work* opportunities. The thrust of our argument is that *Future Work* has to be championed by organizations for it to become viable and robust. For this to come about *Future Work* has to emerge not as an option but as an imperative for the business.

> **Informed and self-motivated organizations may come to determine that the *Future Work* opportunity will become their key aspiration.**

This implies the existence of a business strategy that is supported by a strongly-committed executive within which *Future Work* plays a key role. We have shown the relationship between such a strategy with IT and people at work again in our final drawing, Figure 9.8. This looks remarkably like our first drawing of Figure 1.1. The difference, however, is that whereas Figure 1.1 illustrates the convergence of opportunities, Figure 9.8 depicts how business strategy focuses on and *deliberately selects* desirable opportunities, while it *actively rejects* those that lie outside the scope of its business imperative. Informed and self-motivated organizations may come to determine that *Future Work* opportunity will become their key aspiration.

We do not pretend that the path forward will be an easy one to travel, but the challenges that are being presented are within the grasp of most managers. In order to start the journey the traditional organizations in which these managers work will need to be informed, receptive to change, and willing to act. Simply raising the topic may well encourage some organizations to review afresh their strategic position and awareness. We hope that the knowledge and models we have introduced in this pioneering phase will help managers and organizations to take their first steps forward. We have identified the commitment to an informed strategy, to a business imperative, and to learning as essential ingredients to success.

We believe that many of these organizations and the people both in and around them will achieve their dream of *Future Work*.

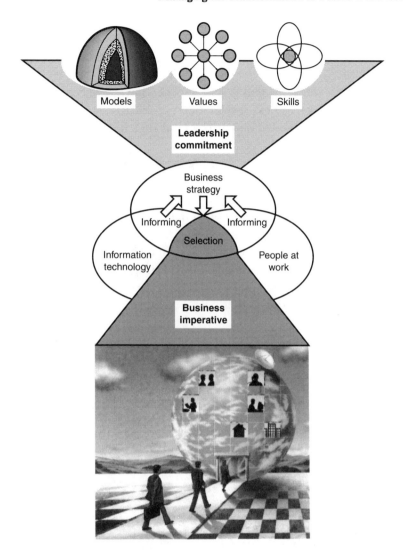

Figure 9.8 The business imperative as the decision-making taxonomy for the organization

Management summary

- Successful change involves the control of context and the management of conflict.
- Quality in decision-making is another key to success and requires change-managers to use special thinking skills.
- Decision-making also makes the vital first link between strategy and implementation.
- There is a current need for a strong theoretical basis for managing major change programmes.
- Organizational MetaLanguage offers a sound theoretical context within which *Future Work*, BPR and other major change programmes can be set.
- Change-managers need to adopt a learning style during implementation.
- Learning may be needed permanently in a turbulent organization. Other organizations will need to learn only during the time that the transformation is taking place.
- The business imperative should be the ultimate taxonomy.

References

1 HARVEY & LEESON, The Management Barrier, Pergamon Infotech Ltd. 1987.
2 HAMMER, MICHAEL AND CHAMPY, JAMES. *Reengineering the Corporation: A Manifesto for Business Revolution*, Nicholas Brealey, 1993.
3 MATTHYSSENS, PAUL AND VAN DEN BULTE, Christophe. 'Getting Closer and Nicer: Partners in the Supply Chain', *Long Range Planning*, 27(1), Feb 1994, pp.72–83.
4 HOLMAN, JIM. Logistics department at Oregon Health Sciences University, Portland, Oregon, in personal correspondence with the authors, November 1994.
5 COULSON-THOMAS, COLIN. in *Management Consultancy*, October 1994, p.4, by David Martin.
6 JONES, DAN. *Companies find that business process re-engineering doesn't work*, in *Personnel Management Plus*, June 1994.
7 GREENSTEIN, DAVID of General Motors Corporation in personal correspondence with the authors, November 1994.
8 HAMMER, MICHAEL & STANTON, STEVEN. 'No need for excuses', *Financial Times*, October 5, 1994, p.20.
9 KONO, TOYOHIRO. 'Changing a company's strategy and culture', *Long Range Planning*, 27(5), pp.85–97, October 1994.

INDEX